Beyond the Lens of Conservation

Studies in Environmental Anthropology and Ethnobiology
General Editor: Roy Ellen, FBA,
Professor of Anthropology, University of Kent at Canterbury

Interest in environmental anthropology has grown steadily in recent years, reflecting national and international concern about the environment and developing research priorities. 'Studies in Environmental Anthropology and Ethnobiology' is an international series based at the University of Kent at Canterbury. It is a vehicle for publishing up-to-date monographs and edited works on particular issues, themes, places or peoples which focus on the interrelationship between society, culture and the environment.

For full volume listing, please see page 245.

Beyond the Lens of Conservation

Malagasy and Swiss Imaginations of One Another

Eva Keller

berghahn
NEW YORK • OXFORD
www.berghahnbooks.com

First edition published in 2015 by
Berghahn Books
www.berghahnbooks.com

© 2015, 2017 Eva Keller
First paperback edition published in 2017

All rights reserved. Except for the quotation of short passages
for the purposes of criticism and review, no part of this book
may be reproduced in any form or by any means, electronic or
mechanical, including photocopying, recording, or any information
storage and retrieval system now known or to be invented,
without written permission of the publisher.

Library of Congress Cataloging-in-Publication Data

Keller, Eva.
 Beyond the lens of conservation: Malagasy and Swiss imaginations of one another / Eva Keller. -- First edition.
   pages cm. -- (Studies in environmental anthropology and ethnobiology; volume 20)
 Includes bibliographical references.
 ISBN 978-1-78238-552-3 (hardback: alk. paper) -- ISBN 978-1-78533-522-8 (paperback) -- ISBN 978-1-78238-553-0 (ebook)
 1. Nature conservation--Social aspects. 2. Nature conservation--Social aspects--Madagascar. 3. Nature conservation--Social aspects--Switzerland. 4. Rain forest conservation. 5. Parc national de Masoala (Madagascar) I. Title.
 QH77.M28K45 2015
 333.72--dc23
                                                                2014029566

British Library Cataloguing in Publication Data
A catalogue record for this book is available from the British Library

ISBN 978-1-78238-552-3 (hardback)
ISBN 978-1-78533-522-8 (paperback)
E-ISBN 978-1-78238-553-0 (ebook)

To Maurice Bloch

In admiration of your intellectual curiosity,

grateful to know you

Contents

List of Illustrations	viii
Acknowledgements/Fisaorana	ix
Notes on Text	xii
Introduction	1

Part I

Chapter 1 A Virtual Tour through Little Masoala	23
Chapter 2 Intention and Perception	58
Chapter 3 Zooming In on Morality	69
Chapter 4 A Kind of People	79
Chapter 5 The Coconut Schema	93
Extract from 'Marrakech' by George Orwell	113

Part II

Chapter 6 Living with the Masoala National Park	117
Chapter 7 The Banana Plant and the Moon	153
Chapter 8 The Island of the Wanderer	173
Chapter 9 Who Are 'They'?	185
Chapter 10 Historical Reflections	197
Conclusions	216
References	225
Index	239

Illustrations

All photographs except 1.9 and 9.1 were taken by Eva Keller

1.1	The Masoala greenhouse at Zurich zoo	24
1.2 and 1.3	Visitors and lemurs looking at one another	28–29
1.4	The 'little house' before it was repaired	30
1.5	The worktable at the research station	34
1.6	Inside the information centre	36
1.7	The Fire Magic wall	38
1.8	On Extinctions and Discoveries	41
1.9	Cover of the audio drama 'Globi'	48
6.1	Ambanizana	119
6.2	Map of Masoala National Park	125
6.3	Women in Marofototra catching fish	146
7.1	A woman with two of her grandchildren	157
7.2 and 7.3	New clothes for the ancestors and elders	160–161
8.1	The Island of the Wanderer	173
8.2	The sacrificial stone amongst the tombs	178
8.3	An empty sarcophagus is being carried to the boats	180
9.1	The balloon over Masoala	192
10.1	Papan' i Lucien's sister holding the bones of their mother during the ritual at the 'Island of the Wanderer'	200
10.2	The gift	206

Acknowledgements

My first visit to Madagascar and my first encounter with some of the people for whom the island is their 'land of the ancestors' go back to 1987. Madagascar has been part of my life ever since. Ultimately, this book is a product of these many years of connection.

In Madagascar, I am grateful to all the people who have contributed, in some way or another, to the research project out of which this book grew. In particular I express my warmest thanks to Harimalala Paul Clément for his outstanding support and collaboration during my research in Masoala, at every stage and in every possible way. I cannot imagine a better research assistant. This book owes much to him.

In the village of Ambanizana, my gratitude extends to many more people than I can mention by name here, but especially Jaorisy and Raharisoa Clémentine who welcome me into their home every time I turn up. I also thank Zandry Bezafy, Razanatsoa Marigritte and Zandry Jean Emile, Marie Gorettie and Fréderic, Faradina Benjamina and Evariste, Rakotondrasoa Ratsitoherina and Simonette, Doko Sel and Jean Clauvice, Razanazafy Modestine, Zarafine and Jean Claude, the late Raharinosy, Ramanitra Jean Batain, Meline and the late Georges Modeste, Be Jacquot, Tombozafy Denis and Benahody Felicitine, Georges Injelina, Zenesy, Randrianasolo Jean, Nazety, Justine Rose, My Be Jean, and the teachers Théodore Tadahy, Velomiarison Francis Bruno, Razafindravola Marie Brigitte and Leonger Michel.

In Marofototra, I express my thanks to Vivienne and Robia Maurice, Volaroa, Rakotoson Nicolas, Toto Simplice and Deliza, the late Sakoty Christine, Jean Victor, Velomora Théodore, Toto Florent René, Miadantsoa and Zaraoely, Bejo Antoine and Germaine, and Margueritte Alain.

In Maroantsetra, the house of Dimilahy Maurice and Rasoamalala Arlette David, whom I have known since my first visit to Madagascar in 1987, has always been my home whenever I am there.

Thank you all so much!

I am also grateful to Salava Haja, director of the Masoala National Park, and appreciative of his openness towards the questions I raised.

In Switzerland, I wish to express my thanks to all the teachers who invited me into their classroom to learn from their pupils. These were, in alphabetical order, Manuela Beeli, Sabina Fricker, Petra Gantner, Dorothea Kellermüller, Martina Kresken, Nadine Künzler, Nicole Leimer, Carmelo Munafò, Annegret Renold, Angelika Rohner, Rosemarie Sattler, Ursula Steiner and the late Brigitta Truniger. My thanks also go to the many people whose names I do not know but who were willing to be interrupted when strolling through the Masoala exhibit at Zurich zoo to answer my questions. I also thank Alex Rübel, director of Zurich zoo, and Roger Graf, from the zoo's education office, for their initial support of the research project.

In the course of the eight years during which I worked on this book, colleagues in Switzerland, London, Madagascar and elsewhere have contributed to the argument's development, among them Rita Astuti, Patricia Purtschert and the late Claudia Roth, as have participants at research seminars where I was invited to present my findings. A special 'thank you' goes to Esther Leemann for her long-standing interest in Masoala, as well as to Nigel Rothfels and Andrew Walsh for extremely valuable comments on early drafts of some of the chapters.

Family and friends also make a significant contribution to any academic research that extends over years. They organised things at home while I was in Madagascar, they brought me to and waited at airports, and they listened to my stories for years on end – for many Madagascar has become a special place, too, despite never having been there themselves. For their support over the years and their interest in (my life) in Madagascar, I thank my parents Alfred and Annemarie, my sister Sibylle and my nephew Janosch Keller, as well as my friends Amir, Andi and Mara, Angela, Annja and Sean, Anne, Artemis and Mali, Bea, Corinne and Sandra, Dorothea, Esther, Iris, Jeannette, Jenny, Luke and Sophie, Martin, Nadja, Natsch, Ninie and Tahina, Patty, Peggy, Petra, Themis, Thomas, and Ursi.

The Swiss National Science Foundation financed the research project between 2006 and 2009, and the University of Zurich for one year at the start (2005/6). I express my thanks to both these institutions for their support.

Ever since I discovered social anthropology in 1991, Maurice Bloch has had a profound impact on my learning and thinking. This book owes a great amount to his engagement with the ethnography presented here and to our continual discussions about almost every aspect of the argument. Maurice's ability to think free from intellectual fashions, his 200 per cent commitment to anthropology and his love of Madagascar have been among the most important inspirations for me throughout all these years. I therefore dedicate this book to him.

Fisaorana

Raha ny teto Madagasikara no itodihan'ny maso sy ny saina omboan'ny eritreritra, amin'ny fahafaham-po feno haravoana ary no amborahako ny fihetseham-poko añatoroako andre jiaby, na ino fomba na ino faniriana narahim-pikarohana nahazoana nankefa ny boky. Tiako ambara miavaka eto ny fisaorana tsy maty vonoina ato am-poko an'i Harimalala Paul Clément tamin'ny fanohanana tonga lafatra sady maro, miaraka amin'ny fiaraha-miasa nandritra ny fikarohana tao Masoala. Tsy haiky eky ny hamantatra ny fañotraorany zaho tamin'izany asa fikarohana izany. Mendrika ho azy tokoa ity boky ity.

Ny fahatsiarovako ombam-pisaorana anareo rehetra vahoakan'ny Ambanizana, dia mahasahana ôlo maro tokoatra, nefa avahako manokana eto I Jaorisy ary Raharisoa Clémentine nahatrañony izay nampandroso zaho an-trano tamin'ny fandalovako sy ny fipetrahako matetika nanao ny asa. Tsy adinoko ihany koa ny mankasitraka an'I Zandry Bezafy, Razanatsoa Marigritte ary Zandry Jean Emile, Marie Gorettie ary Fréderic, Faradina Benjamina ary Evariste, Rakotondrasoa Ratsitoherina ary Simonette, Doko Sel ary Jean Clauvice, Razanazafy Modestine, Zarafine ary Jean Claude, ny nahalasanan'I Raharinosy, Ramanitra Jean Batain, Meline sy ny nenina nahazo an'I Georges Modeste, Be Jacquot, Tombozafy Denis ary Benahody Felicitine, Georges Injelina, Zenesy, Randrianasolo Jean, Nazety, Justine Rose, My Be Jean, anatin'izany koa ireto mpampianatra ireto, Théodore Tadahy, Velomiarison Francis Bruno, Razafindravola Marie Brigitte ary Leonger Michel.

Ao Marofototra tiako ny hanome fisaorana an'I Volaroa, Vivienne ary Robia Maurice, Rakotoson Nicolas, Toto Simplice ary Deliza, ny nenina nahazo an'I Sakoty Christine, Jean Victor, Velomora Théodore, Toto Florent René, Miadantsoa ary Zaraoely, Bejo Antoine ary Germaine, anatin'izany koa I Margueritte Alain.

Teto Maroantsetra nanomboka tamin'ny taona 1987, ho toloranjafy tehina ihany koa I Dimilahy Maurice ary Rasoamalala Arlette David nahatrañony, fao laitry nahatongavako tao amin-jare tamin'io taona 1987 io, tsy nihafahafa zaho fao kara zaho an-tranonahy zaho tamin-jare takao.

Kay mankasitraka mankatelina ay!

Ananako trosam-pankasitrahana ka I Salava Haja, talen'ny Parc national de Masoala, tamin'ny fisokafany eram-po, eran-tsaina namaly ny fanontaniana jiaby napetrako tamin'azy.

Kay, Bingy iribehana ay, Menaka isaorana, Mankasitraka Mankatelina andre jiaby e!

Notes on Text

Glossary of Malagasy Words

andevo	slave, someone under servitude
dina	local, legally binding regulation
fañandevôzaña	servitude, slavery
maromita	servant, bearer of burden
tanindrazana	land of the ancestors
tany fivelômana	subsistence land, land that enables life
tany malalaka	unclaimed land
vazaha	white foreigner, outsider

Spelling and Pronunciation

The dialect spoken in Masoala contains numerous velar nasals. Following other studies of coastal populations of Madagascar, among whom this sound is common, I spell it as /ñ/, pronounced as in English 'long'. Written /o/ is pronounced [u] as in English 'you'. Written /ô/ is pronounced [o] as in English 'lobster'. Written /tr/ is pronounced something like [tch]. Written /z/ is pronounced as in English 'zoo'. Thus 'Masoala' is pronounced [Massuàla], 'Ambanizana' is pronounced [Ambanizàna], 'Marofototra' is pronounced [Marufùtutcha], and 'fañandevôzaña' is pronounced [fangandevòzanga].

List of Abbreviations

ANGAP	Association Nationale pour la Gestion des Aires Protégées
COAP	Code de Gestion des Aires Protégées
EAZA	European Association of Zoos and Aquaria
NGO	Non-Governmental Organisation
V.O.I.	Community committee (Vondron' Olona Ifotany)

WAZA	World Association of Zoos and Aquariums
WCS	Wildlife Conservation Society
WWF	World Wildlife Fund
ZOC	Zone d'Occupation Contrôlée

Introduction

All over Madagascar, small stores sell condensed milk produced by the Swiss company Nestlé. Once the content has been consumed, often to sweeten coffee, the tin itself embarks on a long life as a measuring cup. Nestlé's condensed milk tins have been used for decades in Madagascar for measuring rice and almost any other non-liquid product fitting into a can – a little bit of Switzerland in Madagascar. Travelling from south to north, on the other hand, litchis from Madagascar's east coast have been selling in Swiss supermarkets for many years, now being regularly offered to consumers from December to February – a little bit of Madagascar in Switzerland.

The exchange of goods between far-flung places is certainly nothing new, and has existed for centuries if not millennia, although what we have become accustomed to call 'globalisation' has increased the extent and the speed of such exchange. Contemporary globalisation, however, not only implies the transportation of goods across the planet and businesses of every *couleur* reaching even the remotest of villages, but also involves the idea of universally shared values and visions that are articulated in global agendas. Nature conservation is one such very prominent agenda, and Madagascar is a key site of global Nature conservation interventions.[1]

I use Nature 'capital-N' to refer to the idea of a 'singular global system uniting all life' (Tsing 2005: 91), a self-evident entity of intrinsic, universal worth; the historical and political weight of the concept of Nature has been discussed by numerous writers.[2]

The island in the Indian Ocean is characterised by extraordinarily high levels of species that exist nowhere else on earth.[3] At the same time, Malagasy habitats for rare fauna and flora have been declared to be at a high and immediate risk of destruction. The combination of these two factors has motivated the international conservation community to designate Madagascar as a global 'biodiversity hotspot' – in fact, as one of three 'hottest hotspots' on earth – where conservation measures are required particularly urgently (see Myers et al. 2000).[4]

These measures are rationalised and justified by a narrative that I call 'canonical', referring to it being generally accepted and widely distributed, in slightly different versions, by governmental and non-governmental conservation bodies working in Madagascar (Klein 2002: 195–96; Kull 2004: 11, 56; see also Pollini 2007: esp. 317–22 and chapter 10).[5] According to this canonical narrative, the situation Madagascar finds itself in is, roughly, as follows. Before humans arrived on the island approximately two thousand years ago,[6] Madagascar was a largely forested island providing undisturbed habitats for its numerous endemic animal and plant species. Then people appeared on the scene and, in particular through slash-and-burn agriculture, began to transform forests into grassland. Over the centuries, this process led to most of the island's original forests being destroyed and its landscapes being degraded by erosion, a process that continues today and that needs to be stopped if the last remaining patches of the original vegetation are to be rescued, especially because of an ever expanding population requiring more and more land. The cultivation of rice on forested hills is considered the chief culprit of this detrimental development. Madagascar, in short, is seen as a unique part of Nature that is being wounded by its human inhabitants, as a nation on a suicide track that needs to be rescued through international intervention.[7]

This story is, however, not supported by the evidence provided by scientists from many different disciplines, including paleoecology and -ontology, archaeology, biology, geography and tropical agroforestry.[8] These experts, in contrast, paint a much more subtle and differentiated picture of the emergence of different Malagasy landscapes and of the impact of human activity (see Dewar and Richard 2012). The point is not to deny anthropogenic factors in shaping landscapes; probably all landscapes on the earth have been influenced by the presence of humanity. The problem is, rather, that despite substantial scientific evidence to the contrary, the grossly simplified canonical narrative 'cast[ing] people simply as destructive parvenus, agents of extinction' (Dewar and Richard 2012: 496) continues to be embraced and promoted, in various, slightly different versions, by international Nature conservation players that are active in Madagascar. These, in turn, have, since the mid-1980s, placed tremendous pressure on successive Malagasy governments to implement a strict Nature conservation policy, a fact that has caused analysts to consider Madagascar as being subject to 'global environmental governance' (Duffy 2006: 731).[9] The level of influence of large Nature conservation NGOs (non-governmental organisations) has been observed to be exceptionally strong in Madagascar (Duffy 2006; Pollini 2007: 410–16; Brockington, Duffy and Igoe 2008: 167–70; Corson 2010, 2011a; see also Kremen et al. 2008: 224). As a result of such pressure, Malagasy governments have over the course of the past three decades repeatedly embraced the conservation of the island's biodiversity as their flagship goal (see, for example, Mercier 2006), a prioritisation that has led to an ever-expanding network of various types of protected areas all over the island (UNESCO 2003; Kremen et al. 2008: 224; Corson 2011a: 703–4; Madagascar National Parks n.d.). The rescuing of Madagascar's unique biodiversity has thus become a global agenda said to represent a global value, and the creation of the Masoala National Park, with which this book is concerned, is among the most prominent conservation interventions emerging from this concern. Moreover, the park in Madagascar has got a little brother in Switzerland – a fact that has created a direct connection between two otherwise not directly connected places in the world: Zurich and Masoala.

The Masoala Partnership Project

The Masoala partnership project, which was first conceptualised twenty years ago,[10] involves two locations: the Masoala peninsula on Madagascar's north-east coast and the zoo in the city of Zurich in Switzerland. In both localities, the project is depicted in terms of a partnership in which both sides are interested because of it addressing a shared and pressing concern.

The Masoala peninsula is almost entirely covered by forest, most of which is classified by conservationists as primary rain forest (Merenlender et al. 1998). As much as 1 per cent of the world's biodiversity is estimated to be found on the peninsula and an adjacent area (Wildlife Conservation Society 2013; World Association of Zoos and Aquariums n.d.). In 1997, half of the Masoala peninsula was declared a strictly protected national park, the largest in Madagascar (Allnutt et al.: 2013: 6–7). One side of the story I will tell in this book takes place in two villages on the western shore of the Masoala peninsula. One of these villages is located at a short distance from the boundary of the Masoala National Park, the other is an enclave within it. The local population is not allowed to enter the park although many families' subsistence land has come to lie within it. Production activities inside the park are punishable by fines or imprisonment. The Masoala National Park is co-managed by the Malagasy Protected Areas' Agency created in 1990 (formerly called ANGAP, Association Nationale pour la Gestion des Aires Protégées, renamed Madagascar National Parks in 2011) and the Wildlife Conservation Society (WCS), a New York-based NGO and one of the world's four most influential global conservation players (Brockington, Duffy and Igoe 2008: 157; Brockington 2009: 15).[11]

The other side of the story I will tell takes places in Switzerland. There, I focus on an exhibit at the zoo in Zurich which opened to the general public in 2003, six years after the inauguration of the park in Madagascar. The core part of the exhibit at the zoo is a greenhouse the size of a football pitch (a bit more than one hectare) within which a bit of the rainforest in Masoala has been artificially reproduced. Five hundred plant and one hundred free-roaming animal species live inside the greenhouse (Zurich Zoo 2013a: 7), with the most easily visible animals being the red-ruffed lemurs which are unique to Masoala, chameleons, birds, flying foxes and tortoises. Rather than exposing individual animal species in isolated environments, the greenhouse harbours a tiny ecosystem over which the zoo staff, quite intentionally, do not have full control. Because the zoo exhibit represents a fraction of its natural counterpart in Madagascar, it was baptised 'Masoala Kely', or Little Masoala. The stated purpose of Little Masoala is to alert the Swiss public to the alarming destruction of the world's rainforests in general, and to raise awareness and money for the Masoala National Park in particular. Adjacent to the greenhouse, the heart of the zoo's Masoala exhibit, an information centre has been built for visitors to acquaint themselves with various aspects concerning the island of Madagascar, its people, history and economy, and focusing in particular on concerns regarding deforestation and forest conservation.

Since the inauguration of the Masoala National Park in 1997 and during the years leading up to its creation, the zoo in Zurich has been one of the park's most important supporters, both ideologically and financially, committing itself to provide at least $100,000 (U.S.) annually, that is between a quarter and a third of the park's annual operating costs, via its partner organisation, the WCS (Rübel et al. 2003: 20; Bauert et al. 2007: 205; Rübel 2011). At the occasion of Little Masoala's ten-year anniversary in 2013, the zoo proudly announced that over three million Swiss francs had up to then been donated to the upkeep of the park in Madagascar (Zurich Zoo 2013b). While the zoo provides essential financial means to the park in Madagascar, the cooperation, in turn, contributes crucially to the zoo's reputation as a modern Nature conservation centre, implying not only the sensitising of the general public to Nature conservation issues but also a direct and significant presence in ongoing conservation projects.

A Relationship in Imagination

The Masoala National Park connects the Masoala peninsula to the world beyond Madagascar in a much more direct way than would otherwise be the case, and Little Masoala at the zoo in Zurich brings a little bit of Madagascar to Switzerland. Thus the Masoala partnership project has, through the global agenda of Nature conservation, established a palpable connection between two places at some 10,000 km distance as the crow flies. Global agendas of this kind also imply, as already observed, the existence of shared values and visions. Values are held by people. Does a project such as the partnership between the park in Masoala and the zoo in Zurich, therefore, create a connection between the *people* living at either end? The zoo postulates just that when, for example, its director writes in a leading Swiss newspaper that: 'We hope that over the years a close connection between Zurich and Masoala will develop, that the [zoo] visitors will follow the progress of the project there [in Masoala]. Those who feel like it may travel to Madagascar and get a picture of it [the Masoala National Park] themselves' (Rübel 2003b, my translation). Indeed, the percentage of Swiss tourists to Masoala has risen manifold since the opening of the zoo exhibit (Masoala National Park 2005) so that the Swiss are now among the most numerous of the foreign nationalities visiting, although the absolute numbers are still very moderate.[12] That the creation of Little Masoala is intended to connect *people* is also evident in publications such as one by the World Association of Zoos and Aquariums (WAZA), which the director of Zurich zoo presided over at the time of the opening of Little Masoala, where it is stated that the Masoala exhibit provides 'a window on another culture' (World Association of Zoos and Aquariums n.d.). By 2013, ten million people had visited the zoo's Masoala exhibit (Zurich Zoo 2013b). At the same time, the park management in Masoala regularly highlight their appreciation of the support given by people in Zurich.

Yet, of which nature, exactly, is the contact between people living on the Masoala peninsula and people living in Switzerland? On the one hand, personal, direct contacts are extremely rare, being almost exclusively limited to encounters between tourists and the few local people in Masoala who work in the tiny tourism industry. On the other hand, the people at either side of the partnership project are aware of one another. The farmers in Masoala are perfectly aware of the implication of foreigners in the Masoala National Park, and they reflect about the latter's intentions and the meaning of their involvement. At the other end, the zoo exhibit offers visitors a particular perspective onto Madagascar and the Malagasy people. Thus the park in Madagascar and its mini-counterpart in Zurich have created conceptual windows through which there are possibilities for people at either end of the partnership to gaze at one another and reflect about one another's lives, world views and intentions as well as one's relationship with 'the other'. We are, therefore, looking at a relationship 'in imagination'.

In thinking about this relationship in imagination, I ask what and who do visitors to Zurich zoo's Masoala exhibit reflect about when they look at the Masoala rainforest conservation project presented to them? What and who, at the same time, do Malagasy farmers reflect about when they look at the same project that has led to the creation of a protected area on their doorstep? The stories in this book, told by Malagasy farmers and by visitors to Little Masoala, will reveal that the answers to these questions revolve around entirely different issues, and that there is, in fact, no point of contact.

Outline of Chapters

The study's double focus and its two ethnographic locations also shape the argument's presentation. In Part I, I discuss the issues which visitors to the exhibit in Switzerland, including many school classes, perceive as connected with what is being presented to them. I further examine what looking towards Madagascar through the lens of Nature conservation entails in terms of visitors' imaginations of the Malagasy people. I begin with the Swiss side of the story as the concept of Nature conservation has its origins in the global North.

Chapter 1 takes the reader on a virtual tour through the tropical greenhouse at the zoo, stopping at a Malagasy kitchen and at a research station presented amidst the vegetation in order to reflect about their meanings and significance. Upon leaving the rainforest environment one passes through the adjacent information centre and eventually encounters a shop which sells, besides Malagasy handicrafts and other items, children's books. These include the story of the parrot Globi, a well-known Swiss children's character, travelling to Madagascar in search of a supposedly extinct bird. **Chapter 2** examines the difficult relationship between presented information and its perception by those who encounter it. I first investigate the zoo's mission and goals through an analysis of its own print and online publications. In the second part of the chapter I draw on schema theory to discuss perception from a theoretical point of view, thereby paving the way to consider in detail, in the following three chapters, visitors' perceptions of the zoo's Masoala exhibit. In the first of these, **Chapter 3**, a curious phenomenon crystallizes. For most visitors, the Masoala exhibit, despite its manifold references to the Indian Ocean island, is not a space for thinking about Madagascar but a space for thinking about morality, thereby erasing the focus on saving Madagascar's rainforests that the zoo so ardently attempts to bring home to its visitors. **Chapter 4** examines, partly by analysing school children's understandings of propositions made in the Hollywood animation film 'Madagascar', the role the Malagasy people play in zoo visitors' imaginations of the island. I conclude that not only is Madagascar erased from the picture in visitors' gaze through the window of the Masoala exhibit, but so are, in complicated ways, the people of Madagascar. The final chapter of Part I, **Chapter 5**, continues to examine what visitors have in mind when they think of the people of Madagascar. I investigate this question by analysing discussions I had with a total of twenty-seven school classes of all ages and academic levels in the canton of Zurich. Some of these classes had been to the zoo's exhibit while some had not; I examine the effects of a visit to Little Masoala on these children's and teenagers' perceptions. Drawing on schema theory I argue that, from as early as the age of seven at the latest, the pupils associate the Malagasy people with an evolutionist network of ideas. Moreover, presumed environmental awareness and knowledge has, in the tow line of the global agenda of Nature conservation, become a manifestation of perceived evolutionary progress.

When we turn to the second part of the book and to people at a destination point of global Nature conservation efforts, we encounter an entirely different story. Part II examines which issues the Masoala National Park makes the farmers in Masoala reflect about, and what the park entails in terms of their imaginations of the people connected with it. **Chapter 6** presents the two villages where fieldwork was carried out, introduces the park's history and some of the consequences of its creation for the local population, and details national and local conservation laws and agreements, as well as punishments for transgression of conservation rules. Drawing on a locally told myth about why the Malagasy people prefer to die like the banana plant rather than the moon, **Chapter 7** discusses the Malagasy farmers' 'ethos of growth'. This ethos is intimately linked with the importance and profound meaning of kinship ties and with the aspiration of turning neutral soil into 'land of the ancestors'. This chapter also draws attention to the stark contrast between the Malagasy and the conservationist ethos, respectively. **Chapter 8**, entitled 'The Island of the Wanderer', examines local people's interpretation of, and reaction to, the inclusion into the Masoala National Park of a tiny islet sheltering the oldest burial ground in the region, which has resulted in significant restrictions in the execution of ancestral rituals. The chapter shows that, from the local people's perspective, the park not only puts at risk the fulfilment of their most fundamental aspiration of paving the way for future generations to prosper but that it also represents a potential threat to the safety of the ancestors upon whose blessing their kin's well-being depends. But who, exactly, is responsible for these various kinds of threats discussed in chapters 6 to 8? Who is 'the park'? **Chapter 9** examines this question, showing how the park represents a nebulous consortium of governmental and non-Malagasy outside powers who, in the minds of the farmers in Masoala, merge into one hostile 'other'. The resurfacing of the central Malagasy state and the suddenly increased appearance of white foreigners in the wake of the creation of the park significantly contributes to this interpretation. In the last chapter of Part II, the perceived links between the present situation and former times of servitude, both under Malagasy and foreign rulers, are discussed, and the significance of historically inclined reflections in local people's understandings of the park is emphasised. **Chapter 10** ends with a discussion of how, from an analytically observing perspective, the Masoala National Park threatens to interrupt a historical process through which descendants of slaves have succeeded in shedding the legacy of slave descent by anchoring themselves, over the course of several generations, on the land of the Masoala peninsula. Finally, **Conclusions** provides a comparative analysis between, on the one hand, the reflections of the Malagasy farmers as they look at the Masoala National Park and, on the other, the reflections of the zoo visitors as they look through the window of the Masoala exhibit, including their mutual imaginations of the others' motivations, intentions and situation in life. It will emerge that the bridge between North and South that the Masoala project is said to provide is broken and that instead the project, in fact, widens the gap.

Friction in Imagination

Beyond the Lens of Conservation is not a study about the mechanisms and socio-economic consequences of contemporary globalisation, nor about manifestations of creative, culturally specific agency in its wake. Rather, the book zooms in on ordinary people's imaginations at both ends of a globalised Nature conservation project. This entails a threefold focus: on *imagination*, on imagination at *both* ends of a global agenda (rather than an exclusive focus on a local people in the southern hemisphere), and on *ordinary* people's perspectives, both in the global North and South (rather than contrasting the view of Western experts with that of 'ordinary folk' in the South). By combining these foci, the book offers a novel approach to the study of the global agenda of Nature conservation.

The case I present is an instance of what Anna Lowenhaupt Tsing has coined 'friction', that is 'zones of awkward engagement' that emerge out of 'global encounters across difference' (Tsing 2005: xi, 3).[13] These encounters are sparked by 'aspirations to fulfil *universal* dreams and schemes' (ibid.: 1, emphasis in the original). One such dream – and one that involves a particularly large number of dreamers in the global North and some in the South – is the rescue of Nature from anthropogenic destruction. The fulfilment of such globalised dreams necessitates the movement of particular types of knowledge 'across localities and cultures' (ibid.: 7), and it entails 'spatially far-flung collaborations and interconnections' (ibid.: ix). Yet, while the promoters of such collaborations, of which the Masoala partnership project is a perfect example, imagine the transmission of knowledge to proceed smoothly, in reality the road is full of bumps. The 'cross-cultural and long-distance encounters' (ibid.: 4) that the implementation of universal aspirations trigger are awkward 'interconnection[s] across difference' (ibid.: 4), sparking friction when the ideas and actions of those involved rub each other up the wrong way. It is 'the messy ... features' (ibid.: 3) of such encounters that Tsing suggests we ought to make the subject of ethnographic inquiry, 'grounding one's analysis of global connection not in abstract principles of power and knowledge but rather in concrete engagements' (ibid.: 267). I agree.

I therefore take Tsing's notion of 'friction' as a theoretical anchoring point for the study of the interconnection across distance and difference between a Swiss zoo and a Malagasy national park, and the 'ordinary' people living at either end. Following Tsing, I look at this globalised project through an ethnographic prism, directing the light onto the awkward and messy encounter it produces. My account of the Masoala partnership project, however, differs from Tsing's story of the global connections that manifest themselves through friction in the rainforests of Indonesia, in that my focus lies not on the practical encounters on the ground (although such encounters are not excluded from my analysis). Rather, I primarily investigate how 'the zones of awkward engagement' that have emerged out of the Masoala partnership project are imagined, what the Malagasy farmers and the visitors to the zoo's exhibit think is happening 'at the meeting point'. My focus, in other words, lies on friction in imagination.

Read On!

In the field of social scientific studies concerned with issues related to ecology and the environment, one can, broadly speaking, discern two perspectives (Robbins 2006). 'Symbolic approaches' are concerned with culturally situated ontologies and with examining how relationships between humans and non-humans are mediated through all aspects of human life.[14] In Madagascar, symbolic approaches to the study of the interaction between humans and their non-human surroundings[15] focus on the intimate and profound connection between land and kinship-based identity.[16] Symbolic approaches also discuss the encounter between local ontologies and internationally determined Nature conservation aspirations. For example, the case studies in a special volume of *Conservation and Society* highlight the fundamental 'dissonance' (Campbell 2005: 288) between, on the one hand, the perspective of those who dwell in a place and look at the landscape from within and, on the other hand, the concept of biodiversity that is completely detached from any specific place and involves a perspective as if from space (cf. Ingold 1993) calling for conservationists 'to come back to earth' (Campbell 2005: 302). Chapter 7 of this book stands in the tradition of this line of research.

'Political approaches' examine questions of power in connection with access to, and the use of, natural resources, asking 'Who wins, who loses and through which mechanisms?' This approach is presently very much at the centre of interest in Nature conservation studies, both concerning Madagascar and elsewhere. Among the most prominent issues discussed in the vast body of literature are: the commoditisation of natural resources and the neoliberal character of Nature conservation programmes;[17] new schemes for Nature conservation; carbon trading and its ecological, political and social effects;[18] foreign control over national policies and internationally monitored 'green governance' as well as the tremendous influence exerted by internationally active conservation NGOs;[19] the physical or economic displacement of local communities for the sake of Nature conservation, recently coined 'green grabbing';[20] the strengthening of existing power inequalities within local communities through Nature conservation programmes;[21] the economic and social impacts of large-scale commercial extraction of various minerals or other natural resources, (in Madagascar primarily concerning a large mining project in the country's south-east,[22] as well as the extraction of and trade in sapphires);[23] the history of conservation efforts and the paradigm shift from 'fortress conservation' to participatory approaches (and back), as well as the various difficulties also surrounding the latter;[24] the misinterpretation of local realities and the robustness of 'conservation myths';[25] and finally, local people's skill in rhetorically adjusting their proclaimed identity to fit expectations and to thus earn support by conservation organisations.[26] Most of these topics are not directly discussed in this book although Part II draws attention to the external control over natural resources in Masoala and the resulting economic displacement of local families. The stories told will, nonetheless, be highly relevant also for readers primarily interested in a political ecology analysis, as well as for conservation practitioners, and I therefore urge such readers to read on! Because from whatever angle one wishes to look at contemporary Nature conservation programmes in the global South, it is indispensable to attempt to understand how internationally monitored conservation efforts are perceived by those targeted in situ, and how these perceptions may radically depart from what actors in the North believe them to be. Such a perspective is essential in order to grasp the mechanisms at work when the global agenda of Nature conservation is implemented and, indeed, in order to better comprehend the widespread failure of international conservation efforts.

Methodological Reflections

Because the contexts in Switzerland and in Madagascar respectively required very different methodological tools, it is necessary to say a few words about how I proceeded in gathering the empirical data for this research project and in conducting the analysis.

My principal methodological tool while working in Madagascar was participant observation (as in my earlier work; see Keller 2005). Because readers trained in social and cultural anthropology will be familiar with this method, I will not go into any details about this classical anthropological research tool. For readers less acquainted with anthropology, I would like to briefly point to two of its key aspects. First, participant observation necessitates a researcher spending enough time in a place to become a competent speaker of the vernacular (by 'competent' I mean the ability to converse with ease in daily life); second, it consists in spending long periods of time with local people, in taking part in, and in observing carefully, and as non-judgementally as possible, what they do and in listening to what they say. Once relationships of trust had developed between myself and those people in Masoala with whom I interacted on a daily basis, participant observation was supplemented by recorded interviews about specific topics with selected people and, in the case of one of the two villages where I conducted fieldwork, a household survey concerning the economic consequences of the establishment of the Masoala National Park for the village's residents.

The situation in Switzerland required entirely different methods of data collection. The goal of the Swiss part of the study was to understand what the zoo's exhibit about Nature conservation in Madagascar, and the Masoala rainforest in particular, makes visitors reflect about, and what kinds of images it creates in their minds. Does 'Little Masoala' actually bring to mind Madagascar and, if so, in which ways? Does looking through the lens of the zoo's presentation bring to mind the Malagasy people and, if so, which images emerge? With this goal in mind, I interviewed adult visitors inside the zoo exhibit; I spoke with school classes from primary to grammar school who had, or had not, been to the exhibit together with their teachers, and I accompanied some of them on their visit to the zoo;

I analysed the zoo exhibit's content and took part in guided public tours through it; I examined children's stories about Madagascar and Masoala sold at the zoo; and I analysed the coverage about Madagascar and the Masoala exhibit in the Swiss media (further details will be given in following chapters).

The Implicit and the Explicit

As anthropologists and other scholars have discussed and stressed (e.g. Strauss and Quinn 1997), the relationship between implicit knowledge and language is far from straightforward or clear. It is, therefore, extremely important to be aware that explicit talk is not the same as mental concepts, and therefore what people say is not necessarily a direct window into what they think.

In a situation where one is able to spend a lot of time with the people whose perspectives on things one aspires to understand, and where one can immerse oneself into their lives through round-the-clock and long-term fieldwork as I was able to do in Madagascar, participant observation is likely to yield a much deeper understanding of these perspectives than any kind of interview or survey. I am convinced that participant observation remains the best research method anthropologists have at their disposal, and I therefore use it as my key tool. Bloch has recently discussed the special value of participant observation from a cognitive point of view. He argues that because of our species' outstanding ability to read each other's minds, people who interact in daily life enter into a process that results in 'the mutual colonisation of the related minds' (Bloch 2012: 183) and in mental 'interpenetration' (ibid.: 184). This allows researchers to develop an implicit understanding of the implicit knowledge of those in whose lives they participate. 'The participant observer is simply exposing her mind so that the process [of interpenetration] can take place', thus using the human 'mind reading ability as a research tool' (ibid.: 184). Others' implicit knowledge thereby becomes part of one's own implicit knowledge, thereby producing a feeling in the ethnographer of having grasped 'the native's point of view'. At the same time, it is often extremely difficult to explain in words why exactly one knows what one is so sure to know – a sensation that any ethnographer who has done long-term fieldwork through participant observation will immediately recognise. The challenge then is, of course, to render such implicit and highly complex knowledge into explicit language for the sake of published texts, a process that Bloch (2012: 184–85) suggests is made possible through introspection – that is through the analysis of one's own implicit knowledge that has evolved as a result of the interpenetration of minds. However successful this analytical process may be though, considering it to bring about full congruence between implicit knowledge and knowledge expressed through language would be cherishing an illusion.

In certain cases, the research situation does not offer the possibility of in-depth participant observation. Instead one has no other option but to rely on people's explicit statements they express in interview situations. This was the case with regard to my research in Switzerland which was based on catching people during those moments when 'Madagascar' briefly entered their lives. The question then arises of how to unearth tacit, implicit cultural understandings from speech. The contributors to *Finding Culture in Talk* (Quinn 2005a) suggest a variety of ways. These include paying special attention to recurrent keywords because 'they permit speakers easy reference to the salient cultural concepts that they mark' (Quinn 2005c: 72; see also Strauss 2005). If a specific word or expression crops up frequently and in the talk of many different people, it makes sense to investigate it as a potential explicit marker of an implicit concept. In other words, keywords may point to something important 'beneath'. However, one cannot assume that all concepts will be marked by keywords attached to them like labels to a box. Moreover, in the analysis of explicit talk it is important to take into consideration not only *what* has been said but also *how* it was said. Was a statement expressed with hesitation or assertively? Which emotions accompanied it? Did it appear to be the outcome of conscious reflection or, instead, to represent an almost automatic reproduction of others' talk? Did it seem to spring to mind easily or only after considerable reflection and analysis?

One of the key assertions in *Finding Culture in Talk* is the necessity for every researcher to devise methodological tools that are appropriate and implementable in a given situation (Quinn 2005b: 32–33). By necessity, these will often depart from textbook blueprints. The following sections explicate the way I proceeded at the zoo in Zurich, as well as pointing to inherent and emerging limitations.

At the Zoo

At the zoo, it was only possible to engage visitors in short conversations. Although I had obtained permission from the zoo director to conduct interviews inside the zoo premises on condition that these were not bothersome to visitors, it turned out that the majority of the latter were clearly unwilling to stop and talk for more than a few minutes. Sometimes there were obvious reasons, like impatient children or tiredness after several hours at the zoo. Mostly, however, visitors on a leisure trip simply seemed not to be in the mood or right frame of mind for in-depth discussions about any topic. I approached people randomly at various places along the visitors' trajectory through the exhibit – catching those who were about to enter as well as those who were about to leave it – and asked them for a few minutes of their time. The vast majority consented. I proceeded to ask a small number of open questions concerning my respondents' understanding of the purpose and message of Little Masoala, as well as their imagination and perception of Madagascar and the Malagasy people. I did not record the interviews, nor did I enquire about people's socio-economic background. Had I tried to conduct recorded in-depth discussions with visitors and to get data about their professional and other background, only unusually interested visitors would likely have agreed. This would have produced a highly unrepresentative sample and a consequently distorted picture. Thus the particular 'cultural analysis of discourse' (Quinn 2005b: 3) I undertook at the zoo departs in important ways from the methods presented in *Finding Culture in Talk* which are based on the systematic analysis of lengthy and recorded talk.[27] Immediately after each interview, I took notes on what the interviewee(s) had said, including as many verbatim expressions as I could recall. I also noted clues to socio-economic background that had emerged in the course of the conversation as well as the 'how' of respondents' statements to supplement the 'what'. These notes provided the basis for later analysis.

Some readers might criticise that such a procedure will inevitably result in little more than touching the surface of what might go through people's minds as they stroll through the zoo's Masoala exhibit. Although not entirely untrue, the brevity of most exchanges I had with visitors actually echoes the likely extent of visitors', at least conscious, engagement with what is presented to them at Little Masoala, a point I will come back to later on in this book. In this sense, catching a glimpse of what goes through visitors' minds as they stroll about inside the exhibit enabled me to meet the visitors at *their* level of engagement with the Masoala conservation project rather than forcing onto them my considerably more pronounced interest in this topic (but see the discussion on schemas in chapter 2).

After I had spoken with 125 individuals or small groups of visitors such as couples or groups of teenage friends[28] (I counted such groups as one respondent, although in my notes I differentiated wherever relevant between their individual statements), I realised that I was no longer receiving new information but simply getting more of the same, with many answers being extremely similar. When one reaches such a stage of research, one can either stop or else develop the next research step by investigating certain answers more deeply or developing new questions that lead in new directions. Much to my regret, neither was possible. After having published an article in a leading Swiss newspaper in which

I pointed to injustices the local population in Masoala has to suffer in connection with the Masoala National Park, I was henceforth not allowed to conduct any further research on the zoo premises. As a consequence, certain aspects of my data from Zurich zoo could not be developed as I would have wished. Such are the limitations in the real research world.

At the Schools

Besides speaking to adult visitors at the Masoala exhibit itself, I worked with twenty-seven different school classes in the canton of Zurich at all levels of primary and secondary school education (for more details, see chapter 5). Some of these had visited Little Masoala together with their teachers, others had not; some had had a guided tour by zoo staff during their visit, some had not; in some cases, I accompanied the class on their visit to the zoo; some classes engaged thoroughly with the exhibit, others much less so. In all cases, however, I met with the classes after their visit – between immediately still on the premises of the zoo, and several months (in one case two years) afterwards at their schools – and involved them in conversations concerning their images of and thoughts about Madagascar and the Malagasy people, using open questions as with the adult visitors to the zoo. These discussions were all tape-recorded and later transcribed for further analysis (to different degrees of linguistic detail, depending on the subject of conversation).

Seeking Patterns

In analysing both the adults' words, based on my notes, and the tape-recorded interviews with the children and teenagers, my aim was to investigate *frequently recurrent* ideas and patterns in what respondents talked about in connection with the zoo's Masoala exhibit. Some of these were hinted at by the use of certain keywords. I was particularly interested in those ideas which seemed to spring to mind easily and spontaneously in response to minimal cues such as the word 'Madagascar'. In other words, I wanted to understand which ideas were readily available in people's minds. Research always involves a choice of focus. I decided to pay particular attention to widely shared ideas rather than investigating individual variation which is, of course, not to deny the existence and significance of the latter. I had not chosen to focus on widely shared cultural ideas a priori, however. I did not start out looking for similarities and overlaps between different people's answers to my questions, and I did not start out intending not to differentiate along socio-economic lines, gender, age or similar criteria. On the contrary, I had expected aspects such as formal education to play an important role in shaping people's views. However, early on in my empirical research in Switzerland I was struck by the apparent existence of a relatively small set of extremely widely shared ideas which were voiced by both men and women, of vastly different ages and equally different socio-economic backgrounds (as far as discussions gave me cues to the latter). I was struck and surprised by the far-reaching homogeneity of what children, adolescents and adults said. Below the surface of varying vocabulary and different degrees of eloquence, the gist of a great many respondents' ideas was extremely similar, to the extent of being quasi-verbatim repetitions of one another. Therefore these recurrent ideas – probably reflecting a mixture of tacit 'taken-for-granted-assumptions that are at the core of what is meant by "culture"' and powerful explicit public discourse (Strauss 2005: 203) – became the focus of my study. Schema theory proved to be an important analytical tool that helped me to make sense of what I observed.

Comparing Apples and Pears?

One last methodological point is important to emphasise. It might at first appear that I am comparing apples with pears in that I am juxtaposing the views of Malagasy farmers with the views of visitors to an exhibit in Switzerland, some of whom are children. If I was comparing these different groups of people in any strict sense, I would indeed be comparing apples with pears, but this is not the case. What I offer is a juxtaposition of two different ways of making sense of one and the same Nature conservation project and of the relationships involved in it, a project that has emerged from one of the most prominent contemporary global agendas and that has created a connection between two geographically far-flung places. This juxtaposition allows us to analyse whether, and if so in which ways, the Masoala partnership project also creates connections between the people living in these places. This book is an attempt to find answers to this question.

Notes

1. Since 1990, international donors have invested at least $450 million (U.S.) in Nature conservation programmes in Madagascar (Rabesahala Horning 2008; Allnutt et al. 2013: 2).
2. These scholars, from a range of disciplines, include Nash 1989; Grove 1995; Soper 1995; Escobar 1999; Stepan 2001; and Descola 2005.

3. It is estimated that Madagascar's endemic plant species make up more than 3 per cent of all plant species worldwide, and its endemic vertebrate animal species almost 3 per cent (Myers et al. 2000: 854).
4. The concept of 'biodiversity hotspots' was first formulated by Myers in 1988. By the year 2000, the concept had been slightly modified (see Myers et al. 2000) but the principal idea remains the same. For a critical analysis of the concept of 'biodiversity', see Guyer and Richards 1996; and Escobar 1998. Recently, Kull et al. (2013) have criticised the conservation focus on hotspots, arguing instead for the recognition of the economic, ecological and social value of 'melting pots': smallholder farming landscapes in the tropics where native and introduced plants are mixed and in combination provide the basis for sustainable livelihood and sustainable natural resource utilisation (highland Madagascar is one of three case studies presented in the article). The authors argue that 'wild biodiversity is not the only kind of biodiversity that should be recognized, celebrated, and protected' and that, in fact, 'melting pots are arguably more sustainable than hotspots' (ibid.: 13).
5. It is important to recognise that there is much diversity within the global Nature conservation community in terms of both values and practices, and that it would be unsound to lump together all conservation bodies. However, those which are particularly influential in Madagascar, and certainly the Wildlife Conservation Society (WCS) that shapes matters in Masoala, can be grouped with what Brockington, Duffy and Igoe call 'mainstream conservation' (2008: 9, 154–57; also Duffy 2006; Pollini 2007: 410–16), embracing what I call the 'canonical' conservation narrative. The WCS belongs to those large conservation NGOs that continue to see strictly protected areas from which local people are largely banned as the way forward (Brockington, Duffy and Igoe 2008: 164; see also Escobar 1998: 56–57).
6. A recent study by Dewar et al. suggests, however, a much longer occupational history: 'Past research on Madagascar indicates that village communities were established about AD 500 by people of both Indonesian and East African heritage. … Recent archaeological excavations in northern Madagascar provide evidence of occupational sites … [which date] to earlier than 2000 BC, doubling the length of Madagascar's known occupational history' (Dewar et al. 2013: 1).
7. Consider the following examples of this canonical narrative. On the website of the United Nations Environment Programme, News Round-up 2011 (United Nations 2011), an article is cited which states that 'In it's [sic] pristine condition Madagascar was covered by 85% forest and this has been reduced to just 8%'. Conservation International (2013) states in its online overview of Madagascar that 'people's impact on the land means the curious island is far from pristine. Roughly four-fifths of Madagascar's forests have been stripped bare'. The Durrell Wildlife Conservation Trust stated in 2009 that 'The main threats are slash-and-burn agriculture, mining and logging (either for charcoal or construction wood). The practice of cutting forest to clear for either grazing or cultivation increased dramatically in the 1980s and predictions indicate that unless halted most forest could be removed by 2050'. In 2003 the Zurich zoo

wrote: 'Only 4 per cent of the original rainforests of Madagascar are still intact' (Zurich Zoo 2003: 16; my translation). See also Harper et al. 2007.
8. Scientific research in paleoecology/-ontology and archaeology has shown that the picture of a once (almost) totally forested island, most of which has been reduced to barren landscape by human subsistence activities (a theory that goes back to early French colonial botanists [Burney 2005: 386]), is incorrect and that the extent of anthropogenically induced changes in the landscape since the arrival of humans in Madagascar as well as the role of humans in the extinction of the endemic megafauna have been exaggerated (see Burney 1997, 2005; Dewar 1997; Gommery et al. 2011; Dewar and Richard 2012; Dewar et al. 2013). '[T]he roles played by climatic and anthropogenic drivers remain unclear' (Dewar and Richard 2012: 498). Researchers have also criticised the demonisation of fire as an agricultural technique (Kull 2004) and have discussed the mismatch between representations and realities that lie at the heart of conservation policy in Madagascar (Pollini 2007). The claim that the core cause of deforestation in Madagascar is necessarily population growth has also been challenged by researchers, pointing instead to historical and political driving factors of forest loss (Jarosz 1993; Fremigacci 1998; Klein 2002; Simsik 2002; Horning 2012: 117) as well as, following the pathbreaking study by Boserup ([1965] 1993), to adaptations of farming techniques when population density increases (Pollini 2007: 242–48, 470–72 and chapter 6). Finally, long-term climatic changes (Virah-Sawmy 2009; Dewar and Richard 2012) and seismic activity (Zavada et al. 2009) have been shown to be responsible for landscape transformations in places where the subsistence activities of local people are often postulated as their only cause. These criticisms of the canonical discourse do not, of course, mean that deforestation is not a problem in Madagascar. What they show, rather, is that the narrative used to justify contemporary conservation measures is, in fact, highly contested by expert scientists, and that its presentation as 'uncontroversial' is politically and ideologically motivated (cf. Fairhead and Leach 2003: chapter 2; Brockington, Duffy and Igoe 2008: chapter 3).
9. Concerning Madagascar, see also Kull 2004: 238–40; Mercier 2006; Pollini 2007: 58–62, 89, 410–16; Rabesahala Horning 2008; Corson 2010, 2011a; and Horning 2012. Concerning the emergence of international environmental governance in general, in which conservation NGOs have a crucial role, see Fairhead and Leach 2003, especially chapter 2. Referring to different African contexts, Broch-Due even speaks of 'ecocracy' (2000: 14).
10. For an overview of the development of the cooperation beginning in 1993, see World Association of Zoos and Aquariums n.d.; and Zurich Zoo 2010a.
11. In a study by Brockington and Scholfield on 'Expenditure by Conservation Nongovernmental Organizations in sub-Saharan Africa' (2010) between 2004 and 2006, the WCS ranks third on the list of the 'largest 10 conservation NGOs' behind the WWF and Conservation International (ibid.: 109). Madagascar is among the top five countries in terms of conservation NGO expenditure in sub-Saharan Africa (ibid.: 110).

12. In the peak year of 2007, the Masoala National Park had 2,500 foreign visitors of which 500 were Swiss (Masoala National Park 2009). Most of these only visited the small island of Nosy Mangabe, which can easily be reached on a day's excursion from the hotels in the town of Maroantsetra. See also Ormsby and Mannle 2006: 278, 282.
13. Interestingly, a similar concept of 'friction' was developed independently from Tsing by the authors of the collection of essays entitled 'Museum Frictions: Public Cultures / Global Transformations' (Kratz and Karp: 2006: 27 [note 4]) – the third in a series of books about museums' contemporary roles – to capture the idea of museums in conversation not only with the past but also with 'global flows and articulations' (ibid.: 6). In certain ways, the zoo's exhibit could be seen as a museum exhibit. This line of thought is not, however, further explored in this book.
14. See MacCormack and Strathern 1980; Tsing 1993; Descola 1994, 2005; Hirsch and O'Hanlon 1995; Descola and Palsson 1996; Rival 1998; and Ingold 2000.
15. On the term 'surroundings' instead of 'environment', see West, Igoe and Brockington 2006: 252 and 264.
16. Most ethnographies of Malagasy societies discuss, at some point, the tremendously important link between kin groups and their 'land of the ancestors' (e.g. Bloch 1994a) – including in situations where that link becomes jeopardised (e.g. Evers 2002; Graeber 2007) – or other forms of the inseparability of people and land (Woolley 2002).
17. Special Issue of *Antipode* (Brockington and Duffy 2010); West 2005; Büscher and Whande 2007; Castree 2007; Hanson 2007, 2009; Igoe and Brockington 2007; Duffy 2008; Brockington, Duffy and Igoe: 2008; Igoe 2010.
18. Concerning Madagascar, see, for example: Pollini 2008, 2009; Ferguson 2009, 2010a, 2010b; Bidaud 2012; Larson et al.: 2013; Savaresi 2013.
19. Duffy 2006; Kaufmann 2008; Corson 2010, 2011a; Ramiarantsoa, Blanc-Pamard and Pinton (eds) 2012.
20. Brockington and Igoe 2006; Fairhead, Leach and Scoones 2012; Corson, MacDonald and Neimark 2013.
21. For Madagascar, see e.g. Klein et al. 2007; Pollini 2007; Pollini and Lassoie 2011.
22. For example, Evers and Seagle 2012; Kraemer 2012.
23. Walsh 2004, 2012; Duffy 2005.
24. On the history, see Kull 2004. For analyses of participatory approaches, see Messerli 2006; Pollini 2007: chapter 11; Ratsimbazafy and Kaufmann 2008; Corson 2011b; Pollini and Lassoie 2011; Hanson 2012.
25. See Fairhead and Leach 1998. For Madagascar, see: Pollini 2007; Rabesahala Horning 2008; Scales 2011; Horning 2012.
26. Campbell 2005: 287; Galvin and Haller 2008; Huff 2011.
27. I did attempt to recruit visitors for a longer interview on a different day, but the success rate was virtually nil.
28. Interviews on the zoo premises were conducted between May 2007 and April 2008.

Part I

CHAPTER 1

A Virtual Tour through Little Masoala

The Masoala exhibit at the zoo in Zurich opened in 2003 and was welcomed by the Swiss press with enthusiasm and praise. On the day of its inauguration, the renowned *Neue Zürcher Zeitung* dedicated a special section of eight pages of text and photographs to it.[1] Sometimes, the greenhouse harbouring a mini quasi-replication of the Masoala rainforest is affectionately referred to by zoo staff and in the press as 'Little Masoala' as opposed to 'Big Masoala', the real rainforest in Madagascar. The term 'Little Masoala' was apparently coined by members of the Malagasy delegation who took part in the opening festivities. Soon after Little Masoala had opened its doors to the general public, the Zurich zoo became, according to its own publications, the most often visited 'cultural institution in Switzerland' (Rübel 2004; see also *Neue Zürcher Zeitung* 2008). The number of visitors to Zurich zoo showed a sudden jump in 2003 and a further increase to over 1.8 million annually in 2004 (Zurich Zoo 2004).[2] This number has since remained stable (*Neue Zürcher Zeitung* 2008; Zurich Zoo 2010b).

In what follows I describe the content of the exhibit by taking the reader on a virtual tour through it: through the entrance tunnel and the greenhouse, the information centre, the shop and the restaurant at the other end. In order to evoke the experience of a visit to the exhibit, I will also offer comments and reflections on the prevailing atmosphere, and on visitors' moods and attention spans at various parts of the exhibit. Twice along the descriptive trail I will stop in order to investigate an issue more closely: first, visitors' perception of a kitchen that has been placed among the vegetation inside the greenhouse; and second, two children's books sold at the shop.

One of the main goals of this chapter is to transmit a sense of what visitors encounter in terms of information, without assessing its accuracy or validity. When describing the information provided, I will, therefore, leave it up to the reader to reflect on the messages contained, explicitly

Photograph 1.1 The Masoala greenhouse at Zurich zoo

and implicitly, while offering some reflections of my own at the end of individual sections.

Through the Tunnel

Walking towards Little Masoala from within the zoo premises, the 30-metre-high building is visible from a distance. At the entrance, one is greeted with a 'Welcome' in several languages including Malagasy and is then led towards the tropical greenhouse via a 60-metre-long, dark and cool tunnel. Along the tunnel's black walls are displayed illuminated glass panels depicting photographs and written text about a multitude of topics.

The first panel is dominated by a huge photograph of a section of a lush tropical forest, and a quotation from Charles Darwin expressing the delight that must take hold of every 'naturalist who, for the first time, has wandered by himself in a tropical rain forest' in the presence of the overall beauty and 'the general luxuriance of the vegetation' (see Purtschert 2014).[3] The words 'The great mass. In the realm of plants', written in large red letters on the black wall beside the illuminated panel, point to the fact that, in rainforests, animals are few and far between relative to the masses of plants.

In equally large red letters, the visitor reads above the second panel: 'The uninhabited primary forest: A myth'. This panel is dominated by two very large photographs, one of a crouching Malagasy man looking into the camera, the other showing a couple of simple, thatched houses at the edge of a forest and a few people standing in front of them. A number of much smaller photographs depict various daily activities of rural Malagasy people: a woman making a mat, another carrying a bucket of water on her head and a baby on her back, a man carrying meat slung over a bamboo bar, women washing clothes by the river, a man cutting another's hair. The text beside these photographs cites an indigenous Brazilian leader: 'In the beginning, those who were talking of ecology were defending only the fish, the wild animals, the forest and the river. They had no idea that people live in this forest – and that these people were the true ecologists, because they could not survive without the forest, and the forest could not survive without them'.

The third panel along the tunnel's walls is dominated by a large photograph of a woman amidst some trees, and another one showing a brown hand holding red coffee beans. Again, these large pictures are accompanied by smaller photographs of everyday rural Malagasy scenes. The text beside these photographs cites a representative of the 'Penan rainforest people' of Malaysia as saying: 'Our land means life. The forest gives us food and everything we need for a living'.

The next panel, held in blue and the colours of an evening sky, provides geological information about how the island of Madagascar came into existence, and points to the 80 per cent endemism of the Malagasy flora due to Madagascar's early separation from what are now the African and Asian continents.

The last panel that one encounters as one approaches the end of the tunnel is accompanied, in large red font, by the words 'Endangered living space, Hotspot Madagascar'. This panel presents information about what a 'hotspot' is (the key criteria are a habitat's high degree of unique biodiversity combined with a high degree of it being threatened), locates the eight most threatened hotspots including Madagascar (out of twenty-five worldwide) on a world map, and quotes Norman Myers, who first coined the term, promoting the urgent need to invest in biodiversity conservation. Nowhere in the texts along the tunnel's walls is a Malagasy person cited.

Two points concerning the information provided along the tunnel's black walls need to be mentioned. First, for reasons that are unclear, some of the texts are placed above the visual height of the average person, thus requiring visitors to stretch their necks in order to read them. Second – and this may be partly due to the first point – very few visitors actually stop to look at what is shown and stated on the various displays. Observing visitors on several occasions, it became obvious that the vast majority walk through the tunnel swiftly without reducing their pace and at best throw a cursory glance to the side thus perhaps taking in a vague impression as they make their way towards the greenhouse. Exceptions to this rule are rare. The panel concerning the hotspots – it is placed both at a good height and on the opposite wall to all the other panels – draws a little more attention. The great majority of visitors are thus unlikely to notice much more than some of the large-size photographs. During the winter months, the lack of interest in the detailed information offered along the tunnel's walls might partly be explicable by the cold air that creeps into the tunnel through its open entrance; however I did not observe visitors paying any more attention even on a hot summer's day, when the tunnel offered a welcome cooling.

The tunnel is neither fully in the outside world nor fully part of the tropical greenhouse, but instead represents a link as well as a separation between the two. At its end, one pushes open a heavy metal door and enters a small room that was created to prevent animals from escaping (Bauert et al. 2007: 204), and that also functions as a kind of acclimatisation space. Pushing open another heavy door, one enters the greenhouse.

The Greenhouse

Inside, the atmosphere is humid and warm, and soothingly calm. On very busy days, I observed up to about eighty people inside the greenhouse at any one time, but on less busy days this number drops to around twenty. The silent atmosphere is interrupted only by the singing of the birds and the distant sounds of the waterfall – and, occasionally, by the penetrating cries of the red-ruffed lemurs. Hearing their loud and to human ears unattractive cries by which they communicate with one another is a sure highlight for visitors, making them stop to listen with a mixture of fascination and uncertainty as to what they are hearing, sometimes offering accompanying children explanations such as 'the monkeys are probably having an argument'. The overall auditory impression is a blend of distant sounds dominated by that of water and birdsong.

The visual impression is dominated by lush vegetation with many trees reaching to the greenhouse's top. A tarred path winds through the hall inviting visitors, at various points from where the view is particularly arresting, to stop and look more closely (in order to clear the view, zoo staff regularly cut down the vegetation where necessary). A lizard may be crossing one's path and, if one is extremely lucky, even a red-ruffed lemur. Visitors tend to talk little as they stroll along from one end of the greenhouse to the other. They walk slowly, glancing into the thick vegetation, pointing out to one another what they are seeing. They comment on, or speculate about, which species a particular bird may be and wonder whether the dark spot they have discovered in the distance is an animal or perhaps just a dead leaf? The waterfall in particular attracts much admiration.

The animals are not easily spotted as they are free to move about as they please. The only exception are the giant tortoises. After an initial period when they, too, were left to roam about freely, leaving behind them a trail of destruction that ruined half the plants, they were put in a corner of the greenhouse behind a small pond that functions as a barrier. From the visitors' path, when the animals happen to position themselves 'cooperatively' which they very often do, they can easily be seen resting, eating and mating. Apart from the tortoises, however, luck and patience are required to see any animals, especially chameleons and lemurs. Somewhat unromantically, chameleons can most easily be spotted when they are pacing along the ropes that demarcate the vegetation and the visitors' path. The red-ruffed lemurs, for their part, seem to have developed a particular liking for running along the construction tubes of the building's roof, having realised, it seems, that these offer a much easier route for crossing the greenhouse than jumping from one tree to the next.

Having discovered a lemur sitting high on a branch or a flying fox hanging from a tree, visitors seem inclined to share their luck with others who happen to be standing nearby, often alerting perfect strangers so as to share the pleasure of observing animals 'in the wild'. There seems to be a sense of collective experience. Fairly regularly, one encounters visitors carrying large cameras and who likely visit the greenhouse on a regular basis to take photographs of animals and plants. For brief moments adopting the role of instructors, they at times point out animals to others that their 'expert' eye allowed them to discover, such as a leaf-tailed gecko that is extremely difficult to spot because of its perfect camouflage when clinging head-down to a tree's bark.

From observing visitors on many occasions over several years, my impression is that it is the overall atmosphere that leaves the strongest mark on them rather than any specific aspect of the exhibit. The visitors seem to become enveloped by the physicality of the greenhouse and the humidity, warmth, smells and sounds within it, and it is these physical and sensual impressions that primarily appear to shape the experience. In many cases, a sense of awe for Nature's beauty seems to take hold of

28 | *Beyond the Lens of Conservation*

Photographs 1.2 and 1.3 Visitors and lemurs looking at one another

people as they walk through this tiny make-believe replication of a tropical forest.

As one walks along the path, one passes a small hut on stilts, measuring about two by three metres. Its roof is thatched with palm leaves, its floor is made from bamboo, and its walls are constructed

Photograph 1.3

from other natural fibres. A small space in front of the house provides a kind of mini-yard connecting it to the visitors' path. On three sides, it is surrounded by vegetation. In fact, what visitors mostly call a 'little hut' or a 'little house' [*es Hütli* or *es Hüsli* in the Swiss-German dialect] is a kitchen of the type that is typical for Madagascar's east coast, and it is

Photograph 1.4 The 'little house' before it was repaired

the kind of house that is depicted on the photographs in the tunnel. The particular one exhibited inside the greenhouse at the zoo actually originates from a town near the Masoala National Park. It was dismantled in Madagascar, shipped to Europe and put up again inside Little Masoala (personal communication with zoo staff).

For a number of years after the exhibit had opened, the kitchen's door was left open so that one could easily look inside, and see a couple of mats covering the floor, an open hearth made of three stones on which was placed a cooking pot, a plastic bucket, and a shelf with some plastic and metal cups and plates. It all looked rather worn, the mats torn, the general impression untidy. A majority of those strolling through Little Masoala tended to take the three or four steps away from the path to take a look at the inside of 'the little house', although most people would only stop for a few seconds, turn around without uttering a word and continue on their way. However, the kitchen has now been repaired; its interior still looks very simple, but is not shabby anymore, and the roof's thatch has been replaced where necessary. The bottom half of the previously inviting door opening has now been closed off, leaving but a small space to peek inside. The great majority of adult visitors now walk past it throwing no more than a distant glance at it. Many children, however, continue to be drawn towards 'the little house', quickly running away from the adults and stretching their necks, eager to see what is inside.

Stop 1: About the House

Let us stop on our walk through the exhibit for a moment and reflect on what may go through visitors' minds when they look at the Malagasy kitchen displayed in the midst of all the vegetation inside Little Masoala. As already mentioned, most visitors do not stop at the kitchen but walk past it without uttering a word to one another about it. Occasionally, I have heard people discussing amongst themselves what 'this thing' might be or looking for a sign that would tell them. Not finding one, they would walk on shrugging their shoulders. A large number of adults react in this way when confronted with 'the little house'.

Some visitors, however, do exchange comments with one another as they stand in front of it. Here are some I chanced to hear: 'This is a little tree house'; 'It is a rainforest house. That is how natives (*Ureinwohner*) live, isn't it? Look, they even have plastic!'; 'Is this how people in the jungle live?' Also consider some brief exchanges between adults and children in front of 'the little house':

> *Child to father*: 'Does someone live in here?'; *Father*: 'Perhaps someone used to live in here. This is how people in the jungle live'.
> *Child to mother*: 'Look, this is how it used to be in the past!' *Mother*: 'No, that is not how it used to be in the past, it is still like that. There are people who still live like this these days'.
> *Father to child (grinning)*: 'Look that's a three-star hotel. Fancy a holiday in such a place?'
> *Child to father*: 'Did the natives (*Eingeborene*) use to live in such houses?'; *Father*: 'Yes, of course. There is no internet connection, no television'.

The most frequent exchange consists of children running over to the kitchen and reporting to their parents that they can see nothing but 'an old carpet' or 'a few pots', and the adults replying that 'this is how the people in the jungle live'. Then, people walk on. Visitors' spontaneous comments exhibit a mixture of amazement at the house's tiny size and modest interior, associations with an original *Ur*-state of life (for a discussion of the German notion of 'Ur', see chapter 4), and relief at living differently oneself, as well as mild amusement or irony.

On rare occasions, I overheard comments of a nature that I would never have anticipated. One afternoon, I eavesdropped on two little girls about six to eight years old and a woman, presumably their mother. Passing the kitchen, the girls ran over, looked inside, could not see anything much and turned to their mother with questioning looks. With a slight grin on her face the latter answered: 'The cannibals have gone elsewhere to have a nap'.

Besides eavesdropping on visitors' conversations in the vicinity of the Malagasy kitchen, I learned about what visitors associate with the 'little house' when talking to them directly. Having been asked an open question concerning what came to mind when they thought of Madagascar and the Malagasy people, about 20 per cent mentioned 'the little house' in one way or another. Most frequently, it was perceived as an indication of its inhabitants' poverty or as a window back into humanity's past.

The 'little house' has been placed in the midst of the lush vegetation that makes up the bulk of Little Masoala, and visitors walking past it are surrounded by the distant cries of the birds and the sound of the waterfall. Observing them left me with the impression that, more than anything else, the 'little house' baffles them: they seem unable to place it or to engage with it. Their glances struck me as being of the kind of someone walking through a picture gallery and encountering a piece of modern art that they cannot make head or tail of and that therefore remains meaningless to them, at least at a conscious level. The inability to engage with the 'little house' inside Little Masoala may be due to the fact that while strolling along in this tropical environment, visitors are simply not in 'people mode' and therefore cannot relate to an object that is connected to human inhabitants. The failure to engage with the 'little house' may also be a manifestation of a 'distancing' look that visitors adopt within the context of a zoo in which one looks at living things from a distance – at lions through bars, at monkeys from beyond a separating water canal, at crocodiles through glass panels. Looking from a distance creates a clear separation between observed and observing being (see Purtschert 2014: 12), although, in fact, the Masoala greenhouse is intended to break down that separation as the visitors walk *through* the artificial ecosystem in which the animals are free to roam as they please. Moreover, zoos have a long tradition of conjointly exhibiting animals and the human 'other' (see Rothfels 2002, esp. chapters 3 and 4). Between 1835 and 1964, numerous *Völkerschauen* (people's shows) took place in Zurich in which exotic and at times physically and mentally handicapped people from foreign lands were put on show for the benefit of the European public (see Brändle 2013). Three such shows took place at Zurich zoo in the 1930s. Without wanting to unduly stress the continuity between these people's shows and the zoo's contemporary way of presenting another culture to its visitors, the Masoala exhibit, and especially such aspects of it as the 'little house', stand in the tradition of 'othering' mechanisms as discussed in postcolonial studies (cf. Said 1979; and Hall 1997; concerning Switzerland, see Purtschert, Lüthi and Falk 2012). A distancing, 'othering' gaze is encouraged by the very fact of presenting human beings within a zoo as well as by presenting them as part of a landscape.

The Greenhouse: Continued

Hardly visible among the lush vegetation and at a fair distance from the visitors' path lie a couple of dugout canoes of the kind that people in Masoala use for their daily rounds. They are rarely noticed, especially once they start to be covered with moss. From time to time, zoo staff clear the vegetation to make it easier for visitors to notice the canoes, and once every few years they are replaced with new ones. I rarely heard people make comments about the canoes, and when I did they did not go beyond remarks such as 'look, there is a canoe'.

Inside the greenhouse itself, there is no written information about flora or fauna, such as labels to trees and plants which would tell visitors their popular or scientific names, nor is there anything to be read about Madagascar or rainforests in general. The zoo decided to do without such texts because it wanted people to experience the rainforest 'as authentically as possible' and 'through all their senses'.[4] There are two exceptions. One is the 'weather station', a wooden stand where visitors can check on the greenhouse's momentary temperature and humidity, and consult a catalogue of its animals. The other is the 'research camp', an open but roofed wooden shelter of about two by three metres.

The Research Camp

The research camp presents a jumble of written information and objects that, as the name 'research camp' (*Forschercamp*) indicates, are intended to create the impression of science being done here: a laptop showing a nocturnal mouse lemur climbing about on a tree; a 20-metre measuring tape; a map of Madagascar; pens and pencils; the scientific names of a range of lemurs plus corresponding drawings; a document by the Malagasy Ministère des Eaux et Fôrets concerning the Masoala National Park; a field protocol recording various measurements concerning the behaviour of lemurs; the methods section of a scientific article in English entitled 'Monitoring impacts of natural resource extraction on lemurs of the Masoala peninsula, Madagascar', and many more similar items. All of this is displayed on the imaginary researchers' worktable along with other ingredients of their daily life in the jungle: some Malagasy money, anti-mosquito incense, a coffee mug, an Air Madagascar ticket, bandaging material, a photograph of two researchers sitting sweaty but content on the forest

Photograph 1.5 The worktable at the research station

floor and smiling into a camera. These various items are arranged casually so as to create the impression that one catches a random glimpse into an authentic daily research situation.

Among the displayed items is also a personal postcard addressed to a perhaps fictive WCS researcher named Alex Hürlimann (a typical Swiss name) who is stationed, as the address tells us, in the town of Maroantsetra where the Masoala National Park has its headquarters. The writer of the postcard, whose name disappears underneath another document, informs Alex about the Swiss press coverage concerning the illegal rosewood trade in Madagascar, and expressing her or his hope that Alex's research is not negatively affected by this, as well as sending him news about his godson and assuring him that he is being missed at home. Also under the research camp's roof there are several flasks placed on the beams of the shelter, a fishing net, a cooking pot, a hat, an advertisement for Malagasy beer, a sleeping bag, a T-shirt casually thrown over a rope, and binoculars for visitors to observe the nearby pond with the tortoises. Only a minority of visitors, however, turn off the main path winding its way through the greenhouse to walk up the short staircase towards the research camp, and even fewer pay any attention to the displayed items. Most of those who visit the research camp walk straight to the point from where one has a view onto the pond, have a brief look, turn around and leave without investigating anything of what is depicted on the table.

The intention behind the research camp seems to be the creation of a sense of 'adventurous authenticity', a sense of what it is like to do scientific research in the middle of the jungle and to study animals in the wild. In a number of ways, the research camp provides a sharp contrast with the Malagasy kitchen, the 'little house' discussed above. First, the researchers, whose imaginary work station in the Malagasy rainforest is represented, are highly personified and are brought close to the visitors by being given names and shown to be 'people like you and me' who care not only about lemurs in Madagascar but also about their loved ones left behind in Europe. Visitors can read Alex's postcard and sympathise with the researchers' struggle against the mosquitoes at night. The interior of the Malagasy kitchen, in contrast, gives no clues as to its inhabitants or their occupation but consists only of material items for cooking and eating. Second, the research camp is accessible to visitors allowing them to 'join' the researchers, while the Malagasy kitchen is closed off thus forcing visitors to peek in from behind a physical separation.[5] Third, items displayed in the research camp such as the computer and the air ticket connect the scientific staff to the contemporary modern world while the only sign of 'modernity' in the kitchen is the plastic material of some of the items (some visitors express surprise at this). The Malagasy kitchen thus triggers an 'othering' mechanism while the research camp represents an attempt to break down the separation between researcher and viewer (see Purtschert 2014).

The Restaurant

Approaching the exit of the greenhouse, visitors come to a fork offering a choice of two alternative paths: one leading to the restaurant, the other to the information centre, although the signposting does not seem to make it clear what the choice is. Most people take the route towards the restaurant. Leaving the tropical greenhouse, they slide out of the rainforest environment, leave its humidity and warmth behind to re-enter the outside world. Seated behind the giant glass wall that separates the restaurant from the greenhouse, the panoramic view allows a last glance of the thick vegetation and the birds light-footedly stalking on the pond's water plants. At this point, conversations rarely concern anything to do with the exhibit or with Madagascar. Two percent of the sales at the restaurant are donated to support the Masoala National Park.

According to my observations, visitors spend on average about ten minutes inside the greenhouse, walking through it slowly, glancing around but mostly not stopping anywhere for any length of time. Those who walk through it particularly slowly and attentively may spend up to thirty minutes inside. Most then turn off towards the restaurant, but about a third move on to visit the information centre.[6]

The Information Centre

Coming out of the greenhouse, one enters a suddenly much cooler and semi-dark room. A person taking a careful look at everything exhibited in the information centre would encounter a rich supply of textual, visual and auditory information interspersed with interactive elements.[7]

The first item to catch one's eye is one of three wooden cubes of more than a tall person's height which sports a large heading: 'Madagascar– the 8th continent'. The texts and photographs beneath draw the visitor's attention to the island's varied climate and vegetation zones and include a first mention of the problem of the degradation of the forest through slash-and-burn cultivation. It states that 'Human activities, such as cutting trees to obtain arable land and pastures, destroyed large surfaces of the original vegetation of Madagascar. Wide

Photograph 1.6 Inside the information centre

areas of the once green island are today characterized by savannah-type vegetation forms'.

A second panel on the same cube provides general information such as the name of the capital city of Madagascar, the country's form of government, and the religions adhered to (including 'traditional religions', Christianity and Islam). A third panel describes and illustrates with drawings the laboursome production of vanilla, as well as offering a scent box for visitors to sniff the pleasant smell. The fourth panel of this first cube highlights the affinity between musical instruments found on Madagascar and Borneo (illustrating the historical connection between the two places); a specimen of each is displayed and one can listen to music played on either musical instrument. Directly behind, on the wall of the room, visitors can learn about further manifestations of the close historical and linguistic connections between Madagascar and Indonesia.

If, upon entering the exhibit, one had turned left instead of approaching the first information cube, one would have encountered a large glass panel on the wall depicting the colonial era. A life-size photograph of five Malagasy men dressed in white robes and standing in a straight line, and other photographs of the era – including Malagasy men labouring, a colonial officer being carried on a palanquin – accompany two texts about the pre-colonial Merina kingdom, seventeenth and eighteenth century piracy and slave trade, colonial occupation, taxes and forced labour.

Turning one's head, the visitor is struck by the sight of blazing flames flaring up from within a large stone building against the backdrop of a black wall (see Photograph 1.7).

The rare visitor familiar with Malagasy history would immediately recognise the historic Queen's Palace falling victim to what is believed by many to have been an act of arson in 1995. The word *Feuerzauber* (fire magic) stands out as brightly against the black wall as the flames. The accompanying text deserves to be quoted (but see p. 46). [In the information centre, all written texts are translated into English and French and displayed, in smaller font, next to the German texts. When citing texts from the information centre, I use the English translations provided. Wherever the translation fails to capture the sense or tone of the German version, which is the version almost all visitors are likely to read, I add my own translation in brackets; the translation provided in the information centre is rendered in parentheses].

> [Slash-and-burn cultivation] (Slash burning) has a long tradition in Madagascar. The first immigrants already used this method of cultivation, which they had brought from Southeast Asia. The utilization of fire has its

38 | *Beyond the Lens of Conservation*

Photograph 1.7 The Fire Magic wall

roots not only in agricultural method – the causes of the many bush and forest fires in Madagascar are also of a cultural and political nature.

As an example, in some parts of the country it is taboo to hurt the ground with a hoe. The farmer is supposed to set the field on fire. In some regions the Madagascan creator god Zanahary is revered in connection with fire. The fire is seen as [the bearer of] the immeasurable power of the creator god. The greater the fire, the more power it is thought to contain. And the largest fires are obtained by setting entire forests on fire. The closer and more often one is standing by the fire, the more of this power of Zanahary is conveyed.

One of the motives for arson is also the [belief] (superstition) that there are evil ghosts. The forests are supposed to be the haunt of these creatures. By setting the forests on fire, these [mythical creatures] (creatures of fantasy) can be kept at bay.

It is also quite frequently political protest being manifested in arson. When [people are unhappy with the political situation] (when the political situation is inadequate), frustration has no respect even for cultural [monuments] (landmarks) and replanted forests.

The motives for destroying the forests due to the veneration of ancestors are [almost] impossible to control. For politicians, development activists and nature conservationists, the fire magic of the Madagascans is a perennial (and burning) topic. Essentially, the people are only continuing what their forefathers did before and passed on to them. But [it is urgent] (the fact is): The destruction is going on, and those who live today are the forefathers of those to come.

A text taken from the *Neue Zürcher Zeitung*, which is displayed in the form of a newspaper roll, enhances the allegedly destructive role played by fire in Malagasy cultural and economic life.

To one side of the black Fire Magic wall, children can listen to Malagasy fairy tales. On the other, visitors are told how traditional taboos protect certain animals such as lemurs, crocodiles, chameleons, dolphins and snakes from being killed, as the Malagasy believe these creatures to be connected to the ancestors and thus do not dare to touch them. The text focuses on the positive conservation impact of 'the world of legends of the Madagascans'. Not so with the 'strange-looking' aye-aye though, a nocturnal lemur that the Malagasy kill 'without mercy' because it is 'considered a harbinger of doom and death'.

As one leaves this dark corner of the information centre which is dominated by the photograph of the burning palace, one passes a large, lit-up terrarium and then encounters a Malagasy village shop with multiple products sold locally in Masoala (rice, coffee, cloves, washing powder, *la vache qui rit*-cheese, soap, rapphia, Nestlé's condensed milk cans, oil, Coca-Cola, sweets, etc.; see Photograph 1.6).

Opposite the shop, the visitor encounters a second information cube. This one is dedicated to explaining to the visitors the causes of deforestation. The following issues are discussed at some length and illustrated with photographs, a short video, a comic, as well as material objects: the Malagasy people's poverty in contrast to the country's wealth in natural resources; slash-and-burn cultivation causing an endless cycle of erosion and further deforestation because of the rainforest's extremely thin humus layer and the lack of fallow times due to population growth; cyclones triggering further slash-and-burn cultivation; hunting and animal trade with the text focusing on a Malagasy hunting practice that not only kills lemurs but also necessitates the cutting down of large tracts of rainforest. The texts further discuss the problem of lemurs being illegally kept as pets, as well as chameleons, tortoises and coloured frogs being illegally sold to Europe and North America. Furthermore, the enormous quantities of wood needed by rural Malagasy people for cooking and house construction is emphasised. And finally, the text draws attention to the exploitation of the Masoala rainforest's precious woods destined for export to China, with poor local farmers labouring hard at the bottom of the ladder of this illegal trade. Some historical information about pre-colonial and colonial forest concessions is also displayed.

Turning to the right, one encounters a third information cube which stresses the rainforest's economic value and the many products it yields besides wood. This cube sports the heading 'What is the market value of a rainforest?' One of its panels illustrates the rainforest's wealth for local people, providing them with medicinal plants, roots and lianas or material for basket weaving. Another panel entitled 'The rainforest in the supermarket' makes visitors aware of the many products consumed daily in industrialised societies that contain some rainforest product, including shampoo, perfume, tinned fruit salad, soup and rubber boots. On a panel entitled 'Nature's drugstore' (*Naturapotheke*) visitors are also informed, in an explicit statement against biopiracy, about how the peoples of the global South have for centuries been robbed of their knowledge about medicinal plants which has then become the source of great financial wealth for pharmaceutical companies. One is also informed that the active pharmaceutical ingredients of two Malagasy plants are presently used for the treatment of leukaemia. The last panel on this cube discusses the detrimental effects of local fishing methods vis-à-vis 'the potential abundance of fish in the waters around Madagascar'. The text is written across a large photograph of Malagasy people holding up a fishing net.

On the wall behind this third wooden cube, Madagascar's unique biodiversity is described and illustrated. The same area in the room also harbours a second terrarium, inside which one may spot the Madagascar Tree Boa (and, sometimes, a member of staff cleaning the terrarium).

Photograph 1.8 On Extinctions and Discoveries

Taking a few more steps, one finds oneself in front of a massive plastic creature that children often run towards right from the entrance door, screaming to their parents something about dinosaurs.

In fact, the over two-metre-tall bird is a life-size replica of the extinct elephant bird that was indigenous to Madagascar until a few hundred years ago. On the wall directly behind it is drawn, again life-sized, a Malagasy boy holding an elephant bird's giant egg. This corner within the information centre is dedicated to indigenous Malagasy animal species, in particular lemurs and birds, and the danger of further extinctions. Human activity is highlighted as the chief cause:

> Since the first settlement by humans, the number of species existing on Madagascar has been drastically reduced. The destruction of the original habitats in order to obtain arable land and pastures, but also hunting, are the main reasons. About 90 per cent of the original cover of vegetation has been destroyed since people came to Madagascar for the first time. Since 1960, the destruction of the rain forest has been going on at an alarming rate.

And:

> Within only a few centuries, all lemur species with a body weight of more than eight kilograms were exterminated. Excessive hunting and the destruction of habitat were their doom.

The skeleton of a lemur hangs from a beam above the three glass cabinets where this information is presented.

The information about the disappearance of lemur and bird species is juxtaposed with a list of newly discovered lemur species (both their German and scientific names are given) as well as the date of their discovery, a list so long that after having run the full height of the wall it continues its course on the floor thus forming an L-shaped text moving towards the centre of the room. A similar list gives the names of newly discovered Malagasy frog species.

Adjacent to this information about extinction and discovery of endemic animal species, the visitor is informed about the existence of numerous protected areas in Madagascar and about the organisations that manage, support and finance them, including the zoo itself. It is stated that half the tourist entry fees go towards development projects for the local population (but in the case of Masoala, according to the director of the Masoala National Park, this has yet to be realised). The zoo's partnership with the Wildlife Conservation Society (WCS) is furthermore highlighted, the WCS representing the zoo in all matters concerning the Masoala National Park in Madagascar.

Having almost reached the end of the information centre, visitors encounter a relief of the Masoala peninsula and are invited to put on headphones in order to be taken on a virtual 'control flight' over the park. The pilot informs the passengers that the flight has been 'commissioned by the Malagasy Nature protection authorities in order to supervise that no anthropogenic destructions are taking place within the borders of the national park'. After asking the passengers to fasten their seat belts, the aircraft 'takes off'. Throughout the eight-minute virtual flight, the pilot addresses the passengers in direct speech, informing them, in a somewhat authoritarian tone, about the good and bad things to be seen below, including: the illegal slash-and-burn cultivation, lemur hunting and rosewood lumbering inside the park; the park's buffer zones and the devastating effect of a recent cyclone; a palm oil plantation on the peninsula's east coast; overfishing of the sea; authorised lumbering outside the park's boundaries by small enterprises and the necessity to regularly check that they do not illegally enter the park; a research camp and the beauty of the rainforest's giant trees; and humpback whales coming into the large bay in September to give birth to their young. To illustrate the atmosphere 'on board', I have chosen the following extract of the pilot's explanations to his virtual passengers:

> Aha! Do you see the clearing down there in the forest? A chopped down tree trunk leads right across the clearing so that the lemurs walk straight into the snare trap. Illegal hunters were at work here. We have to pass this on. Our rangers will go to check up on this. The village below us is not inside the protection zone but the forest aisle with the trap lies inside the park's

boundaries. I know exactly where the boundary of the national park is. Ok, we are now flying in the direction of the Indian Ocean. The reserve down there protects mangrove forests and the coral reefs in the sea. Whenever we see fishermen inside the reserve we have to act swiftly. Fishing is strictly forbidden in this area. Now we are flying over Cap Masoala. Dugongs live here in the marine reserve. These are rare sea mammals that feed on sea grass. Do you see the big ship out there at sea? That's possibly a foreign fishing fleet. Unfortunately, I cannot recognise the flag. There, ahead of us – smoke! And there as well! We continuously have problems with illegal slash-and-burn cultivation in this region. Mostly, the fires are within the park's boundaries. Of course, we cannot tolerate such things. The rangers will intervene here as soon as possible. The small settlement below us is called Antalavia [sic] ['Antalaviana']. There still exists an old saw mill overgrown by the rainforest in this place and old rails that have gone to rack. About a hundred years ago, wood was still lumbered in these forests and transported to the saw mill on small freight cars. Now we are flying directly over the research camp of Andranobe. Here, the primary forest (*Urwald*) still grows right down to the coast. Red-ruffed lemurs (*Rote Varis*) live here, an endangered prosemian species (*Halbaffen*). Hiking trips in this part of the national park are beautiful and really to be recommended.[8]

Upon landing on the airstrip near the town of Maroantsetra, the pilot ascertains with satisfaction: 'Apart from a few slash-and-burn fires, the transport of rosewood and the illegal lemur trap, there are fortunately not many negative things to be reported today. Our projects and the work of the rangers seem to be effective. Let's hope it will continue this way'. The headphones are taken off and the passengers disembark.

Turning around, one now stands in front of an aquarium with colourful exotic fish. Most visitors stop and admire it. At this point, they have the option of entering a small black room, 'the cinema', seating some twenty people, where three documentary films are screened alternately throughout the day: one presents beautiful scenes of daily animal and plant life inside the zoo's Masoala greenhouse with gentle music playing in the background, one informs about the illegal rosewood trade, and the third concerns the threats posed to the rainforest by local people.

Coming out of the cinema and moving towards the exit of the information centre, the observant visitor may notice a large glass panel offering information about 'How to protect rainforests' at the regional, national and international levels. The information, however, only lights up if one touches the screen, so that most visitors are unaware of it.

At the exit of the information centre one is confronted with a prominently displayed board that would be hard to miss, on which is written in big, illuminated red letters: 'In Madagascar, an area of rainforest as large as the entire Masoala Hall [Little Masoala] is destroyed every 5 minutes!' This board is complemented with information about how the Zurich zoo supports conservation and development efforts in Masoala, and various leaflets about a zoo-affiliated association called 'Friends of Masoala' as well as travel information for tourists. Finally, visitors have the opportunity to donate money. Astonishingly, nowhere in the information centre is any information given about lemurs as a species (except for the names of extinct and newly discovered ones) despite the fact that especially the red-ruffed lemur is the zoo's and the park's flagship species being otherwise showcased on every occasion.

What Do Visitors Actually Look At?

A majority of visitors do not find their way into the information centre. When meeting the fork that offers the possibilities of either going towards the restaurant or else towards the information centre, they take the former route. This may be partly due to the fact that the signposting towards the information centre is easy to miss. On average days, there are only a handful of people inside the information centre at any given time, and sometimes not a single soul. On busy days, however, there is a steady trickle of visitors moving through it. Most of those who do visit the information centre spend but a few minutes inside it. The majority of those I observed walked through it fairly swiftly without paying much attention to the detailed information that is available, merely throwing a glance here and there. If they do stop to look more closely, this tends to be in front of the aquarium or one of the two terrariums.[9]

In October 2005, the zoo itself conducted an 'undercover' study whereby a student was employed to observe a total of one hundred adult visitors to the information centre. Each visitor's trajectory was recorded as well as each object which she or he had visibly stopped at, even for a few seconds. The results highlight the outstanding attention received by objects that 'are easy to look at' and require little or no reading, especially the village shop, the two terrariums, the aquarium, and the relief of the peninsula. The zoo also concluded that visitors are particularly interested in topics with which they are already familiar or which may affect the emotions: illness (especially the information about the pharmaceutical use of medicinal plants), poverty (the Malagasy's low income), nutrition (shop/supermarket products containing rainforest ingredients) and natural disasters (cyclones). The average visitor was found to spend ten minutes in the information centre. The shortest visit recorded lasted seventy seconds, and the longest forty minutes.[10]

My own observations a few years later suggest that visitors spend even less time in the information centre – mostly no more than five minutes – and that they pay attention to fewer objects than the zoo's study had found. One statement, however, catches almost everyone's eye and causes alarm in many of those who read it: 'In Madagascar, an area of rainforest as large as the entire Masoala Hall is destroyed every 5 minutes!'[11] Visitors often stop beneath this sign in a state of great concern, exchanging comments about the tragic dimensions of deforestation and the urgency to act against it.

Why is it that visitors pay relatively little attention to the mass of visual, auditory and written information displayed? There are surely many different reasons, most of which I can only guess at. Firstly, people have, after all, come to visit a zoo and so many might simply not be in the mood for taking in much information about anything but animals' behaviour. Visiting the zoo is a leisure activity during which most people seem disinclined to delve into complicated issues. Secondly, the Masoala exhibit is located in an area of the zoo that many visitors walk through on their way out,[12] and many of those to whom I spoke who had walked through the information centre without paying any attention to what is displayed said that having spent several hours at the zoo they were simply too tired. Thirdly, quite a lot of the written information is presented on horizontal slates similar to drawers that need to be pulled out from the cubes before the texts can be read. Many visitors do not appear to realise this. Moreover, similarly to part of the information presented in the entrance tunnel at the other end of the exhibit, some of the texts are placed well above the eye level of the average visitor, and even a tall person would have to be on tiptoe to read them. These texts concern the colonial era and slavery, the unique flora and fauna of Madagascar, new discoveries of species, and the Masoala National Park itself, as well as information about its partnership with the zoo and the Wildlife Conservation Society. Why this information is so poorly displayed is somewhat mysterious, as it would seem to be an obvious mistake.

Disputable Facts and Contradictions

As noted at the beginning of this chapter, the accuracy and validity of the individual statements and propositions offered in the information centre are not my main concern here. Nonetheless, I would like to draw attention to a few questionable points regarding its contents. In many ways, the information centre mirrors the general public discourse on Madagascar in Switzerland, which is highly standardised in the sense that the messages carried forth over many years through a multitude of media channels have been extremely homogeneous and often quasi-identical. Again and again the same issues are raised, the same questions asked, the same answers given. This leads, including in the information centre, to certain propositions being presented as undisputable facts in spite of them being discussed highly controversially among the scientific community, including among experts in paleoecology and tropical agroforestry. For instance, it is far from being universally accepted by natural scientists working in Madagascar that '90 per cent of the original cover of vegetation has been destroyed since people came to Madagascar for the first time', as is stated in the information centre, or that it was humans alone who caused the extinction of the Malagasy megafauna (see Introduction, endnote 8). No visitor reading the information available at the zoo would, however, suspect any such debates.

Moreover, at times, reliance on the media and other popular sources has led the zoo to make statements that are clearly incorrect. The most striking example is the text provided with the image of the burning palace under the heading of 'Fire magic'. Many of its assertions are questionable but one is particularly problematic, namely the claim that Malagasy farmers set forests on fire to harness the power of the creator Zanahary. After close to three years of fieldwork in Madagascar and having read extensively on the island's cultures, I had never come across this explanation. I thus enquired among the people in the villages in Masoala where I work, as well as asking eight anthropologists working in different regions of the country. None of them had ever heard it either. On doing some research on the statement's origin I discovered an almost verbatim rendering of it in an online publication by a German journalist who, in 1996, had been sponsored by a German foundation to spend three months in Madagascar. Subsequently, the claim found its way into a travel book,[13] again rendered in remarkably similar and at times identical words, under the heading of 'Ethnological causes of slash-and-burn'.

I would like to finish our tour through the tunnel, the greenhouse, the restaurant and the information centre by pointing to a contradiction between the information provided in the tunnel at one end of the exhibit and that provided at the other end in the information centre (see also Purtschert 2014). In the tunnel, no Malagasy person is cited. The pictures of Malagasy people engaged in rural chores are accompanied and framed by citations of indigenous leaders from Brazil and Malaysia emphasising that it is indigenous people who are 'the true ecologists, because they could not survive without the forest, and the forest could not survive without them'. The association of the Malagasy with these indigenous 'eco-goodies' (Köhler 2005) contradicts, almost totally, their representation in the information centre as 'eco-baddies' (ibid.). There, the rural Malagasy are in numerous places explicitly identified as the key obstacle to sustainable Nature conservation, and as the main cause of the forest's disappearance and the impoverishment of sea species, with much emphasis being placed on their irrational beliefs and the immense force of their often destructive traditions. At first sight, these contradictory representations seem a manifestation of the double image of natives as 'noble savages' and 'primitives' that has been well researched in the context of evolutionist thinking and colonial imagery, and of the 'simplification' and 'generification' of the complex and place-specific realities of non-European lives (West, Igoe and Brockington 2006: 265). However, there is more to it than that, and I will come back to this double representation of the Malagasy farmers in the following chapters.

The Shop

Coming out of the information centre, one encounters a shop where a great variety of products are on sale of which a considerable number are Malagasy, including herbs and spices, coffee, nuts, cooking pastes, colourful animal figures of all sizes for decoration or children's play, endemic Malagasy plants sold in small clay pots, precious stones, bags and shawls. Potential buyers are informed on tags attached to products as well as on large boards on top of shelves that, as is the case with the restaurant, 2 per cent of the returns of the shop are donated 'to support the sustainability and the living space of the animals in the Masoala National Park' (see also Bauert et al. 2007: 205). The sentence 'Your purchase at the Masoala shop creates living space' greets the visitor from all sides. Also on sale are a number of DVDs and books about Madagascar and Masoala, among them travel guides, a cookery book, and illustrated books about Malagasy fauna, flora and culture. At the bottom of the bookshelf, the small children might spot *Globi*, the blue parrot.

Stop 2: Globi, the Blue Parrot

Globi is a highly popular Swiss children's book character who came to life in 1932 and is still regularly on bestseller lists. He features, for example, in family wagons of the Swiss Federal Railways where children can play during a train journey and on non-alcoholic drinks advertised as 'Globi champagne'. His stories are designed for children up to the age of about nine. Globi is a blue-coloured parrot (addressed as a 'he') wearing red and black chequered trousers, whose many adventures and good deeds take him to places all around the world. The stories are told in nursery rhyme accompanied by illustrations. The dozens of Globi books that have to date been published include titles like *Globi among the Celts*,

48 | *Beyond the Lens of Conservation*

Globi at the Airport (where he rescues a Brazilian monkey), *Globi and the Polar Researcher*, *Globi with the Rhinos*, *Globi in the Alps*, *Globi with the Red Cross*, *Globi's Adventures in Space* – and, first published in 1995, *Globi and the Madagascar Bird* (Heinzer and Strebel 1995). This story is sold in three different formats at the zoo in Zurich: as a book (nursery rhyme with illustrations), as an audio drama, and as an accompanying colouring book. It is worth looking at it in detail.

Globi and the Madagascar Bird

The book and the audio drama, the latter being told in the Swiss dialect, are slightly different versions of the same plot: Globi goes off to Madagascar together with the enthusiastic ornithologist Professor Pinfeather (*Federkiel*)

Photograph 1.9 Cover of the audio drama 'Globi' (copyright Globi Verlag, Imprint Orell Füssli Verlag AG, Zürich)

in search of the extinct (but in the story, only *supposedly* extinct) elephant bird (in reality, it *is*, of course, extinct). The story as told in the audio drama unfolds as follows.

Globi and Professor Pinfeather are in the middle of a game of chess when the door bell rings and a mysterious parcel is delivered. It turns out to be a giant egg sent to the professor by a fellow ornithologist. In the midst of the ensuing excitement, the egg breaks into a thousand pieces revealing, to the professor's unspeakable joy, a still fresh yolk. Immediately, the two friends decide to go off to Madagascar in search of the 3.5-metre-tall *Aepyornis maximus* as clearly, but contrary to the professor's up-to-then knowledge, it must still be alive. And what a sensation this will be! Globi and Professor Pinfeather proceed to fly to Mozambique from where a dark-skinned pilot takes them across the Mozambique Channel to Madagascar in a tiny propeller-driven aircraft. Their first adventure occurs when they are caught in a storm and have to parachute down to Madagascar where Globi makes the acquaintance of a kind snake that has rolled itself into a soft cushion for him to land on. Professor Pinfeather for his part, his parachute having got stuck on top of a tree, is rescued by a bunch of frisky lemurs. Their first night in the tropics proves to be mosquito infested, a problem that is solved with the help of spiders quickly weaving a net around the travellers' sleeping place to protect them against the unwanted insects. Globi and the professor thus enjoy a restful night listening to the jungle's mysterious animal voices. After trekking across the terrain for a number of days, they eventually arrive in Madagascar's capital city where they intend to buy all the necessary equipment for the expedition (and where the pilot leaves them to go back to Mozambique). Globi and Professor Pinfeather venture into a hotel bar and ask for some coconut milk which is served to them in a container that turns out to be precisely the eggshell of the elephant bird they are looking for! Having given the friendly waiter a large tip that the latter receives with grateful astonishment, they set off towards the south of Madagascar where they hope to discover the last living specimens of the *Aepyornis maximus*. Travelling on bumpy dirt roads, their oxcart soon breaks down. They thus continue their adventure on foot, singing their 'Madagascar song' (periodically recurring throughout the story) to keep up the stamina they require to achieve their goal. The song goes like this (my translation; in the Swiss dialect, it rhymes):

> We are walking through Madagascar
> Far away from home
> We are looking, here in Madagascar
> for the bird with the giant egg

Here in Madagascar, there are wild animals and primary forest trees (1st verse) / there is rice and sugar cane (2nd verse)
Here in Madagascar, one experiences a boy's most exciting dreams (1st verse) / you feel like a king (2nd verse)
Each day an adventure
Each night a campfire
The blood of a researcher in the veins
The courage of an explorer in the heart
That's why we like it here in Madagascar
Far away from home
We are looking, here in Madagascar
for the bird with the giant egg.

At one point of their trek through the jungle, Globi and the professor encounter a monkey cup. Upon discovering that the carnivorous plant is pale from hunger, Globi feeds it the only tin of sardines they have, the one luxury that Professor Pinfeather had insisted on taking with them. Alas, it is gone, sacrificed to the hungry plant! After many days of trekking through the landscape and at the brink of giving up from exhaustion, they eventually arrive at a tunnel from which they emerge at an extinct volcano with a beautiful lake in the middle – 'a paradise!', as Globi and the professor exclaim at the breathtaking view. Before long, they meet the elephant bird they have been looking for all along. It is a male who at first is scared of the professor's flashlight camera, but being assured that Globi and the professor are his friends and do not intend any harm, he takes them to be introduced to his wife, *Frau Madagaskar-Vogel*. To the professor's immense joy, she is presently hatching three eggs, and as she politely stands up to greet the honourable guests he begs her to please, please sit down again at once! Globi and the professor spend a number of happy days with the elephant birds, but on the day of witnessing the eclosion of the three young ones, they announce that it is time for them to leave. Before they depart, however, the elephant birds beg them not to tell anyone about their secret existence at the other end of the tunnel, lest 'masses of people will come and exterminate us'. Disappointed at not being able to tell the world about their sensational discovery, but recognising the need to comply with the birds' request, Globi and the professor say farewell to their new friends promising them not to breathe a word to anyone. Back in the capital city of Madagascar, they – naively as it will soon turn out – entrust the waiter at the hotel bar (the one who had served them the coconut milk before) with taking their expedition photographs to be developed at a nearby shop. The next morning, the two friends sit unsuspecting at their breakfast on the hotel terrace when suddenly there is great agitation in town, and lots of hunters with guns, trappers with spring traps, and animal catchers with large cages are out and about in the streets. (In the audio drama, listeners are likely to assume these hunters to be Malagasy as the story is set in Madagascar and nothing indicates that they should not be local people. In the book version, the text speaks of 'men' and 'rambos' while the accompanying drawing depicts a wild-looking cohort of men with European facial features, some looking like gangsters with grim faces and dark moustaches, others like cowboys, and one is dressed like a stereotypical Native American.) In the midst of it all, a newspaper boy shouts: 'Special edition! Special edition! Great sensation: the Malagasy giant bird is alive! Globi discovers the *Aepyornis maximus*!' The waiter, upon discovering that the pictures he took to be developed revealed sensational news, had brought them straightaway to the newspaper. 'Of course you got a lot of money for this, didn't you?', Globi interrogates the waiter, turning away from him in disgust (in the book version of the story, the photographs are brought to the newspaper by the shop assistant). This is obviously a disaster but Globi, never short of a brilliant idea, knows what to do about this unfortunate turn of affairs. The premises of a scrap dealer, where all sorts of junk lies about, happens to be nearby, so using old stove pipes, rain barrels and the like, Globi and the professor quickly construct a fake elephant bird and present this creature to the agitated crowd in the streets. They are easily fooled into believing that the whole story was just a joke and that this metal construction is, in fact, what they saw on the front page of the newspaper rather than a living bird as they had believed. (The following final twist to the tale is missing in the book version.) However, the crowd is now filled with indignation at this joke and declare they will take revenge. Attempting to calm the situation, Professor Pinfeather makes the following suggestion: 'Why don't we all keep quiet about this whole giant bird story? Then nobody will know that you were fooled and then nobody can laugh at you'. This suggestion is greeted with relief by the previously angry crowd, but Globi has an even better idea, namely to place the bird in the middle of the square 'so that everyone can see that you have a sense of humour and are funny guys'. The crowd cheers Globi for this ingenious solution, and Professor Pinfeather and his parrot friend depart for Switzerland where they finish the game of chess that they had left behind upon their departure.

Woven into this plot is a considerable amount of information about the size and weight of the *Aepyornis maximus* and the date of its (in the story, alleged) extinction, about chameleons, the Madagascar boa, lemurs, carnivorous plants, orchids that exist nowhere else in the world, as well as about the fact that the capital of Madagascar is a large city with (at the time) a million inhabitants and that it sports a modern, international airport.

By 2011, forty thousand copies of the book *Globi and the Madagascar Bird* had been sold, very largely in the German-speaking part of Switzerland.[14] There are no figures available for the audio drama.

The story of Globi and Professor Pinfeather travelling to and across Madagascar in search of the elephant bird is saturated with images of a colonial *couleur* (for a discussion of postcolonial features in Globi and other Swiss children's stories, see Purtschert 2012; and Purtschert and Krüger 2012). The Malagasy are presented as naive and childish (being so easily fooled) as well as lacking in morality (wanting to kill the elephant birds, selling the secret for money), while Globi – he occupies the moral high ground in all his stories – and the paternal figure of the professor are portrayed as superior in a number of ways: they discover the bird that everyone thought to be extinct; they want to do good (they feed the carnivorous plant with their only tin of sardines; they forfeit the revelation of their sensational discovery of the elephant bird for the sake of rescuing it from extinction); and they are clever, as they fool the Malagasy crowd into believing a pretence story. They are superior intellectually and morally. The morality on the Malagasy side lies with the anthropomorphised animal world helping Globi and Professor Pinfeather wherever they can, while the only Malagasy people one meets in the story are the waiter and the mob in the streets intent on going off to kill the elephant birds. That such representations continue to inform public discourse and many people's imaginations of the African continent has been shown in numerous works in the postcolonial studies tradition (cf. Purtschert, Lüthi and Falk 2012) and is thus not surprising. What is noteworthy, however, is the fact that these images are so bluntly present in a story first published in 1995. As Purtschert, Lüthi and Falk highlight in their overview of the existence and absence respectively of a public discussion of the colonial legacy in different European countries (ibid.: 21–31, 49–52), in Switzerland 'one can discern a glaring gap' (ibid.: 51, my translation). This can only partially be explained by the fact that Switzerland never had any formal colonies;[15] the authors also observe such 'amnesia' (ibid.: 23) in countries that once were colonial powers, especially Germany and Italy.

More important for the present context, however, is another observation. Globi and Professor Pinfeather are motivated to go off in search of the *Aepyornis maximus* by the prospect of scientific discovery. In fact, the professor's excitement and enthusiasm is a key element in the story. The very fact that the story involves a professor of ornithology who knows the Latin name of the elephant bird and all sorts of details about it, locates the story, from the very beginning, within the realm of scientific discovery and knowledge. Globi and the professor are not only motivated by scientific zeal, however. They also want to do good, and are motivated by altruistic ideals (which is why they do not give away the birds' secret even though this would have made them famous). Equally strong is the sense of adventure throughout the story which is an exciting expedition into unknown territory. Globi's 'Madagascar song', which is repeated several times over the forty-five minutes of the audio drama, illustrates this particularly well: 'Each day an adventure; Each night a campfire; The blood of a researcher in the veins; The courage of an explorer in the heart'. In short, the story is based on the combination of science, adventure and recognising one's moral responsibility towards Nature.

Quite another question is what children listening to the story actually pick up, learn and later on recall. Although my evidence in this regard is limited to discussions with three primary school classes (1st and 2nd grade), they allow at least a glimpse into the way children perceive and process the story. When meeting with the pupils of these three classes, I first talked with them about their ideas concerning Madagascar and the Malagasy people before providing any input. We then together listened to the audio drama, after which I asked them to retell the story. Finally, I asked them whether they had learnt anything new from it and, if so, what.

On the whole, listening to Globi's adventures in Madagascar did not alter the children's explicit ideas about how Malagasy houses look, what people in Madagascar are like, or what they wear and live off. But there was one point that many children mentioned as having realised for the first time, namely that there are *a lot of people* living in Madagascar. Recall that the story partly takes place in the capital city where 'a million inhabitants' are said to live. Many children had thought before that there were only very few people living in Madagascar, and some that there were none at all, because they had either all been eaten by wild animals or else died from hunger. I will return to these issues in chapters 4 and 5.

Globi Experiences Masoala

Globi and the Madagascar Bird is not the only Globi item sold at the zoo. In fact, the zoo has produced, in cooperation with the Globi publishing house, its own Globi story entitled *Globi Experiences Masoala* (Ammann and Müller 2004). This pocket-sized children's book was first published in 2004 shortly after the opening of the Masoala exhibit, and by 2011 had sold 9,400 copies. Like *Globi and the Madagascar Bird*, it is designed for primary school children.

In the zoo director's foreword we encounter the same combination of moral responsibility, science and adventure that is also present in *Globi and the Madagascar Bird*.[16] The zoo director first tells the children about the biodiversity prevalent in rainforests and that 'scientists have discovered that about 1 per cent of our planet's species live on the Masoala peninsula in Madagascar' and that many species are endangered. Then he proceeds with the zoo's commitment to help to safeguard these animal and plant species by showing 'the rainforest's miracles' in the Masoala greenhouse, imploring the children to also help in saving the rainforest and to support the Masoala National Park. The text goes on to say that 'through our knowledge and our support, we here in Switzerland want to contribute to enabling the people [in Masoala] to live without having to cut down the forest because they are hungry' (my translation). The foreword ends by announcing that Globi's many adventures in the Masoala rainforest can be found in the book, and encouraging the children to come and visit the zoo themselves and to make their own discoveries.

The story then begins with Globi standing in his kitchen ready to make vanilla pudding for some of his friends who are due for a visit. Upon discovering that he will need vanilla pods and that these grow in Madagascar, he reads up about various facts and figures concerning the island, including its size and early separation from Africa and India, the existence of thirteen thousand plant species many of which exist nowhere else in the world, and about the first people arriving in Madagascar from Indonesia fifteen hundred years ago. Then the Masoala National Park in Madagascar is introduced, and Globi suddenly finds himself inside the zoo's Masoala greenhouse. (At first, one is not quite sure whether Globi is presently in Masoala proper or in the zoo greenhouse, but as the story proceeds it becomes clear that he is in the greenhouse.) Having arrived at Little Masoala in Zurich zoo, Globi meets Stradi, a friendly red-ruffed lemur who offers to help Globi in looking for the vanilla he needs for his pudding. On their way, Globi and Stradi encounter various animal and plant species, and the reader is informed about the characteristics and scientific names of carnivorous plants, the common screw pine, the Rodriguez flying fox, the elephant ear plant, the black bat flower, various palm species, fern and algae, the giant Aldabra tortoises, the African jacana, several lemur species, millipedes and cockroaches, bamboo, the olive bee-eater, the kingfisher, the traveller's tree, and about how the council tree reproduces by strangling its host. All of this is presented as strictly factual/scientific information (illustrated with colourful drawings) that is inserted into the fictional story about Globi's search for vanilla. Also inserted in the story are facts and figures about the greenhouse itself (its size, construction materials, etc.), about the nature of ecosystems and why it is wrong to think of certain insects as vermin, and about why plants need light. In a couple of places the reading child is encouraged to do some maths, such as calculating the number of days needed for the bamboo to reach the greenhouse's top.

After fifty-two pages of rich information about flora and fauna in general and in Masoala in particular (though there is not much on a page), there are six pages, also interspersed with information about animals and plants, but primarily dedicated to explaining how the people in Masoala live. The reading child learns that most Malagasy live in very small, isolated villages in the countryside; that there are hardly any paths or concrete roads and that the railway has ceased to work so people have to either walk or travel in dugout canoes; that young families go off in search of a piece of uninhabited rainforest which they then burn to build a house on the cleared land – a house that is no larger than three by four metres, and is constructed of palm leaves and bamboo; that Malagasy families have lots of children, many of whom suffer from malnutrition and have no shoes or any money to buy Globi books; that the Malagasy mainly eat rice and sometimes a little fish, but meat only on special occasions; that the village schools often lack books and pencils and that people have to walk a long way to reach the nearest hospital; that in most villages there is no electric light, thus no televisions, CD-players or telephones; that the Malagasy are afraid of the aye-aye – a species of lemur that was introduced in the previous pages – and immediately kill it upon seeing one, as well as being afraid of chameleons as these are thought to bring illness and worries. After another few rounds through Little Masoala during which Globi and Stradi come across more animals and plants, they eventually arrive at the shop next to the information centre where Globi can finally buy the vanilla pods he needs. He proceeds to make his pudding and the book ends with the recipe.

The information about human life in Masoala (often phrased as 'in Madagascar') is little more than a list of deficiency and insufficiency pointing to all the things the Malagasy lack. A pinch of superstition is added. Some information is patently wrong, such as that the Malagasy do not drink coffee but instead chew the coffee beans, or that the occasional radio one may find in a village will be one with a crank handle.

Towards the end of the book, some explicit moral instruction is added. The two friends pass an oil palm which gives occasion to state that a lot of rainforest is regularly cut down to grow oil palms, and that if one wishes to help the rainforest then one ought to eat Swiss butter, of which there is too much anyway, rather than margarine.

As in *Globi and the Madagascar Bird*, the plot is embedded in the tripartite frame of moral responsibility, science and adventure. The child learns the scientific names of fauna and flora, and is told about its duty to save the rainforest (which is said to be done, inter alia, by helping the poor in

Madagascar); and a sense of adventure prevails in Globi's learning about many rather bizarre creatures.

This first chapter of Part I has provided an introduction of what meets visitors at the zoo's Masoala exhibit. Chapters 3 to 5 will examine in detail how visitors perceive what they are presented with and what, for them, the exhibit is about. Connecting what is offered and what is seen, the following chapter discusses the relationship between intended message and its reception.

Notes

1. The 'technical life span of the Masoala Rainforest building' is estimated to be thirty years, after which time 'the exhibit will have carried out its promotional work' (Bauert et al. 2007: 205).
2. After business hours, the zoo offers guided tours inside the greenhouse which take participants along narrow paths through the forest that are normally closed to visitors. The numbers have hovered around an astonishing fifty thousand a year since 2003, with 2004 forming a peak of sixty thousand (Bauert et al. 2007: 205). During one hour on Saturday mornings, such tours are also open to the general public. Tour guides are students of biology, zoology and related subjects, as well as zoo staff and volunteers. Some of the latter are often present within the greenhouse to answer visitors' questions and to point out animals to them.
3. All texts at the exhibit are provided in German and also, in smaller font, in English and in French. Unless otherwise specified, I quote the English translations provided at the zoo.
4. Personal communication with Roger Graf, a key member of staff involved in designing the Masoala exhibit at Zurich zoo.
5. I thank Patricia Purtschert for highlighting this point.
6. Ten years after the Masoala rainforest exhibit opened to the general public, an additional attraction was added to the greenhouse in 2013: a canopy walk linked by two cocoon-shaped towers of ten and eighteen metres height respectively, from which visitors are able to view the rainforest and life within it from above (see Zurich Zoo 2013a). The present study was conducted prior to this addition.
7. Since its opening in 2003, the information displayed in the tunnel and the information centre has not been changed or updated.
8. My translation from the German original. The audio material in the information centre is provided in German only.
9. According to a review of visitor tracking studies at zoos, 'a large proportion of a visitor's time in an exhibit is spent passively walking between exhibit elements' (Francis, Esson and Moss 2007: 24). Exhibit items that include live animals have a higher attracting power than those without (ibid.: 23).

10. As mentioned in the Introduction, the zoo was at first supportive of my research. During that time, the zoo was kind enough to share the results of this small observation study with me. Later on, however, my request to conduct another systematic observation study inside the information centre was declined.
11. The area of the information centre containing this board was not included in the zoo's observational study because the shape of the room would have made it difficult to observe 'undercover'.
12. The exhibit can be approached from two sides, either via the tunnel from within the zoo premises or from a parking space outside the shop on the opposite side of the overall exhibit. Three-quarters of the visitors arrive through the tunnel. On very busy afternoons, I counted up to 170 people walking in through the tunnel within 15 minutes, while only 66 came in through the shop.
13. *Iwanowski Insel-Reiseführer* by Susanne Rössler (edition 2001).
14. Personal correspondence with the publishing house (November 2011).
15. In contexts of countries without a direct colonial history, postcolonial studies focus on 'colonial complicity' (Purtschert, Lüthi and Falk 2012: 25).
16. According to Nigel Rothfels who has examined zoo history, the word 'zoo' was coined in 1869 by a songwriter connoting 'amusement and pleasure' (2002: 38).

Chapter 2

Intention and Perception

One cannot assume that the messages the zoo intends to transmit to visitors are what they actually 'take home'. This chapter therefore draws attention to questions regarding the relationship between the intention of messages and their perception.

The first section reviews the messages that the zoo intends to get across to the general public and to visitors of the Masoala exhibit. Keeping in mind the contents of the tunnel, the greenhouse and the information centre, I investigate this issue by looking at various print and online publications by the zoo in which it explicates its mission and goals. Other possible agendas that may also motivate the zoo's involvement in the Masoala project, such as a concern for its own reputation or economic interests, are not the subject matter of this book. In the second section I discuss perception from a theoretical point of view, drawing on schema theory which is relevant for understanding visitors' statements that will be explored in detail in subsequent chapters.

Intention

As the exhibition of exotic animals becomes increasingly controversial, sensitising the general public to the beauty of our planet's biodiversity and thereby making visitors inclined to support Nature conservation projects offers contemporary zoos a compelling way of justifying their existence. In the early 1990s, the World Association of Zoos and Aquariums (WAZA) defined modern zoos' new raison d'être and long-term goal as acting as Nature conservation centres, highlighting in particular their role as conservation educators. The Zurich zoo has embraced this strategy wholeheartedly. Stressing its new identity in public discourse, the zoo director routinely recites the words of the Senegalese poet Baba Dioum: 'In the end, we will conserve only what we love, we will love only what we understand, and we will understand only what we are taught' (Baba Dioum speaking to the general assembly of the International Union for Conservation of Nature in New Delhi in 1968). Regularly in the course of the past decade, the zoo director has publicly referred to the Masoala exhibit as the heart and the flagship of his vision of turning the zoo into a modern Nature conservation centre.

Ever since the opening of Little Masoala in 2003, the zoo has presented the goals of the Masoala project, both in Madagascar and in Switzerland, in a large number of its own publications.[1] These publications form the basis of my presentation in this chapter of the zoo's intended messages to visitors; however, I do not consider the numerous media reports published in a wide range of Swiss newspapers, magazines, and radio and television programmes, because there is no guarantee that they truthfully represent the zoo's own views (albeit that they very often closely mirror the zoo's own statements). As an exception to the above, I include in my data a special dossier of some eight pages of text and photographs about the Masoala exhibit which was included in an issue of the renowned newspaper *Neue Zürcher Zeitung* shortly before Little Masoala opened its doors to the public. As it was handed out to the participants of the opening symposium which formed part of the festivities in 2003, it is reasonable to assume that the zoo saw its goals and intentions presented in a satisfactory way. The special dossier contains several long articles. These introduce the zoo's overall Masoala project, provide facts and figures about the greenhouse, emphasise the importance of the sensual experience awaiting visitors, and discuss the evolutionary emergence of lemurs as well as possible reasons for their almost unique existence in Madagascar. Also reported is the sweaty experience of being inside the greenhouse in Zurich and, in an article entitled 'A paradise for pioneers', an equally sweaty and additionally wet and adventurous trip to the Masoala peninsula mentioning 'stresses and strains', 'rudimentary infrastructure' and 'bush-hotels'. The special dossier's articles further introduce a number of animal and plant species present in the zoo's greenhouse, emphasise the importance of 'environmental education' and present a lemur zoo run by two American scientists in Madagascar, as well as giving voice to the zoo director's vision of the Masoala project having a profound learning effect through 'educational work' in Madagascar (in particular concerning population control).

The intended goal of the Masoala exhibit is stated explicitly, clearly and repeatedly as: (a) ensuring the long-term conservation of the Masoala rainforest, and (b) sensitising the population both in Switzerland and in Masoala for Nature conservation. The zoo presents itself as an 'authentic ambassador for the Masoala National Park' (Bauert et al. 2007: 203) and for the beauty of the Malagasy rainforest, and as an educator towards a 'change of awareness' in the general populations of both Switzerland and Masoala.

In Switzerland, the zoo's explicit goal is to motivate visitors to actively contribute to the conservation of the Masoala rainforest, for example by way of a donation. For instance, it is explained that 'With the Masoala rainforest, the zoo in Zurich wants us to experience, understand and enjoy the rainforest, despite being far away from its actual location. The rainforest is intended to impress visitors and to thus motivate them to contribute towards the conservation of the rainforest in Madagascar' (Rübel 2003a: 7), and 'The Masoala rainforest at the Zurich zoo is also a plea to all visitors to contribute towards the preservation of Madagascar's irreplaceable treasures' (ibid.: 13) and the protection 'of one of the last untouched paradises on this earth' (ibid.: 7).

This motivating experience is intended to happen at three stages in a person's visit. Firstly, while approaching Little Masoala through the entrance tunnel, visitors are able to 'tune in to the Nature experience' awaiting them by seeing 'beautiful photographs', reading 'quotations from famous scientists' and getting 'key facts and figures' (IRBIS 2003: 6). Secondly, while inside the actual greenhouse, the 'authentic impression' (Bauert et al. 2007: 204), and 'the close-to-reality Nature experience is foregrounded' (IRBIS 2003: 6), enabling visitors to experience this 'near-authentic piece of Malagasy rainforest' (Zurich Zoo 2003: 7) 'through all their senses' (special dossier of *Neue Zürcher Zeitung* 27 June 2003: 3). Thirdly, visitors leave the humid environment and enter the information centre, where 'we get to the bottom of things' by investigating 'the causes of, and possible solutions to, the destruction of rainforests by way of the example of Madagascar' (IRBIS 2003: 7). Experience and information are strictly separated within this concept, leading visitors through the three consecutive stages of tuning in, sensual experience, and in-depth information.

The zoo's commitment to the Masoala project extends beyond its own premises to Masoala itself. There, the $100,000 (U.S.) or more that the zoo annually donates is used by its partner organisation WCS and the park authorities: (1) to finance the upkeep of the park (wages of rangers, marking of the boundary, maintenance of the park's infrastructure such as paths for tourists); (2) to educate the population in Masoala in matters of sustainable use of natural resources; and (3) to finance micro-projects in villages aimed at promoting Nature conservation (e.g. plant nurseries, small irrigation damns).[2] Furthermore, the zoo intends to support the conservation of the Masoala rainforest by promoting 'tourism in the, so far, not widely known national park' (Bauert et al. 2007: 203).

As in Globi's children's stories, one encounters in these publications a mixture of pleas to responsibility, science/know-how, and adventure.

Many contain all three elements.[3] The overall message could be paraphrased thus: 'We are not merely talking about Nature conservation, we are accepting our responsibility to act in the world and we actively initiate and support Nature conservation projects in Masoala; our commitment and our activities are based on scientific expertise and know-how of implementation; and supporting Nature conservation is also exciting and fun.'

In terms of accepting responsibility, which is closely related to the zoo's stated purpose of acting as educator, the zoo magazines report, for example, that 'with our plant nursery on the Masoala peninsula, we are showing the local population how to use the rainforest without burning it down' (Zurich Zoo 2003: 9), or that through its 'educational work concerning Nature conservation in the circumjacent villages' the zoo helps to 'stop the plundering of the rainforest' (ibid.: 13). In its annual report of 2004, the zoo announced that 'together with the surrounding village communities, we will develop new cultivation methods that make slash-and-burn unnecessary' (Zurich Zoo 2004: 5), adding a year later that it also fosters eco-tourism so that local people will come to recognise the economic value of the rainforest providing them with an alternative source of income (Zurich Zoo 2005: 11). On the zoo's website it is stated that 'A lack of expertise concerning more sustainable cultivation methods as well as cultural traditions such as the socially higher prestige when owning more land, contribute to the continuing deforestation of the tropical rainforest' and that the zoo is therefore committed to 'the education of the population concerning ecologically meaningful ways of cultivating the land'.[4] In its online press kit of 2011 (Zurich Zoo 2011a), the zoo claims that it has succeeded in 'create[ing] an awareness for the significance of an intact rainforest among the local population' in Masoala, and that since 2003 it has financed target-oriented projects in the surroundings of the Masoala National Park that allow the population to cultivate their land sustainably without destroying the rainforest.

The scientific basis of all these efforts is highlighted by repeated references to various research projects that the Zurich zoo is involved in, in cooperation with the renowned Swiss Federal Institute of Technology and the University of Zurich, as well as other research institutes. On the one hand, these research projects study animals and plants inside the zoo's greenhouse and concern such topics as the behaviour of the geckos, the reproduction strategies of the panther chameleon, and lemur habitat use. On the other hand, they take the reader to Madagascar where the zoo has, for example, conducted seed collections in order to 'research and document plant diversity in Masoala' (Zurich Zoo 2004). The Zurich zoo also considers one of its duties to function as a 'Noah's ark' of threatened

Malagasy frog species (Zurich Zoo 2006: 5) and reports to co-finance a long-term monitoring research project concerning the tomato frog which is endemic to the Masoala region (Zurich Zoo 2008). Recent publications draw attention to the Zurich zoo's active involvement in a research project concerning the DNA of rosewood (Zurich Zoo 2011b and 2012).

The exciting side of supporting Nature conservation in Masoala is primarily presented in reports about journeys into 'an unknown world' in order to 'discover the rainforest's secrets', during which members of staff from the zoo encountered various adventures such as the prop aircraft's bumpy landing on the local airstrip or learning how to form a spoon out of a leaf (Zurich Zoo 2003: 11–14). In recent years, the zoo has begun to offer tourist trips to Madagascar, with a member of staff acting as tour guide, which promise the experience of 'primary [urtümlich] animal and plant species' and 'explorative trips on foot, in boats or on ox-carts' (Zurich Zoo 2012: 16). A touch of adventure is also offered in the greenhouse back home in Zurich, especially during the annual Madagascar days at the zoo – they have been taking place since 2004 and last between two and three days – when visitors can undertake 'wanderings in the dark, in the rain and on adventure paths' (Zurich Zoo 2011b: 6).

If the zoo represents the Masoala project as being about taking responsibility for Nature conservation, about scientific knowledge, but also excitement/adventure/fun, what do visitors perceive the Masoala exhibit to be about? Before I address this question, I offer some theoretical reflections on the nature of perception.

Perception

How someone perceives a particular phenomenon is not only the result of a dynamic process. It also involves a process that continues throughout life making it impossible and indeed nonsensical to try to think of a point of origin or to isolate particular moments within it. This also applies to the ways Swiss people perceive Madagascar and the Malagasy. Thus trying to grasp visitors' perceptions as they walk through the tunnel, the greenhouse and the information centre is not to look at a moment in isolation but to look at an event within a life-long process. Still, the specific event of visiting the zoo's Masoala exhibit is for the average visitor likely to be an exceptionally prominent and input-intense moment within that process. This, I believe, makes it meaningful to ethnographically investigate visitors' perceptions at the moment they are actually exposed to this input. Thus I ask: What does the exhibit make people think about? Does it actually make them reflect about Madagascar, and if so, which images emerge?

Schemas

Perception is likely to be strongly influenced by schemas. As a prelude to this point, imagine a family on a rainy Sunday afternoon. They decide to go for a visit to the zoo which, like other zoos, offers a number of attractions for children. They stroll about, visit the children's favourite animals, check out the new lion enclosure, have a bite in one of the restaurants and round off their stay by visiting Little Masoala. They approach the rainforest exhibit through the tunnel and then enter the greenhouse's pleasant warmth. Taking off their jackets, they start strolling along the tarred path that leads visitors from one end of the greenhouse to the other, admiring the giant tortoises on the left, spotting, if they are lucky, a chameleon in the bushes or a group of noisy lemurs in the trees, throwing a glance at the waterfall. They might briefly stop at the 'little house', peak into the interior and perhaps have a version of the following conversation:

Child: Daddy, does someone live in here?
Father: Not here in the zoo, but that is how people in the jungle live.
Mother: If you look at how these people live, we really should be more grateful for what we have.

… and then they move on. Most people I spoke to inside the exhibit admitted that although on arrival at the zoo they had intended to properly visit Little Masoala rather than simply walking through it on their way out, they now felt too tired after several hours visiting other parts of the zoo to engage with it thoroughly.

But even for those visitors who are still in good shape when they arrive at the greenhouse, like the imaginary family above, their time at Little Masoala is but a brief moment in their lives, an exotic world they enter and leave within the space of a quarter of an hour, and the thoughts that might cross their minds or the emotions that might take hold of them while strolling about in the tropical heat are likely to soon be forgotten until revived at another occasion. When trying to understand visitors' perceptions of what they encounter in the exhibit, it is important to realise that many fail to engage with it deeply, at least at the consciously reflexive level. Most visitors stroll through the exhibit without looking at anything in any depth but merely glance at things that happen to meet their eye. Thus by urging those I spoke with to consciously gather their thoughts, I might have constructed a deeper engagement with the content of the exhibit than they would otherwise have had. At the same time, a person visiting the exhibit does not enter it with an empty mind. Even if someone has never before consciously thought about Madagascar or the Malagasy people, her or his mind will already be equipped with ideas and assumptions about such notions as 'the tropics', 'the jungle', 'rainforests', 'wilderness', 'science', 'the Third World', 'civilisation', 'development', 'Nature', 'aesthetics' or 'Africa' as a result of previous inputs and influences throughout their lives. Such ideas and assumptions will bear on how people process what they meet at the Masoala exhibit.

Schema theory has shown (see Bartlett 1932; D'Andrade 1995: chapter 6; Strauss and Quinn 1997; Quinn 2005c, 2011) that the human mind tends to perceive and process information on the basis of already established schemas.

> A schema is a generic version of (some part of) the world built up from experience and stored in memory. The schema is generic – . . . simplified and prototypical – because it is the cumulative outcome of just those features of successive experiences that are alike. Although schemas can change, those built on repeated experiences of a similar sort become relatively stable, influencing our interpretations of subsequent experiences more than they are altered by them. (Quinn 2005c: 38)

In simpler words, a schema is what one considers to be typical of, and thus assumes about, and expects of, a particular phenomenon, activity, place, time, event or any other concrete or abstract entity on the basis of what one has already learnt about the world. Schemas are clusters of established ideas about something, 'networks of strongly connected cognitive elements that represent the generic concepts stored in memory' (Strauss and Quinn 1997: 6) which have developed in the course of one's life on the basis of experiences in the world.

Schemas operate largely at an unconscious level. For example, probably close to everyone who has grown up in Switzerland will have a zoo schema in their mind. Thus a Swiss family visiting the Zurich zoo does not need to be told upon arrival that a zoo is a place where one goes to see animals, that one runs no risk taking small children to see lions or crocodiles as all dangerous animals will be kept safely behind bars, that one has to pay to be allowed in, that there will likely be a playground and places to have a bite to eat, and so on. Having this kind of knowledge about the world enables us to act competently and at appropriate speed in everyday life. It is uncontroversial that schemas are a central human mechanism for processing and storing information (cf. Quinn 2011). Schemas are like '"scaffolding" [Clark 1997: 46], that reframe and assist our performance of everyday cognitive tasks' (Quinn 2005c: 45). Schemas are 'already in the air, and available to think with' (Quinn 2011: 38). On the less uplifting side of things, these very same, life-necessary schemas make us inclined to only 'take in' what we already believe to be true about a specific phenomenon in the world, while tending to make us somewhat blind towards that which does not fit our expectations. Schemas thus prompt us to be, automatically and unconsciously, mentally conservative.

Not only do schemas greatly influence what we are inclined to perceive and to store as relevant information, they also come into play rapidly. One of the key features of schemas is the fact that they are activated by *minimal* input – by a word, a physical object, a visual representation, a sound, a smell, the humidity of the air. For example, even a cursory glance at the African-looking faces among the photographs displayed on the walls of the entry tunnel to Little Masoala can activate multiple, interrelated schemas (cf. Strauss and Quinn 1997: 48–54) and spark a firework of thoughts and assumptions in someone's mind. This means that the inferences we make from minimal input go well beyond the information actually provided, with the activated schemas filling in gaps and missing links. From seeing a photograph of a dark-skinned woman carrying a bucket on her head and a baby on her back, for example, a visitor to the zoo's Masoala exhibit may assume or believe to know all sorts of things about that person's way of life, abilities and world views.

Schema theorists like Naomi Quinn and Claudia Strauss emphasise that although schemas are impressively robust, even in the face of contrary information, they are not carved in stone but can be modified and changed. Schemas 'are rooted in experience without ever hardening beyond all possibility of change' (Strauss and Quinn 1997: 84). Emotions and 'social evaluations' about what is good and what is bad play a key role with regard to both the durability and modification of schemas (ibid.: 90–108). However, it seems to be considerably less clear how and under which circumstances schemas actually do change than it is why they do not (cf. ibid.: 90–101). The overall evidence points to a remarkable robustness of schemas which is precisely what is so noteworthy about them. Thus when we encounter information that fails to fit a schema we have in our mind, we are much more likely to ignore it or to interpret it as an exception or to otherwise neglect its potential than we are to modify the relevant schema.

Coming back to my initial observation that for many people a visit to Little Masoala represents but a brief and, in certain ways, 'on the surface' engagement with it, I now have to qualify that. It is true that many visitors walk through the exhibit – the tunnel, the greenhouse, the information centre – without ever pausing to have a closer look at anything in particular, thus often missing the things they have probably come to see in the first place like a lemur dozing on a branch right above their heads. Nonetheless, at the implicit level at which schemas operate, even the least observant visitors *are* engaging with the exhibit's content by the very fact that certain of their deep-rooted, unconscious mental representations are being activated by way of association with whatever they perceive while walking through Little Masoala.

Modification?

While recognising that a visit to Little Masoala is but one event within a continual process of the formation of ideas about things in the world that visitors associate with the exhibit's content, and also recognising that explicit talk is rarely a direct window to thought, as well as taking into account that two-thirds of the people I spoke with had visited the exhibit on one or several previous occasions and were thus not being exposed to it for the first time, I nonetheless wanted to understand whether being exposed to explicit and focused information about Madagascar and being exposed to the sensual impressions inside the greenhouse might have an effect, albeit perhaps only short-term, on people's ideas about Madagascar and the Malagasy people. Would an exhibit that is explicitly presented as being about Madagascar, and that offers a wide range of information about the island's flora and fauna, human population, geography, history, economy and politics, actually bring Madagascar home to visitors, and if so, in which ways? And what would be the effect of Madagascar being presented through the lens of Nature conservation on visitors' imaginations of the country and its people?

In order to address these issues, I approached visitors randomly at various places along the path through the exhibit, in particular at the two entrances/exits (the tunnel and the shop) in order to catch both those about to enter Little Masoala and those about to leave it. It turned out that there was no systematic difference between these two groups of visitors with respect to their responses to my questions. The difference between 'before' and 'after' was no greater than that between the individual statements of different visitors at the same spot. It therefore appears reasonable to infer that a visit to Zurich zoo's Masoala exhibit does not modify pre-existing schemas but activates and further nourishes them. Actually, this is hardly surprising. As we have seen, the information provided at the zoo does not in any way challenge the dominant Madagascar discourse in Switzerland. Rather, it exemplifies it. Moreover, my data indicates that when there is a mismatch between what visitors expect and what they find at the zoo's exhibit, they react as schema theory would predict: they tend not to 'see' the ill-fitting information. Such an incongruity between what the zoo seems to want to get across to visitors, on the one hand, and what the latter take in, on the other – a mismatch between intention and perception, in other words – can be observed with regard to the question of who are the culprits of deforestation in Madagascar. In the zoo's own public statements concerning its commitment to rainforest conservation in Masoala, the chief reason leading to deforestation in Masoala is claimed to be the local farming practice of slash-and-burn rice cultivation, a practice that is furthermore said to be caused by poverty and cultural traditions. Additionally, the zoo also points a finger at illegal timber trade causing massive destructions within the Masoala National Park. These two purported causes of deforestation in Masoala have received different amounts of attention in different zoo-related publications over the course of the past ten years, but on the whole, the former (i.e. naming local farming practices as the chief cause) clearly prevails. In the Masoala exhibit's information centre, too, both causes are explained and illustrated in several places, but if one were to judge which one of the two messages is more prominently highlighted, the scales would clearly be tilting again to local farmers being the chief culprits of deforestation. However, the visitors do not seem to take this message on board easily (although my sample with regard to this specific point is admittedly small). Those visitors who have not yet been to the information centre often attribute deforestation in Madagascar to local people in search of agricultural land as much as they do to large-scale commercial plundering of the forest. For visitors who have visited the information centre, illegal logging that is often orchestrated by criminal groups, chiefly from outside Madagascar, becomes more salient than local farmers' agricultural practices, despite the fact that in the information centre the latter is given considerably more space.[5] I suggest, therefore, that the message that local farmers are to blame is not easy to embrace for many visitors, because denouncing poor subsistence farmers as culprits violates the visitors' sense of morality. It is morality to which I now turn.

Notes

1. These include: a special magazine entitled *Masoala Regenwald. Ein Naturschutz-Projekt des Zoo Zürich* published in the opening year (Rübel 2003a); the 2003 edition of the periodical of the Zoological Society Zurich (IRBIS 2003); regularly published zoo magazines (*Zooh Journal, Zooh Magazine, Zooh News*) in which the Masoala project has already featured several times as the cover story and which, in almost every edition, give readers news about various aspects of the Masoala project in Switzerland and/or Madagascar (the zoo magazines are sent to the members of the Zoological Society, which includes all visitors with an annual entry ticket, and they are available at every ticket counter at the zoo for very little money); the zoo's website in which the Masoala project has a prominent place, including over the years only slightly changing information about a wide range of issues; the zoo's press releases as well as a press kit (Zurich Zoo 2011a); an article entitled 'Three years of experience running the Masoala Rainforest ecosystem at Zurich Zoo, Switzerland', published in the *International Zoo Yearbook* 2007(41): 203–16, co-authored by

four people of whom three work at the zoo in Zurich. All quotations below are my translations from the original German.
2. During the first ten years of the exhibit's existence (1997–2006), the zoo provided an additional $10,000 (U.S.) per year as part of an agreement with the Malagasy political authorities (personal communication with the director of Zurich zoo, Dr Alex Rübel, 3 July 2006).
3. Stepan (2001: 35) has noted that 'writing that mixture of adventure and scientific fact' was characteristic of the period during which the concept of 'the tropics' emerged (see pp. 90–91).
4. Retrieved 16 May 2006, 12 June 2009 and 5 August 2012 (the cited texts have remained identical) from http://www.zoo.ch/xml_1/internet/de/application/d1/d1971/d72/f73.cfm
5. My sample with regard to this specific question comprises 39 visitors; at the time I spoke to them, 24 had not yet entered the information centre while the other 15 were about to leave it. Of those yet to visit the information centre, 8 considered local people to be the culprits of deforestation, 9 blamed multinational illegal logging, and 7 both. Of the 15 about to leave the information centre, 4 considered local people to be the culprits, 8 multinational illegal logging, and 3 both.

CHAPTER 3

Zooming In on Morality

Before examining, in this and the following two chapters, visitors' perceptions of the Masoala exhibit at Zurich zoo, it is useful to briefly give some information about their background.

Visitors' Background

I am not aware of any available systematic information as to which socio-economic groups tend to visit the Zurich zoo, or Swiss zoos in general. The European Association of Zoos and Aquariums, EAZA, has launched a 'Visitors Studies Working Group', but there are no results available as of yet (EAZA 2010: 11–13; 2011). International studies suggest that 'by and large, museum visitors are of higher than average socioeconomic level. These findings apply equally to visitors of art museums, science museums, arboreta, and zoos; they apply as well cross-culturally, to visitors in the U.S.A., Canada, Sweden, and Great Britain' (Falk and Dierking 2002: 21). Furthermore, the same authors have found that the more popular a museum, the more 'people in low socioeconomic brackets tend to visit' it (ibid.: 22). Thus, if these observations are also correct for Switzerland, and if it is true, as the zoo itself claims, that since the opening of Little Masoala it has become the most often visited cultural institution in the country (Rübel 2004), it would seem that visitors to Zurich zoo belong to the lower socio-economic levels within a socio-economically higher than average section of society. On the basis of my own research (see below), I consider it very likely that visitors to the zoo in Zurich include people from a broad range of backgrounds and that they are a fairly good mirror of Swiss society at large. This suggestion requires two qualifications, however. First, with extremely few exceptions, those strolling about in Little Masoala are white (international studies confirm this observation; see Falk and Dierking 2002: 23). Second, first-generation immigrants are strikingly absent among the visitors to Little Masoala. Randomly approaching people at the exhibit, I hardly ever hit on someone (except for tourists from places like Germany, the U.S.A. or Japan) who was not fully competent in the Swiss dialect or spoke it with a foreign accent as would likely be the case with first-generation immigrants. It is possible that the high entrance fees to the zoo are prohibitive to this section of Swiss society or that other, perhaps cultural reasons play a role. The history of zoos in general is closely linked with the history of Western Europe (Rothfels 2002), and it is at least a reasonable thought that visiting a zoo on a Sunday afternoon may be less of an obvious thing to do for people originating from the Balkans, for example (they form a large section of Swiss immigrant society), than for those who have grown up in Switzerland.

Saving Nature – Helping the Poor

For most of the 125 visitors or small groups of visitors I spoke with, the key message promoted at the exhibit relates to a universally applicable ecological message against the destruction of Nature by humankind, and the moral imperative to act against it. The exhibit is perceived as asking people to appreciate the intrinsic beauty of Nature and to make them aware of what we stand to lose if the destruction of the planet's natural environment continues at its present pace. Statements like the following by a couple in their mid-fifties are typical: 'It's very nice how Nature is brought close to children here. One learns to observe. And it's good to show what still exists so that one realises what is being destroyed.' For many visitors, the message is specifically about the world's threatened primary forests (*Urwälder*, see chapter 4) and rainforests, and the need to put these under protection. Almost half the respondents specifically mentioned the destruction of the rainforest as an issue.

Close to a third of the visitors I talked to failed to realise that the exhibit concerns Madagascar. Having walked through the tunnel and the greenhouse, and sometimes even after having passed through the information centre, these visitors speculated that the exhibit might have concerned Amazonia or perhaps the jungle in Borneo, or else they had no idea which country the exhibit might be connected with.[1] About half the people who answered in this way had been to Little Masoala at least once, and in some cases many times, before the day I met them.

Even among those who recognise the connection between the zoo's Masoala exhibit and Madagascar, only a comparatively small number perceive its central message to be Madagascar-specific as opposed to 'about the rainforest in general'. Those who do, tend to emphasise the island's unique flora and fauna and extraordinary levels of endemism and to rapidly turn to the topic of deforestation. Doing so, visitors identify and variously weigh and highlight two major causes leading to the loss of rainforests in Madagascar, as briefly discussed in the last chapter: (a) unscrupulous industrial logging of precious wood for export, positing the Malagasy farmers as victims who must be protected against such schemes; and (b) destruction caused by local farmers themselves who are in need of agricultural land.

The farmers, for their part, are thought to act unsustainably for one of two reasons. Many visitors consider the core of the problem to be their failure to envisage the consequences of their agricultural practices, especially slash-and-burn cultivation. According to this line of thinking, farmers therefore need to be educated and instructed about methods of sustainable land use, as suggested in the following statement by a young woman: 'A certain percentage of the money raised at the restaurant is donated in order to educate people there so that they take better care of Nature, and to help them to make environmentally friendly plantations, and sustainable tourism, too – perhaps also in order to support them against poachers. But the main point is schooling.' If not because of a perceived lack of environmental foresight, Malagasy farmers are thought to cause deforestation due to dire poverty and the lack of alternatives. This situation is interpreted as calling for development projects helping the poor to find new means of income so that they no longer *need* to destroy the forest.

A Doubly Moral Act

The various ways of reasoning – about Nature conservation in general and deforestation in Madagascar in particular – that zoo visitors put forward carries a clear message that supporting Nature conservation serves a double purpose: saving endangered fauna and flora from extinction while, at the same time, helping the poor.

> [The Masoala exhibit] is about the diversity of animals and plants. It's impressive. It's a poor country. It's about the support by the zoo for this particular region. The people there also benefit from this, from the support for the rainforest; they get jobs for example. (Couple in their thirties)
>
> The zoo makes sure that the primary forest is being protected but also that the people there are able to make a living without having to cut down the forest. (Elderly couple)
>
> The Zurich zoo does both: Nature protection and development aid. They also give money. (Man in his fifties)

Both elements of this double purpose – to protect Nature and to help the poor – are invested with great moral weight for many a zoo visitor. This became especially clear in the *way* people talked about the purpose of the Masoala exhibit, more than by *what* they said. Their tone of voice and other hard-to-pin-down indicators of the quality of their statements seemed to me to clearly suggest that for them Nature conservation was, first and foremost, a *moral* imperative.

There is an interesting question to be thought about in this context which, however, my data does not allow me to answer: Is the notion of Nature conservation as a moral duty connected with Protestant ethics which, in Switzerland, obviously play a significant role, and if so, in which ways? Also, following Weber's seminal essay (1988, first published in 1904/5), there is evidently a vast body of philosophical and other literature on the topic of European Protestant morality. It would, however, go beyond the scope of this book to engage with the extensive discussions on this issue. Suffice it to say for our purposes here that I employ the term 'morality' to refer to a sense of having an inner obligation to adhere to certain incontrovertible values – an obligation to ask oneself 'What is right and what is wrong?' and to act in compliance with the answer to this question.

The following quotation from a discussion I had with a woman of about seventy years of age expresses the moral aspects of Nature conservation more directly than most other visitors did. I approached her at the exit of the information centre. She had both listened to the virtual flight over the Masoala peninsula and seen the film on rosewood logging that is shown in the information centre's small cinema area. She was one of the few people I ever met at Little Masoala who were visiting the Masoala exhibit for the first time the day I met them. My questions are in italics:

What do you think the Masoala exhibit is about?
It's about Madagascar, about the cutting down of the rainforest.
When you now, after having visited the greenhouse and the information centre, think of Madagascar, what comes to mind?
The rainforest there is being cut down. It's crazy how everything is being destroyed. Nature is being destroyed completely. One heard this from this pilot [the virtual flight], he discovered slash-and-burn fires (*Brandrodungen*).
Who do you think causes these fires?
Well, those who want to make profit! The workers hardly earn anything, I think 250 Swiss Francs per year, but those who make all the profit earn 250,000 Francs! [This information is given in the film on rosewood logging that she had just seen]. It's not the people; it's those wanting to make profit. It's all about corruption. It takes nine men nine days to cut down just one of those pieces of rosewood [shown lying on a pile in the film]. But others will make the profit.
'In Madagascar [she reads from the text on the board we are standing beneath], an area of rainforest as large as the entire Masoala Hall is destroyed

every 5 minutes!' You see, the two of us have perhaps been talking for five minutes now and already within this short time another piece of rainforest has disappeared. That makes one really sad.
And what comes to mind when you think of the people of Madagascar?
Poverty. I feel so sorry for them. Only because of profit! These people are being totally exploited.

Later on in our discussion, she said:

> It is good that such information is provided, like this Swiss man who is missing . . . [looking for the name of Bruno Manser, a famous Swiss rainforest activist who went missing several years previously – I suggest his name] . . . Bruno Manser, that's it. Why did he go missing? Because he stood up for the rainforest! There are such people also in Madagascar, like this pilot that we heard [she seems to have understood the virtual flight's pilot to be a real person]. That takes courage, that's a dangerous job. One needs such people.

Other visitors expressed views like: 'The Malagasy are a very poor people and therefore need development aid so that they can lead a better life'; 'One ought to help the poor peoples much more often, especially in Africa, so that they also receive better education and proper laws'; or 'The Malagasy need help to protect the rainforest because their infrastructure is bad'. These statements were made without any further qualification of why one ought to provide such help. Indeed, there is no need to further qualify why one ought to help if one considers doing so to be a self-evident moral imperative.

Visitors' inclination to see profit-oriented big business as the chief cause of deforestation in Madagascar, even though the available information at the zoo points more strongly to local farmers as the immediate culprits, is another indication that their understanding of the purpose of Nature conservation is strongly moralised. First, they are reluctant to point a finger at poor peasants in a poor country. Moreover, when visitors do hold farmers responsible for the loss of rainforest, they often excuse them by reference to poverty, tradition or ignorance,[2] as in the following examples:

> The population is poor, they have no alternative but to cut down the *Urwald* (primary forest) in order to gain agricultural land, perhaps also to sell expensive woods. (Couple in their early to mid-twenties)

> The people are backward-oriented. The traditions are very important, the ancestral cult. This is an obstacle for development aid. Because even if the people understand that they ought to practise a new way of cultivation, they don't do so because the ancestors don't want them to, because it doesn't correspond to their traditions. They think in a very short-sighted manner, they don't understand that they are destroying their own living space. They have different values. That renders development aid really difficult. (Man in his mid-forties whose colleague is married to a Malagasy woman and who

had been in a team from the Swiss Federal Institute of Technology working in Madagascar)

The population who lives there is causing the deforestation. They have to live off something you know. And they would first need to develop an awareness of what is bad for them. (Woman in her mid-fifties)

There is no environmental awareness among the Malagasy. They don't know that if they continue like this, the resources will be exhausted at some point. (Couple in their mid-twenties; he intended to study eco-tourism)

It seems that holding poor peasants 'truly responsible' for something deemed bad is counter-intuitive for many visitors. This is, I suggest, because it violates their sense of morality.

As mentioned above, not everyone who visits the Masoala exhibit realises that it is to do with Madagascar. However, the difference in perception between those who recognise the connection to Madagascar and those who do not is not as big as one might at first assume. Both those who are mentally looking towards Madagascar when inside Little Masoala and those who may be looking towards Brazil or some other distant, unnamed tropical country see, when looking at whatever rainforest conservation project they imagine the exhibit to represent, just that: namely, *a* rainforest conservation project. Even those who recognise the exhibit's connection to Madagascar or, in many fewer cases, to the Masoala peninsula, appear to think of it primarily as a reminder of the urgent duty to contribute towards saving Nature. Madagascar thereby becomes a means to the end of passing on the message that to support Nature conservation is to act morally. In other words, for many people Little Masoala is a space for thinking about morality rather than a space for thinking about Madagascar.

Emotionally Charged

Not all ideas carry the same force. Thus, what is it that renders certain ideas or networks of ideas (i.e. schemas) particularly solid and powerful? Certainly, strong schemas are not merely the cumulative outcome of a lot of input of a certain kind, and to view schemas in such arithmetic terms would be to grossly oversimplify matters. In their discussion of the force of schemas, Strauss and Quinn highlight the importance of emotions (1997: 92–93, 101–8). '[E]motional arousal ... helps make learning "stick"' (ibid.: 93). Furthermore, issues that are associated with '[i]deas about goodness and badness' (ibid.: 94) are especially likely to be emotional (ibid.: 103). If one follows these insights, the notion of Nature conservation is particularly powerful because it is strongly linked with evaluations of what it means to do good, and is, therefore, emotionally charged. In fact, I believe that the reason I perceived visitors' statements to be, more than anything else, statements about 'morality' was precisely because I could sense the emotionality of their statements.

Moreover, when emotionally charged ideas are learnt during early childhood, the force of what has been learnt is further enhanced: '[T]he feelings activated by very early experience will be strong ones, and to the degree that these early feelings are tied to emerging ideas about being good and being bad, these ideas, the emotions attached to them, and the motivations to be good and not to be bad that these emotions activate, will also be exceptionally powerful' (Strauss and Quinn 1997: 101–8). Most children growing up in Switzerland will learn from an early age that 'it is a bad thing to wilfully harm Nature'. Toddlers are taught not to carelessly tread on, for example, an earthworm, and older children are scolded if they are seen inflicting pain on animals, however small. When having an outdoors picnic, parents are likely to tell their children not to leave any rubbish behind as this 'is not good for Nature'. Children hear adults exchanging remarks about the beauty of butterflies and flowers, and many are taken to mountain tops to admire the view.

The idea of protecting Nature as a moral imperative thus has all the ingredients that would, according to Strauss and Quinn, render it exceptionally solid and powerful: it is learnt in early childhood, it is coupled with a social evaluation of what it means to be a good person, and it therefore carries enormous emotional force.[3]

A Timeless, Quasi-religious Truth

The visitors to the zoo in Zurich are not alone in considering Nature conservation an act of morality. The notion of Nature conservation as a moral cause amounts to a powerful paradigm in contemporary Swiss society as elsewhere in the global North (besides other reasons for embracing the global agenda of Nature conservation). Living in Switzerland one is, through various media channels, routinely presented, not to say bombarded, with the message that to save Nature is to act morally. Since the opening of the Masoala exhibit in 2003, Swiss media coverage about Madagascar and especially Masoala has skyrocketed,[4] and has promoted, in an astoundingly consistent manner, the following basic message: 'By educating the Malagasy and making them understand and consequently embrace Nature conservation, one not only saves the rainforest and many extraordinary animals found nowhere else in the world before it is too late, but one also rescues a nation on a suicide track: one stops the Malagasy from destroying the very habitat upon which the survival of both the island's wonderful wildlife and they themselves depend'.

Given the omnipresence of the Nature conservation paradigm, it is hardly surprising that a great number of the visitors to the zoo's Masoala exhibit with whom I spoke (re)produced the idea of Nature conservation being an act of morality, often in the kind of blueprint language that Candace Slater (2003: 19) has coined 'Environmentalese'. I do not mean this ironically; the quest for morality is genuine on the part of people like the visitors to the zoo's Masoala exhibit.

Roderick F. Nash (1989) has traced the historical trajectory of the idea that Nature has certain intrinsic rights and that it is our moral responsibility to respect these. He proposes that 'the rights of nature' are the conceptual extension of the originally European idea (going back, in its explicit formulation, to the seventeenth century) that certain beings have certain intrinsic rights. These rights were first granted to white men and then gradually extended to include all humans. Eventually, they were also assigned to certain animal species and, finally, to all non-human living things, including plants. The idea of intrinsic rights is, according to Nash, the basis of Euro-American morality. The zoo visitors' perception of the Masoala exhibit as, above all, a moral cause fits this view well.[5]

Not only is the conservation paradigm centred around the notion of acting morally. The notion of Nature's intrinsic, axiomatic worth entails a commitment to Nature conservation as a 'timeless standar[d] of truth' (Tsing 2005: 120), a truth beyond any particular time or place. The conservation paradigm is thus invested with universal moral authority. From this perspective, the Masoala biodiversity conservation project is self-evidently a moral enterprise which, therefore, requires no further justification.

The timeless, axiomatic worth of Nature, on which the Nature conservation paradigm is based, gives it a transcendental, quasi-religious quality, thereby continuing a long historical pedigree of visions of Nature as embodying God's creation, of Nature as sacred (concerning this idea in the Swiss context in particular, see Harries 2007: 124–30). 'The rain forest . . . is a concentrated form of a nature in which very different people have long perceived religious meanings and which often acquires the force of the sacred in an increasingly secular world' (Slater 2003: 9). In today's conservationist vision, Nature is a coherent and 'singular global system uniting all life' (Tsing 2005: 91), a strangely beautiful chain of predator–prey relations in which every species has its rightful place. Nature exists beyond human time, space and endeavours – it just *is*, like God is for believers.

The quasi-religious, awe-inspiring quality of the contemporary concept of Nature was brought home to me when I watched the BBC's 2011 four-part documentary on Malagasy Nature, 'Madagascar: The Land Where Evolution Ran Wild', an abbreviated German version of which was also shown on the first channel of the Swiss public broadcasting corporation at prime transmission time. It is hard to imagine anyone who has been socialised in a country like Switzerland not being awestruck when watching the pictures of wondrous creatures like the giraffe-necked weevil, or seeing a sifaka lemur jumping from one seriously thorny tree to the next without hurting its feet; nobody knows how it does it. Reflecting on my own emotions as I was watching the documentary, I sensed precisely that quasi-religious awe taking hold of me that is so difficult to put into words.

Conclusion

Because contemporary Nature conservation projects are perceived as attempts to respect a timeless moral truth – namely the sanctity of Nature – for many visitors, Little Masoala, which presents Madagascar through the lens of Nature conservation, is a space for thinking about morality and a space for reflecting about one's own moral duties more than anything else. Consequently, the exhibit's focus on Madagascar and on the Masoala peninsula is lost in many visitors' perception of it. In other words, by zooming in on questions of morality, visitors to a certain extent erase Madagascar and Masoala from the picture. This is somewhat ironic if we consider the fact that rescuing the rainforest on Masoala was chosen as the zoo's flagship project precisely because of the peninsula's biological uniqueness.

In her insightful study of development schemes in Indonesia, Tania Murray Li (2007) examines the Western 'will to improve' people in other places. She questions the nature of this agenda, and points to the historical tradition of the idea that 'trustees' – a position defined by the claim to know what is best for others (ibid.: 4) – from Canada, for instance, should travel all the way to Sulawesi in order to reform the 'hill tribes' there. She finds that the basic concept underpinning 'the will to improve' has little changed since the colonial era (ibid.: 282), and that it is always coupled with the notion that those to be reformed are in some way or another deficient (ibid.: 122), often, interestingly, in terms of their use of natural resources (ibid.: 21). 'The will to improve' is a manifestation of power relations, as its inherent claim to be in possession of what those in need of being improved lack is a claim to superiority. These aspects are recognisable in many statements made by zoo visitors. I have met a few who consciously reflected about the power relations inherent in wanting to educate the Malagasy about Nature conservation. For the vast majority, however, improving Malagasy agricultural practices through education (thereby removing ignorance and traditionalism) and improving farmers' lives through development aid (thereby removing poverty) is an uncontroversial, doubly moral act, no more, no less.

At the same time as recognising inherent power asymmetries, it is important, Li emphasises, to understand the morality underlying 'the will to improve' as reflecting *genuinely* felt moral obligations on the part of most of those who embrace it. 'The will to improve' is not necessarily a cover-up for 'hidden motives of profit or domination' (ibid.: 9) but is often a real force driving 'an earnest desire' to help (ibid.: 134). This, too, makes a lot of sense when we think about the zoo visitors. Their support of the Masoala Nature conservation project as a matter of moral duty is clearly genuine, and is neither cynical nor dishonest.

Notes

1. Thirty-seven per cent of those I interviewed *before* they entered the greenhouse were unaware of the exhibit's connection with Madagascar. This number dropped to 30 per cent in the case of those visitors I interviewed *after* their visit to the greenhouse and to a still remarkably high 25 per cent of those who had also visited the information centre.
2. Of the twenty-two respondents who referred to local farmers as (also) being responsible for deforestation, fourteen provided such an explanation.
3. A different line of thought with regard to the question of why it is that certain ideas or schemas are more powerful than others is offered by Sperber in his theory of the 'epidemiology of representations' (1985, reprinted in Sperber 1996). Sperber asks why it is that certain cultural representations spread more easily than others so that we find them time and again in unrelated societies around the world. He argues that when a cultural representation corresponds well with a particular 'psychological susceptibility' (1996: 57, emphasis removed), a hardwired cognitive predisposition in the human mind, it becomes 'catchy' (ibid.: 58) – that is, easy to adopt and to remember.
4. Since 2003, I have collected 60 media items from daily newspapers, local neighbourhood journals, sports newsletters, Nature and travel magazines, and television (school) programmes and documentaries.
5. I am aware that there is a vast body of literature on the topic of 'rights' of human and of non-human life, but it does not fall within the scope of this book.

CHAPTER 4

A Kind of People

A People-Free Land

Approaching visitors at various points in and directly outside of the Masoala exhibit, I engaged them in conversations about their understanding of the purpose of Little Masoala, as well as asking their thoughts about Madagascar and the Malagasy people. My questions brought to the surface slumbering ideas and images and, at the same time, revealed what visitors do *not* seem to reflect about in connection with the exhibit. When I asked visitors, without any further specification, what came to mind when they thought of Madagascar, references to lush rainforests and rare, endangered animals came bubbling out and were quite obviously readily available in most visitors' minds. In contrast, when asked about their ideas and images concerning the *people* of Madagascar, a great many visitors were at a complete loss to say anything at all, admitting – in fact, discovering – that they had never before thought about the human population of Madagascar. Large numbers answered – often after a few seconds of silence and mental head-scratching – that they had absolutely no idea. In other words, a 'Madagascar schema' is easily activated but it often has no people in it. One young man expressed this explicitly: 'One doesn't know anything about the people there. When one thinks of Madagascar, one thinks of animals. One gets the impression that there are no people there at all. They are probably *Urvölker* (aboriginal peoples). But whether they are yellow or red or . . .? Ever since hearing about Madagascar even as a child, one only hears about the biodiversity there'.

Visiting the information centre does, however, have an impact in this respect. Of those visitors in my sample who had not (yet) visited it, about a quarter (25 out of 93) mentioned the population in some way or another without any probing on my part. In the case of those visitors whom I spoke to as they came out of the information centre, this number rose to about half (17 out of 32). Many of the mentions in both cases were, however, but brief references to the Malagasy's poverty and their assumed simplicity of life. The absence of people in the imaginations of Madagascar of large numbers of zoo visitors is one of the most striking findings of the present study. I argue that because for visitors Nature conservation is strongly associated with the idea of 'doing good', the exhibit becomes a space where they reflect about their own morality, rather than being a space for thinking about Madagascar. When I then came along enquiring about their images concerning the people of Madagascar, they were, more than anything else, astounded and somewhat bewildered. In these cases, their first reaction was almost invariably of the kind: 'Oh, the *people* there, gosh, I never thought about *them*!'

In the school classes with whom I spoke, too, human beings played an utterly marginal role in the pupils' imaginations of Madagascar. A sixteen-year-old pupil in a grammar school class explained:[1]

> I always feel that there are no people living in Madagascar, that's my impression.
> *Can you say why you have this impression?* I enquired.
> Because the only thing one hears is that researchers go there and what they have discovered, that's probably why.

A classmate of hers added:

> I think one just always only hears about animals and trees, but never about people. One never talks about the people of Madagascar. For example, in the Masoala Hall people are not mentioned – or in the animation film *Madagascar*, or things like that, there are never any people.

With some of the primary school children, discussions at times took a truly unexpected turn.

Of Skeletons and 'Dead Bones'

At the beginning of my discussions with the pupils of various school classes, I always asked them, without further specification, what came to mind when they thought of Madagascar. Similar to the adult visitors to the zoo, pupils from all age groups saw Madagascar as 'a jungly place', as their spontaneous responses to this question almost invariably mentioned animals, palm trees, the jungle or the rainforest, and the hot climate. The human population was simply not part of the picture or only to a very limited degree. When I asked the pupils explicitly whether there was anything they knew about the *people* of Madagascar, often their first reaction was silence; some children, especially at the primary school level, kept sliding back to the world of animals and plants despite my prompting them several times to talk about what they knew about the people.

Many pupils, in fact, believed that there are only a few people living in Madagascar, and were utterly astonished when they heard that there are big towns and millions of inhabitants – this was not how they imagined a 'jungly place'. In five out of six primary school classes who had not visited the zoo's Masoala exhibit, the question as to whether or not there were *any* people living in Madagascar was raised by the children themselves, with many among them being uncertain and some asserting that there were none. Consider the following conversation I had with the children of a 1st-grade primary school class (aged about seven). Their answers to my opening question were thus:

> Denise: There are giraffes and things like that.
> Véronique: There are lions and animals.
> Jenny: And often, there are monkeys, too.
> Véronique: There are also black people, kind of.
> Elisabeth: And many trees and palms trees.
> Gentrit: Zebras.
> Alfrid: Dead people.

I asked Alfrid what he meant; it turned out that he thought that the people had been eaten by animals such as lions. The conversation continued:

> Luna: There are tigers, too.
> Asma: There are bones everywhere.
> *What do you mean by that?* I asked.
> Asma: Well, bones, dead bones.
> Luca: I know what she means. She means skeletons.
> Alfrid: I also meant skeletons.
> *Skeletons of what?* I asked. *Of animals or of what?*
> Luca: Of people.
> Asma: Yes.

I asked the children where they had learnt this, to which Alfrid responded that he had a DVD at home about 'Madagascar lions and big fish' and in which he had seen an aircraft and a pilot, and 'one pilot up in a treetop'.

> Ismael: There is this film!

At this point, all the children started to scream excitedly about the film, and Alfrid repeated: 'Only dead people'.

Clearly the children were referring to the Hollywood animation film *Madagascar* which was screened in Swiss cinemas in the summer of 2005 – the above discussion took place in 2008 – and which was extremely successful internationally (followed by two further films in 2008 and 2012 continuing the story).[2]

The storyline of the first part of the trilogy goes like this. Four animal friends from the New York Central Park Zoo – a lion, a zebra, a giraffe and a hippo – decide to run away in search of 'the wild'. After a number of adventures in New York City, the four friends end up packed in individual boxes on a ship headed for Africa. By accident, they are thrown off from the deck of the ship and are washed ashore in Madagascar where they, unexpectedly and happily, reunite. The first sight they get of the place they have ended up in is a sandy beach lined by a thick jungle of palm trees and baobabs making the zoo animals assume that they have landed in the zoo of San Diego. Feeling lost, they decide to go and look for the people who would surely be able to help them to return home. Soon they encounter a large group of lemurs engaged in a swinging party in honour of their king that is presided over by the royal spokeslemur. The two groups of animals have the following conversation (original English version):

> Lion (to his friends): We just have to ask these bozos where the people are.
> Lemur king: Excuse me, we bozos have the people, of course!
> Lion: Hey, the bozos have the people! Oh, well, great, good!
> Lemur king (pointing up into the treetops where a human skeleton with a helmet hangs from a tree): They are up there.

The zoo animals look up greatly astonished.

> Lemur king (grinning): Don't you love the people? Not a very lively bunch though.
> Lion: Oh, wow! So do you have any live people?
> Lemur king: Eh, no, only dead ones.
> Spokeslemur (laughing): I mean if we had a lot of live people here, it wouldn't be called 'the wild', would it?
> Lion: The wild?! Hold up there a second ... fuzz bucket, you mean like 'to live in a mud hut and wipe yourself with a leaf' type wild?
> Lemur king (laughing): Who wipes?

Horrified, the zoo animals run away. The story continues along several narrative lines. Eventually, they depart from Madagascar, continuing (in *Madagascar 2*) their adventure on the African mainland.

Throughout the film, Madagascar represents 'the wild'. At first, 'the wild' is scary to those from the civilisation of New York, but with time the zoo animals start to appreciate its beauty, and later on in the story they are informed by the lemur king that they have arrived 'In paradise! In Madagascar!' At the same time as being both dangerous and stunning, 'the wild' is marked by the absence of human beings. While the first part of the film, which is set in New York, involves various encounters with people, not a single human being ever appears once the zoo animals have arrived in Madagascar except in the shape of skeletons which are seen at various points in the course of the story. Who these skeletons once were is unclear, though it is suggested that they were the pilots and passengers of an aircraft, the wreck of which is shown lying in the jungle providing a meeting hall for the lemurs' gatherings. As a royal sceptre, the lemur king uses a human skeleton arm. It is 'nature' against 'culture', animals against humans, 'the wild' against 'civilisation', with Madagascar representing the 'natural, uncivilised wild' throughout the film.

In a 4th-grade class (pupils aged ten), there was a consensus among the children that 'Madagascar is intended primarily for animals' and that there were only a few people living there, while in another class of the same age group, the children (with the exception of one boy) associated 'the people in Madagascar' primarily with tourists and filmmakers.

> Jan: In Madagascar, there are no people.
> *Why do you think that?* I enquired.
> Jan: Well, there are tourists there, but nobody lives there.

This view was shared by an eight-year-old girl in another class:

> The animals are kind of at home there but the people are not there very often. Sometimes they are there, sometimes not.
> *And where would they be when they are not there?* I asked, not quite understanding at this point what she meant.
> Well, then they are at home or they travel to another country.

Obviously, the only people this girl could imagine in connection with Madagascar were tourists. In a 6th-grade class (pupils aged twelve), I asked the children what they had learnt from the animation film. One boy asserted: 'That there are no people there, well, only a few', and one of his classmates added: 'The people who are in Madagascar, well those who went into the jungle, they didn't emerge anymore, well, there were skeletons'.

In four out of the five primary school classes where the presence of human beings in Madagascar was controversial, the idea of Madagascar being primarily a place for animals was explicitly linked to the animation film.

Ambiguities

It seems rather astonishing that children as old as twelve would be willing to take literally the proposition suggested in the film's narrative that 'there are only dead people in Madagascar'. In order to better understand this phenomenon, I briefly turn to the studies by the developmental psychologist Paul Harris.

In his book 'The Work of the Imagination', Harris (2000) examines how children from as young as two enter into worlds of imagination, in particular through the pretend play that they engage in with adults, other children and by themselves. Harris shows that children move masterfully and competently between the world of imagination or fantasy and the empirical world, without getting muddled about what is imaginary and what is real. For example, they have no problem 'suspend[ing] objective truth in favour of make-believe truth' (ibid.: 10), and can 'wash' a teddy bear with make-believe water and make-believe soap while being perfectly clear that the teddy bear is not going to be empirically wet at the end of the procedure (ibid.: 9–10). They know that one can pretend things, and they know that one can agree with others to jointly enter a fantasy world and that everyone is aware that they are within a fantasy world without it being necessary for anybody to say so explicitly. Having the capacity to distinguish reality from worlds of imagination from early on, children are continuously on the lookout for signals that indicate to them what kind of phenomenon a particular entity is. In doing so, they screen information they encounter against their knowledge of the principles that apply in the world, and identify as fantasy anything that violates any such principle. This would explain why the primary school children easily identify a talking lemur king as a fantasy character without any explicit statement to that effect, because they know that animals do not speak human languages. When, however, their knowledge of the empirical world does not clarify things, children follow adult testimony very closely unless they have good reason not to trust the source of information (this last point is elaborated in Harris et al. 2006).

The information that children are offered in the animation film *Madagascar* is, however, ambiguous. On the one hand, some aspects of the film clearly identify it as being set in a fantasy world, especially the fact that all the animals can talk. None of the children in the classes I worked with ever suggested or wondered whether perhaps it was true that lions and zebras can speak German. On the other hand, the story is not set in 'Wonderland' or some distant galaxy that would be easily identifiable as a fantasy place. Rather, it is set in New York and Madagascar. Although it is possible that not all children would be entirely clear whether or not Madagascar is a real place,[3] it seems very likely that they would have heard of New York as a real place in the world. Thus the input as to whether the story is set in a fantasy or the real world is ambiguous. Furthermore, much of the information about Madagascar, such as that it is an island and that it represents 'the wild', is not presented in a way that would qualify it as a fantasy equivalent to talking animals. Overall, the input provided in the animation film is unclear: some information qualifies it as fantasy, while other bits qualify it as being set in real places. This mixture apparently makes it difficult for young children to decide which information is to be understood literally and which not. Thus some children are willing to accept the proposition that 'there are only dead people, only skeletons of human beings in Madagascar' as a real fact about the real world. After all, why should they know that there are people in Madagascar if this is not part of their world knowledge and if they are told the opposite? As Harris and his collaborators have shown (Harris et al. 2006), children closely follow adult guidance as part of the continual process of mental differentiation between reality and fantasy unless propositions offered by adults violate a principle of the world that the child knows to exist (such as that animals do not speak human languages). The proposition that 'Madagascar is a place where there are no living people' does not constitute such a violation. On the contrary, it fits the children's imagination of Madagascar as a 'jungly place' where people are at best of marginal significance perfectly well. Within such a framework, it seems possible to accept the proposition that Madagascar is a place *entirely* without people, leading some children to imagine that the only people present in Madagascar are tourists or filmmakers, or that the earlier inhabitants have all been swallowed up by the jungle.

Interestingly, listening to the story of Globi and Professor Pinfeather travelling to Madagascar in search of the supposedly extinct elephant bird, and hearing therein of a town with a million inhabitants, had the effect that many children recalled this information afterwards because it had challenged their previously held assumption that Madagascar was a place with almost no people. Schema theory would predict such recall because completely unexpected features tend to catch one's eye: 'under certain circumstances schema-*inconsistent* behavior will be especially noticeable and memorable, and especially likely to change a stereotype. One such circumstance is when schema-inconsistent behavior is exhibited by an otherwise good exemplar' (Strauss and Quinn 1997: 98, emphasis in the original). The story of Globi in Madagascar would have been such a case. Whether unexpected features change a schema in the long run, is, however, another question.

A Kind of People

After this first excursion into the world of the primary school children, I return to the adult visitors at the Zurich zoo's Masoala exhibit. Having at first been stuck for any answer to the question of how they imagine the people of Madagascar, many visitors attempted, after a few moments' reflection, to verbalise their thoughts. In doing so, the vast majority, including those who had visited the information centre, said things like: 'They are poor people', 'They live a very simple life', 'They are not civilised like us, not industrialised, but they are happier than us', 'They are poor people, they don't have schools or infrastructure', 'They are dark-skinned, it's a poor country', 'Like in Africa, they are dark, hardly modern, still close to Nature, backwards. They don't have hotel chains and luxury and so on'. One man, aged about sixty, classified the Malagasy as 'half-savages or savages' (*Halbwilde oder Wilde*) as did three young women (*eher wild, noch Wilde*). Others referred to the Malagasy as *Eingeborene* (natives), *Ureinwohner* (aboriginal inhabitants) or as *Urvolk* (an aboriginal people). These are different German expressions that are used interchangeably by many people and that in terms of meaning encompass the entire spectrum of the double image of the primitive/backward and the noble savage. The idea of an *Ur*-state is of particular importance here. The German prefix *Ur-* represents the idea of authenticity referring to something that has remained in a pristine and unspoilt state since time immemorial.

A considerable number of visitors rapidly turned to comments about other populations elsewhere in the world with whom they associated the Malagasy. The young man cited at the beginning of this chapter continued:

> It's like when the tsunami happened. There were these tiny islands where they then flew over to see whether the people there had survived or not. These are still *Urvölker*, they don't live within civilisation. They were shooting at the helicopters with their bows and arrows. One doesn't know anything at all about these people either [just as little as one knows about the Malagasy]. Perhaps these people sensed the tsunami coming as they are still *Urvölker*; they feel more than we do.

Having been asked about her images and ideas concerning the Malagasy, another person, a young woman, began to speak about a book called 'Child of the Jungle' (*Dschungelkind*) in which a daughter of German linguists and missionaries recounts her youth among the Fayu in West Papua – 'a lost tribe still living like in the stone age' [*einer vergessenen Stammesgesellschaft, die noch wie in der Steinzeit lebt*], as it says on the book's cover text. Another woman in her fifties wondered whether the people in Madagascar were perhaps pygmies? There were many more examples of this kind in which, in their imagination, visitors to Little Masoala merged the Malagasy with other populations from around the world, such as the 'tribes of the Amazon', the 'American Indians' [i.e. Native Americans] or the 'Australian Aborigines'. In other words, the Malagasy are imagined as an example of a category, as representing a 'kind' of people. As a member in a category of people, the Malagasy are substitutable by other examples of people who also qualify as members of, and represent, that same category.

I ended the last chapter by concluding that zoo visitors' zooming in to questions of morality when reflecting about what they encounter at the zoo leads to the perceptual erasure of Madagascar from the picture. In this chapter, I have thus far investigated what visitors to Little Masoala say about the Malagasy people when pushed to consciously reflect about them. The evidence suggests that they primarily reflect about the human population of Madagascar in terms of a *type* or a *kind* of people rather than thinking about the Malagasy as a specific group. As such the Malagasy are interchangeable with other representatives of the kind they stand for.

On the basis of my experience as a Swiss citizen, I consider it extremely unlikely that the same people who view the Malagasy as representatives of the category of *Ur*-inhabitants would think of, say, the Japanese or the Indians in the same way. The latter would likely be perceived as specific groups, as groups that have specific characteristics and specific histories, even if one knows very little or nothing about either, rather than as representing a type of people found in many different parts of the world. The difference lies not with unequal amounts of specific knowledge about specific others. The difference lies with the perceived presence or absence of the other's specificity, and an awareness or lack thereof of the historicity of a particular place. In many zoo visitors' imaginations, the Malagasy are seen as people *like* the Native Americans, *like* the *Ur*-inhabitants of Amazonia, *like* the pygmies, so that the human population, too, is erased from the picture. Despite the unprecedented visibility Madagascar has obtained thanks to the Zurich zoo's Masoala exhibit and the immense public attention paid to it, Madagascar and the Malagasy people are, in fact, 'invisible' to many of those from the general public who look through the lens offered by the zoo.

Walsh (2012: chapter 4) makes a related point with regard to the question of what Westerners are looking for when they travel to Madagascar to experience its 'natural wonders' (sapphires and ecotouristic resorts in particular). He argues that the tourists are in search of authenticity rather than anything specifically to do with Madagascar, and that the kind of authenticity they are looking for on the Indian Ocean island they may equally well find elsewhere in the world. Madagascar appears to 'fit on a pre-existing shelf in the European imagination – that is, as one among many distant, distinctive, exotic, and unusual places' (ibid.: 87), occupying but one place on a 'list' of 'last great Edenic homes to animals on the edge of extinction' together with other 'oases of "wilderness"' (ibid.: 88). For those in search of authenticity, Madagascar is among many 'places of a certain kind' (ibid.: 88) making it 'fairly generic and largely interchangeable with others of their kind' (ibid.: 92).[4] In certain ways, the visitors to the Zurich zoo's Masoala exhibit can be said to make a mini-ecotouristic trip to Madagascar – or rather, a place *like* Madagascar – as they stroll through the greenhouse; and like the tourists studied by Walsh, they perceive Madagascar and especially the Malagasy population as representatives of a certain *kind*.[5]

Early Ideas

The perception of the Malagasy as representatives of a type of people rather than a specific people is already established at an early age. In the school classes I worked with, children from about the age of ten began to talk about the Malagasy in this way, irrespective of whether or not they had been to the Masoala exhibit with their teachers. Children below this age claimed to know all kinds of things about the Malagasy, such as that they live in straw huts or that they wear torn clothes; but they did not, at least not explicitly, merge them with other, similar peoples they had heard about.

When I asked the 10-year-old children of a 4th-grade primary school class – they had been to the zoo with their teachers one week prior to our conversation – what kinds of images they had of the Malagasy people, a stream of ideas came bubbling out without any interruption or further encouragement on my part:

> They walk barefoot, they don't drive in cars / They are tanned / They are peaceful people / They don't have any clothes, well, no T-shirts / They have holes in their teeth. Don't they have dentists? / Sometimes, they make holes through their back teeth. I saw this on TV / They are not used to sweets and the like / They are nice people, perhaps because they don't have television [or] the kinds of things that we have in our play rooms / They live in a natural way. They don't go to the hot dog stand, they produce their food themselves. They hunt animals and things like that. If one compares us and those in Madagascar one notices that they make all their things themselves. We go shopping, buy our clothes ready-made. When they need clothes, they make them all by themselves. They make perhaps one or two pieces of clothing in one day and there is no label attached like 'style hip-hop' or anything like this. It's perfectly normal / They help one another / I am not sure that this is right, but perhaps they never argue / They have to live modestly / They always have to be careful because danger lurks everywhere, like poisonous animals or scorpions or things like that / They eat healthily / There, the law of nature still prevails, the law of the jungle [*fressen und gefressen werden*, meaning literally 'to eat and be eaten'] is more important there than here with us.

One pupil asked: 'The people there, do they also paint their faces and things like that?' I answered that the Malagasy do not do this, and enquired why she had asked. She replied: 'Most of them have their faces painted you know, the American Indians [Native Americans] for example, or the Africans, too, they . . . have their faces painted'.

In a 5th-grade class (children aged eleven) who had also visited Little Masoala, one child remarked during a similar conversation: 'It's similar to the Caribbean – it's basically rainforest. There, the people are poor as well and they live similarly, though their houses are made of stone, but still. Once you have been to the Masoala Hall, you know exactly what it's like'. Similar statements were made by children in primary school classes who had not visited the Masoala exhibit together with their teachers. In a 6th-grade class (children aged twelve), a discussion ensued as to whether or not there were cannibals in Madagascar. At least four pupils (out of some twenty) agreed with this idea. In the following extract, my questions are put in italics.

> Takschan: I think there are cannibals there, I think, the people, like they eat the flesh.
> *Why do you think that, where did you learn this?*
> In a film.
> *A film about Madagascar?*
> No, a South African film.
> *You are talking about people eating other people?*
> Yes.
> *What do the other children think? Is Takschan right?*
> Justin: Yes.
> *Why do you think so?*
> Justin: I don't know, because there are *Indianer* [American Natives] there.
> Marko: About the cannibals, I think there are perhaps cannibals there, because there are surely *Ureinwohner* [aboriginal inhabitants] who live there, too.
> *Is that the same?*

There is a murmur in the class indicating that not all the children agree with the suggestion that *Ureinwohner* are the same as cannibals.

> Marko: Perhaps some of the *Ureinwohner* are cannibals.
> *What do you think an Ureinwohner is? What do you imagine an Ureinwohner to be like?*
> Marko: Someone who lives in a hut and things like that, and in the rainforest. Without clothes.
> Lundrin: I think that Madagascar is not a rich country, it's more like poor. And because of the *Ureinwohner*, I also think that there might be cannibals living there.
> *What do you understand by 'Ureinwohner'?*
> Lundrin: People who have grown up there.
> *Like you and I have grown up in Winterthur* [name of the town where the school is located]?
> Lundrin: No, not like that, those who were the very first people there.
> *What do you imagine the lives of Ureinwohner to be like? If one is an Ureinwohner, how do you think one lives?*
> Lundrin: A little bit poorer than others, in huts, on straw.

Similar notions were expressed by older pupils as well. In a grammar school class (pupils aged sixteen to seventeen) – they had spent a considerable amount of time in the Masoala exhibit's information centre – my question 'What comes to mind when you think of the Malagasy people?'

triggered, amongst other answers, the following: 'I think they are like tribes, like in Africa. Well *Ureinwohner*. They live just from Nature, naked so to speak, well no clothes, and they hunt, and live off plants'. Just like many of the adults I had talked to at the zoo, these pupils clearly had in mind a *type* of people thought to be living in different parts of the non-Euroamerican world, a type which seemed to come to mind extremely easily and quickly as soon as they tried to think of the people of Madagascar. Some pupils, as well as adults, used expressions like *Ureinwohner* or *Urvölker*, but the concept of a type of person is clearly much more widespread than the explicit use of such linguistic labels. Moreover, pupils made statements about the Malagasy that went way beyond what they were likely to actually know, thus inferring 'knowledge' about the people of Madagascar by way of association with other populations considered to be similar. This was especially clear in the case of young children who had neither been to the Masoala exhibit with their teachers nor were likely to have been exposed to any explicit information about Madagascar elsewhere (except for the Hollywood film), but who nonetheless said things like 'The people in Madagascar have torn clothes' and 'They eat coconuts and bananas'.

Obviously, there are age-specific differences in the way children, teenagers and adults talk about the Malagasy, especially in terms of the vocabulary employed. But beneath such inevitable differences, there exists an astonishingly consistent undercurrent of ideas that appears to have great influence throughout child- and adulthood. In other words, the fundamental perception remains surprisingly stable once it is established.

Seeing the Generic in the Specific

One can observe a double process of perceiving the specific as generic. As we saw in chapter 3, visitors perceive so much of what they see at the zoo as a call for acting morally that the Madagascar-specific aspects of the exhibit get shifted to the margins of conscious reflection. At the same time, the Malagasy people, too, are seen through a generic lens when they are perceived as an example of a 'type' of people – a type that is associated with the notion of an *Ur*-state of humankind. Indeed, the perception of the Masoala project as a generic rainforest conservation project goes hand-in-hand with the idea of the Malagasy as a generic people.

In her study of the emergence of 'the tropics' as spaces of European imagination, the historian Nancy Stepan (2001) highlights the intimate connection between the imagination of 'tropical nature' and the imagination of 'tropical people', both constructed as 'the other'. Stepan begins her analysis with an observation that many previous and subsequent studies confirm: all representations of the non-human world are intimately linked to the history and contemporary circumstances of the societies in which these representations emerge. This is also true for the idea of 'the tropics' to which Stepan's study is dedicated (investigating in detail the case of Brazil). The tropics are 'imaginative spaces as much as empirical ones' (ibid.: 50). 'Tropicality' as a set of ideas associated with specific parts of the world emerged in the eighteenth and, in particular, the nineteenth century in the context of European colonial expansion. The combination of a set of characteristics of European societies at the time – including the popularity of travel, the availability of affordable illustrated books, and technical developments such as steamships and railways (ibid.: 31–35) – provided the ground on which the idea of 'the tropics' as out-of-the-ordinary spaces grew.

From its beginnings, the European imagination of 'the tropics' was strongly coloured by the idea of the latter's 'radical otherness to the temperate world' (Stepan 2001: 17), with the European perception oscillating between seeing the spaces identified as tropical as either heavenly or devilish. At first, travellers and explorers emphasised the tropics' purity and abundant vegetation. Later on, the fascination for the tropics as a lush and aesthetic paradise gave way to seeing all sorts of dangers lurking in tropical environments – diseases first of all, but also other gloomy elements of 'wild nature', in particular the backwardness of the inhabitants which, amongst other things, was detected in the lack of European-style agriculture (ibid.: 54). Both in moments of admiration and in times of contempt, the tropics' otherness included tropical peoples as much as tropical Nature. To demonstrate that this has historically been the case is Stepan's main point.

The association of particular kinds of landscapes with particular kinds of people manifests itself in visitors' perceptions of Little Masoala. As mentioned earlier, most visitors' spontaneous answers to the question of what came to mind when they thought of Madagascar consisted of references to lush rainforests, exotic fauna and flora, humidity and heat. As this image of a tropical paradise was the first to spring to mind and was domineering in the majority of the conversations I had with people at the zoo, it stands to reason that their subsequent reflections about the Malagasy people at least partly derived from imagining them as rainforest dwellers. The 'little house' (the Malagasy kitchen inside the greenhouse) that one passes as one walks along the visitor trajectory (see Photograph 1.4 on p. 30), and which was put there in order to indicate the presence of humans in rainforests, is particularly conducive to this association. In the end, the vision of most zoo visitors when they look at what is being presented to them is one of generic rainforest dwellers living in a generic rainforest environment. Thus a key effect of the zoo's exhibit about Madagascar, and Masoala in particular, is that in visitors' perceptions the specificity which the zoo set out to highlight is obliterated.

Ureinwohner (and similar terms) denotes a category, comparable to, say, 'hill people', rather than a specific group embedded within a specific context. Words like *Ureinwohner*, and by inclusion the Malagasy, label a cluster of interrelated ideas and, as such, are adequate and meaningful for those who employ them. But the imagination of the Malagasy as a 'kind of people' makes it impossible to imagine them as specific others with whom one stands in some kind of a relationship. Indeed, one cannot have a relationship with a category of people. As we will see in the second part of this book, this generification of the Malagasy people contrasts sharply with the way the farmers in Masoala imagine people like the Swiss.

Notes

1. All interviews with school classes were recorded and transcribed. When citing pupils, I translate from the original Swiss German or German. I render the children's words as closely as possible, but eliminate grammatical mistakes.
2. The trilogy is reported to have been one of the biggest commercial successes of the company DreamWorks Animation, and has earned hundreds of millions of U.S. dollars (see Los Angeles Times, 1 November 2012; http://dreamworks.wikia.com/wiki/Madagascar).
3. In a 2nd-grade primary school class, one girl explained that she had thought that Madagascar was an imaginary place; five of her classmates confirmed that they had thought the same.
4. On processes of 'generification' in the context of Nature conservation, see also West, Igoe and Brockington 2006: 261.
5. I also conducted interviews with eight Swiss people/couples who had been to Masoala as tourists, but this part of my data is not included in the present analysis.

Chapter 5

The Coconut Schema

In the previous chapter I discussed how human beings are rarely part of the mental images that easily spring to mind when people think of Madagascar and that when pushed to reflect about the human population of Madagascar, adults and children tend to view the Malagasy people in generic terms as representing a 'kind'. In this chapter I want to investigate how, exactly, this kind is imagined. I will do so by looking at the evidence from discussions with pupils. Between June 2006 and December 2009, and again in 2012, I worked with a total of twenty-seven school classes in the canton of Zurich, including all age groups from 1st-grade primary school classes to the final year of secondary education (three academic levels, see below). Thirteen of these classes were primary school, and fourteen of them secondary school. Recruiting school classes who had *not* been to the zoo's exhibit with their teachers turned out to be difficult. Thus of the twenty-seven classes, eighteen had visited Little Masoala; in eight cases I accompanied them on these visits. Of the remaining nine classes who had not been to the exhibit with their teachers, six were primary and three secondary school classes.

The chapter consists of three parts. In the first and second sections, I will investigate and compare the mental images of the Malagasy people of pupils at the primary and secondary levels of schooling. The third part will examine specifically the issue of deforestation which was raised as a topic in almost all classes.

As mentioned in chapter 2, no systematic difference was discernable between the statements by adult visitors about to enter the zoo's Masoala exhibit, on the one hand, and people at the end of their visit, on the other. Thus with the adults the exhibit appears primarily to activate and reinforce already existing images and ideas. This is also true for the children. There was no systematic difference between the answers of those children who had visited the zoo's Masoala exhibit – as mentioned earlier, my discussions with the pupils took place between immediately and two years after their visit to the zoo – and those who had not. There is one exception, however: with regard to the issue of deforestation, a school visit to Little Masoala does make a difference, a point I will discuss below.

The following presentation of pupils' imaginations of the Malagasy people cannot possibly do justice to all the details and subtleties in their statements and the differences between individual pupils' ways of voicing their thoughts. However, the discussions I had with them reveal a relatively small set of prominent and recurrent themes that were talked about again and again, often in strikingly similar language and using regularly employed key words (cf. Quinn 2005c: 43–47; Strauss 2005: 205–8). It is these recurrent themes that I will focus on in what follows.

The features that I will highlight cannot be arranged along the lines of a ranking order. However, some crop up so spontaneously, quickly and consistently that – following the basic insight of prototype theory according to which concepts are built around best exemplars (Rosch 1977) – these regularly recurrent features can be said to form part of the core of pupils' imaginations of the Malagasy people, while other features appear from time to time and much less frequently on the fringes or the periphery.

Primary Education

Among primary school children, four features, all interrelated and often intertwined with one another in the way they were presented, formed their core of ideas about the Malagasy people.

Almost invariably, they listed what they thought the Malagasy *lacked*, such as (in random order): money, good/decent clothes, proper houses, electricity, machines, shoes, cars, medicine, banks and credit cards, dentists, shops, airports, jobs, tools, television sets and other electrical equipment, factories, schools or proper schools with blackboards, glass panel windows, pen cases and books. It is worth recalling at this point that the imagination of the Malagasy through the lens of deficiency is echoed in children's stories like *Globi Experiences Masoala* that I discussed in chapter 1. Deficiencies of various kinds were often mentioned in the same breath as the idea that the Malagasy are poor, an assumed feature that was also regularly mentioned by the primary school children (see Strauss 2005: 204–7 on the importance of investigating which keywords are used in conjunction with one another).

For many children, clothes are a major issue, as in these extracts from a discussion in a 1st-grade class:

Jenny: The people there wear torn clothes. (Lots of her class mates scream: Yes!)
Elisabeth: No, they don't have torn clothes, they have clothes made of leaves.
Jenny: The people there have dirty clothes. (Several other pupils agree with this.)
Véronique: They also make their clothes themselves. Because when they don't have any clothes, and no money to buy any, they have to make them themselves out of things they have.

In two other classes, 2nd and 4th-grade (children aged eight and ten respectively), it was asserted by individual children that the Malagasy wear clothes made of straw or hay. Other suggestions included that the Malagasy wear the fur from hunted animals, loincloths and raffia skirts.

Another significant feature of the primary school children's imaginations of the Malagasy was their being hunters and gatherers, an idea that is closely related to the Malagasy's imagined *Ur*-state. Many children I spoke with assumed that the Malagasy live in the jungle and take 'from Nature' whatever they need, gathering berries, bananas and coconuts, and hunting animals for food.

Next to these four features – deficiencies, poverty, clothes, hunters and gatherers – that are particularly central in these children's imagination of the Malagasy people, a whole range of ideas float around this core of representations, among them: the idea that the Malagasy live in straw houses or houses with roofs made of straw or leaves; that they are not modern or civilised; that they are nice and peaceful; that there are many things they do not know; that they have dark skin; and that they learn skills from animals. These views are exemplified in the following quotes from 4th- and 6th-grade primary school classes respectively:

> I think they learn most things from the animals, they copy things from animals, such as climbing (a boy remarked), or getting a coconut from a tree (a girl added).
> Perhaps there are schools, but perhaps these are not so much schools for language and maths like here with us but more like schools for learning how to hunt and things like that – because there aren't so many jobs in offices where you need to know maths.

The Coconut Schema

The word 'Madagascar' seems to trigger a whole range of ideas and mental images in these children's minds. It triggers a schema that I will call 'the coconut schema', one that, amongst other features, has the idea of 'jungle' in it, of jungle dwellers, of poverty and deficiency (material and in terms of knowledge), of jungly activities and of what is thought to be jungly food, especially bananas and coconuts. In fact, coconuts were specifically mentioned by children in six out of thirteen primary school classes. Consider the following example (5th grade):

> Miguel: They don't have any money.
> Ilenya: They are nice people.
> Mike: They are not so white.
> Ignesa: They don't have clothes like us.
> Julia: More like cloths really.
> Mateo: They are black.
> Julia: Most are poor because the people in Africa are poor, too.
> Berk: They cut wood, as a job.
> Dilay: They climb up trees to get down coconuts or bananas.
> Agnesa: Coconuts. They often eat coconuts.

As discussed in chapter 2, the activation of one or several features of an established schema triggers the activation of the whole. In the case at hand, the association of 'Madagascar' with 'jungle', for example, or a child having heard that Madagascar is a place in Africa may, therefore, lead to a great number of inferences about Madagascar and the Malagasy people that go way beyond what the child actually knows or the information she or he has been given. Thus, when asked to reflect about the people of Madagascar about whom the primary school children I spoke with actually knew next to nothing, they drew on a network of interconnected ideas built up in the course of their lives which I name 'the coconut schema'. This schema being activated by the word 'Madagascar', the children then apply all the features of that schema to the people of Madagascar – for example, that the Malagasy live in straw huts, hunt animals and eat coconuts.[1]

The coconut schema is not a schema *of* the Malagasy people or *of* Madagascar. Rather, it is a schema that is activated by the word 'Madagascar' and that, like every schema, has fuzzy edges and is interconnected with other schemas and, therefore, can be applied to a limitless number of contexts. In other words, though it is not a schema of the Malagasy people, the cluster of ideas that are part of the coconut schema is readily available and can easily be retrieved in order to help to imagine who the Malagasy might be and how they might live. The coconut schema is 'available to think with' (Quinn 2011: 38).

A Cultural Schema

No two individuals ever encounter exactly the same input or have exactly the same experiences in the course of their lives, thus the extent to which the contents of the schemas people carry around in their heads overlap is by necessity always partial. At the same time, 'experience is often substantially shared, not the least because the environment in which a given group of individuals lives – including their institutions, practices, and responses to these – is already extensively culturally shaped' (Quinn 2011: 39). As Strauss and Quinn write in their influential book: 'It is not necessary that two people have exactly the same experiences . . . for them to arrive at some of the same schemas' (Strauss and Quinn 1997: 123). Especially if a schema is activated in many different contexts in a given society, most individuals growing up in this environment will develop a common general pattern of understanding the issues that the schema is associated with. The primary school children's ideas about the Malagasy people appear to be such a case, in which one can confidently speak of a cultural schema, an *'intrapersonal*, mental structur[e]' (Strauss and Quinn 1997: 6, emphasis in the original) which is extremely widely shared.

The recognition of widely shared schemas that are nonetheless different from person to person rests on an understanding of culture as 'a fuzzy concept' (Strauss and Quinn 1997: 7) in which 'cultural representations . . . are more or less widely and lastingly distributed, and hence more or less cultural' (Sperber 1996: 58, cited in Strauss and Quinn 1997: 7). It rests on a view of culture that neither assumes any kind of clearly bounded cultural entities – hence its fuzziness – nor denies the fact that people who (grow up and) live in very similar environments and life-situations will develop many shared understandings of the world.

The features discussed above, both those at the core and on the periphery of the coconut schema, are as much present with the 1st- as with the 6th-grade primary school children. Thus the overall data from the thirteen primary school classes with whom I worked suggests that the coconut schema is established at the age of seven (and possibly before) and that it remains stable throughout primary school up to the age of twelve.

Stability

The stability of the coconut schema is exemplified by the following case. My meetings with school classes usually consisted of two parts. During the first part, I enquired about the pupils' ideas concerning Madagascar, the Malagasy people and other issues that came up in the course of the conversations, for example the Hollywood film *Madagascar*. When the pupils had nothing else to say and the discussion had run its course, we took a break following which I made a presentation about Madagascar and certain aspects of Malagasy daily life and culture. Much of what I said, and what I showed on photographs that I had taken in Madagascar, disturbed the children's previously held assumptions. Many of them expressed surprise at seeing Malagasy children wearing 'proper clothes', for instance, or seeing pictures of tall, modern buildings in the capital city. In a 2nd-grade class (they had not been to the zoo), the children's narratives about the Malagasy at first included many references to houses made of leaves, wood or straw and many other typical features of the coconut schema. After my input, several of these ideas became shaky and new ideas entered into negotiation with old ones. Some of the children now emphasised that they had learnt that not all Malagasy were poor, that many had good clothes and that not all houses were made of straw, while others still held on to the 'straw hut' narrative. One year later, the same children were asked by their teacher to write an essay with the title 'What do I know about Madagascar?' Of the twenty-two children, eleven wrote exclusively about animals and plants. In eight essays, the only mentions relating to the human population were 'houses with straw roofs', and in the remaining three the information about the Malagasy people related solely to what they lack, their poverty and their dark skin. The short-term effect of the new input, that at the time had surprised them and challenged some of their previously held assumptions, had evaporated. It was not that the children had forgotten the visit as such. They remembered many particulars, such as that I had shown them a photograph of myself with a Madagascar boa around my neck, that I had brought lemur toys and that I had told them that I have 'like a family' in Madagascar, but the information that had been new to them at the time had since been lost.

The 'Little House'

Not only words may trigger schemas. 'Schemas can include words, but are hardly limited to these. They can include experience of all kinds – unlabelled as well as labelled, inarticulate as well as well-theorized, felt as well as cognized' (Quinn 2005c: 38).

How a Swiss child 'pictures' the Malagasy people may, for example, be triggered by a quick glance to the side while walking through the tunnel that leads up to the Masoala greenhouse. Catching a glimpse of one of the photographs displayed along the wall might be enough to activate a complex network of ideas.[2] Within the greenhouse one object seems to be particularly effective in triggering the coconut schema and especially the notion that the Malagasy provide a window into the past of humankind, namely the Malagasy kitchen ('the little house') that one passes as one strolls through the artificial rainforest (Photograph 1.4 on p. 30).

Consider the following conversation I had with a 2nd-grade primary school class (8-year-old children); the conversation took place two weeks after their visit to the zoo. After the children had brought up a number of issues including naming various animals to be seen inside the greenhouse and the difference between Africa and Europe 'where there is no country with only brown people', and also having discussed amongst themselves, without reaching a clear conclusion, whether or not there were any people living in Masoala, I asked them to tell me – assuming there were people living in Masoala – how they thought these people lived.

> Till: The people there live primitively, fairly primitively.
> *What do you mean by that?* I asked.
> Till: Old fashioned. Old, a bit like the cave-dwellers used to live. The cave-dwellers also used to build kind of tents. More like primitive, like the cave-dwellers.
> *What do the others think? Do you agree or do you have any other ideas?*
> Kevin: No, they have houses, they don't live in tents.
> Till: What I meant was the way they cooked, and the way they lived and so on. I knew they had houses. And also I made a mistake: I should have said like stilt house-dwellers, because they did have houses while the cave-dwellers still lived in caves.
> *What do the other children think, how do the people in Masoala live?*
> Uguraycan: In Madagascar, they also live in huts. And they don't have . . . they collect wood so that they can make a fire. They need a lot of wood, they make fires.
> Till: They live in huts and in there, they live very simply. Not like us, all modern, not really modern.
> *How do you know these things* (addressing the children who have given the above answers)?
> Uguraycan: We saw it in the Masoala Hall at the zoo. We saw a hut.
> Till: Me too, I also saw it in the Masoala Hall. I also saw the house there.

In another, 4th-grade primary school class (10-year-old children), our conversation one week after their visit to the zoo took the following turn. In this case it was the teacher in fact who spoke of the 'little house' as a window into the distant past. After one of the girls had mentioned the 'little house' and that it looked 'nice and calm', I brought the conversation back to it, asking the children what they had thought when they had seen it.

> Nicolas: There are beetles inside. It's not comfortable, there is no sofa. But perhaps, because it was just for demonstration, if it was real I think it would be much nicer inside.
> Julian: It's made in a simple manner and there are posts because of the heat of the floor.
> Silvan: It's not inhabited.

I confirm that nobody lives in that particular house in the zoo exhibit and ask the children whether they can imagine people living in such houses?
Alen: Natives.
Jolanda: There are people who live in houses like that. They don't know anything else.
Sascha: Most of those who look inside think nobody could live in such a house, but those who actually live in there have never seen blocks of flats with sofas and television sets, they are used to living like this. We are used to electronic things.
Aldin: They sleep on the floor.
Teacher: The house reminded me a bit of our house from the New Stone Age. (Teacher to me:) Before speaking about the rainforest, we talked about the New Stone Age, and we had a picture of a house which looked similar.

In another, 5th-grade primary school class, one girl said: 'The people there are quite poor. They don't have as much money as we do. And they don't live in houses but in something like straw huts. I think so because there is such a hut also in the Masoala Hall'.

Later on in our conversation, I asked the children what they thought the Malagasy did in terms of work. One boy answered: 'They are hunters and gatherers, who still live in huts somewhere in the forest, in huts that they have built themselves'.

Contradictions

None of what has been said so far implies that individual children's imaginations of Madagascar and the Malagasy people are necessarily coherent or without contradictions. Following the propositions of one particular child throughout a conversation makes this clear. Take the example of the 10-year-old Lukas. In the course of my discussion with him and his classmates, his contributions were these:

(a) My guess is: Madagascar lies on the east coast of Africa.
(b) I think, Jan is right [Jan had said that there were no people living in Madagascar, only tourists] because I have seen the film *Madagascar* and there, too, there were no people, but only lemur-like monkeys.
(c) A quarter of Madagascar is threatened by deforestation. One can see this on pictures, in books at home, one often sees pictures of forests that have been cut down.
Do you have any idea as to who cuts down these forests? I asked.
Probably the people of Madagascar, who then send the wood to another country.
(d) I think the Masoala Hall has to do with Madagascar because the rainforest temperature is almost exactly the same and the animals, too, are probably the same as in Madagascar.

(e) Answering the question: *What do you think people in Madagascar are busy with all day long?* Lukas said: Outside of the city they have to build high houses as a protection against carnivores.
(f) I don't think that they have the same kind of clothes as we do, more like loincloths. [Explaining what a loincloth is:] Clothes made from animal fur, almost like a bag that one wraps around oneself.

Statements (b) and (c) flatly contradict one another, with the first claiming that there are no people and the second talking about what the people of Madagascar do. Lukas made these two statements within the space of three minutes, and he voiced statement (c) before any consensus had been reached among the children of his class that there *were* people living in Madagascar other than tourists and filmmakers. In statement (e), Lukas continues to differentiate between urban and rural people thus acknowledging the existence of cities, *pace* statement (b) that there are no people living in Madagascar. Reflecting on the coexistence of competing ideas held simultaneously by one and the same person, Strauss points to different strategies whereby people often deal with these. Lukas's different statements within a short period can be regarded as an instance of 'compartmentalization' – that is a mechanism whereby a person simultaneously holds conflicting ideas without being aware of 'the conflict between them' (Strauss 2005: 223).

Secondary Education

If the coconut schema is already well established at the beginning of primary school, when children are about seven years of age, and if it remains stable until they reach the age of about twelve, do pupils' ideas about the Malagasy people develop further, getting modified as they grow older and enter secondary education?

In the Swiss system, pupils are divided into four levels of secondary education after completing six years of primary school. The three levels (A, B, C) of what is called *Sekundarschule* last three or optionally four years; grammar school lasts six years. In presenting the data from the secondary school level, it is necessary to distinguish between *Sekundarschule* and grammar school. Of the fourteen classes at the secondary level I worked with, seven were *Sekundarschule* classes and seven grammar school classes.

At the Sekundarschule

In all seven *Sekundarschule* classes the coconut schema was clearly present. As in the primary school classes, these teenagers spoke of the Malagasy being like *Ur*-inhabitants, bush people or *Indianer* (a German word for indigenous North American groups that covers both the notion of backwardness and of the nobility of those who are thought to still live 'close to Nature'). They spoke about the Malagasy people as 'primitive', as 'not being civilised yet', as 'less developed than us'. They spoke about poverty and the lack of electricity, cars, running water, computers, industry and proper clothes, as well as about a simple lifestyle, living in huts, hunting and gathering for food, and about the people having dark skin. A 15-year-old girl, for example, said:

> They don't live in luxury but, well, like *Ur*-inhabitants.
> *What do you understand by that term?* I asked her.
> Well, that they live simply and off what they produce themselves or catch fish and other food.

One 13-year-old girl told me after I had provided input that challenged many of her assumptions that she had thought that the Malagasy were 'savages' (*Wilde*) and that previously she had not realised that they were wearing the same kind of clothes as people in Europe.

My data from the *Sekundarschule* classes (pupils aged between about thirteen and sixteen) suggests that the coconut schema is present with these teenagers as much as with the younger children at primary school level, and that for them, too, thinking of 'Madagascar' triggers that schema rapidly.

At Grammar School

Moving to the higher academic level of grammar schools, the picture becomes more complicated and less clear. All seven classes I met had visited the Masoala exhibit at the zoo with their biology teachers. In two of them, the pupils painted the familiar 'coconut picture'. One of these was a class at a grammar school for adults (aged 20+), the other a regular grammar school class (16- to 17-year-old pupils). The remaining five classes were different in that their visit to Little Masoala was embedded within a so-called 'project week' during which they had engaged thoroughly with questions concerning the world's rainforests and their protection. In several cases students had been asked by their teachers to discuss whether or not the zoo's Masoala exhibit could be considered a genuine contribution to Nature conservation. Because of this special focus in these classes, the discussions always very quickly turned to deforestation, and little was said about Madagascar or the Malagasy people that was not connected to rainforest conservation. Thus the comparability of the data from these five classes with the other classes at the secondary education level is limited. Nonetheless, some interesting observations can be made.

On the whole, the students in the five grammar school classes who had had a project week had a vision of the Malagasy as a people who are destroying their own livelihood by cutting down the rainforest for a combination of three reasons: ignorance, poverty and traditionalism. We are already familiar with this tripartite concept from the adult visitors to the zoo. The Malagasy were thought to be failing to understand the consequences of their agricultural and other practices, to have no alternative to exploiting their natural resources due to poverty, and/or to act as they do even if this is a road to ruin because their forebears have always done so. Closely linked with these notions was a sense of moral responsibility on the part of people in industrialised countries like Switzerland to educate the farmers on the Masoala peninsula about sustainable ways of using their environment, exhibiting a pronounced 'will to improve' (Li 2007) on the part of these grammar school teenagers. The combination of the three explanatory frameworks of the causes of deforestation and what ought to be done about it is exemplified in the following extract of a conversation. The pupils were between sixteen and eighteen years old.

> Pupil 1: They are still much more connected with Nature, they hunt. On the other hand, they perhaps don't know that they are destroying the forest when they keep making new fields.
> Pupil 2: I think they know what they are doing but they have to do it in order to survive. For them the question is: 'Do I want to survive or do I want to protect the rainforest?' and, of course, one's own existence is more important in the end. One ought to do something against poverty.
> Pupil 3: I think they don't care. I can imagine that this is just natural for them because one's grandfather did the same and one's father and then one does it oneself, cutting down the wood and then cultivate something.
> Pupil 4: I think for these people there, the rainforest is nothing special, it's just forest – they have no awareness that the rainforest will be gone one day.
> Pupil 5: My godmother was in Madagascar six months ago and she told me that the people there harvest rice just for the next day. They only look as far as the next day, not into the future; they live day by day.

In another class, the discussion took the following turn:

> Pupil 1: The Malagasy are friendly people and there is great natural wealth but there is also a lot of devastation, and the people there probably cannot see yet that they are destroying themselves by cutting down or overusing the rainforest. They cannot see yet that continuing as they do leads them into ruin. But other than that, it's a really beautiful country.
> Pupil 2: The countryside is extremely beautiful, and the country has a lot of potential. If one really helps these people a lot of development can happen. I am glad that the country gets support and that one tries to educate them, in terms of sustainability, that one doesn't just think 'It's your business to

find solutions, you destroy your own livelihood anyway' but that one really tries to help them; that's really important. I think it's nice that they have this national park there and that they [those running or supporting the park] are really trying their best and that they also show tourists around, show them the national park, the locals themselves.
How exactly do you think one should help these people? I enquired.
Pupil 2: Just like one already helps them now, through the cooperation with the Zurich zoo, with money and donations, and the WWF and things like that; and that one tries to teach them not to cut the wood because that's bad for them themselves; that one tries to enhance their environmental knowledge; that one teaches them things but still leaves them the possibility to get enough wood for themselves because they can't suddenly live without wood; that one shows them a different way such as, well I don't know, perhaps there are ways that we know of here in the West that would be useful for them, too, that we could show them; that one kind of educates them though it sounds stupid to say 'We are the Westerners and we will educate you now', I don't mean it like that but in the end, it is a question of education.

In a third class the following conversation ensued:

Pupil 1: Compared to us, they are extremely poor people, they hardly have any money, they live off the natural resources. Sometimes perhaps, they can sell something and then buy something else they need from a shop, but there is a shortage of money. I imagine them to be living in large families with each member contributing to support the family. There is little money, one can't afford to get ill and go to hospital; one just lives from day to day and in order to be able to support one's family.
Pupil 2: No, I don't think it's a fight for survival, it's more like, this is just their way of life, I don't know how much they know about the world around them. (. . .)
Pupil 3: For them it's normal, they are *Urvölker* and they have lived like this since time immemorial and it was always ok. But the population grows and needs more, but they probably don't see that.
Pupil 2: I think it's more that they have a different awareness than us, that's probably also due to their culture.
Pupil 4: I think it's difficult to make them aware of the fact that their environment is threatened and that it is worth saving, because for them it's natural to use what there is, and they have lived like this for generations; and then the Europeans come and say: 'Your environment is in danger and you must protect it now and you are only allowed to cut this much wood'. It's probably not so easy to make this clear to these people.

The continuation of the conversation focused on the question of whose duty it was to educate the farmers in Masoala – Europeans or Malagasy park rangers?

Many aspects of the coconut schema were also in place with the grammar school classes who had had a project week concerning rainforest conservation and who had been looking at the issue through the example of the Masoala partnership project between the zoo in Zurich and the park management in Madagascar. The notions of backwardness and deficiency, in particular, persisted in these classes, although words like 'primitive' and 'uncivilised' were used much less often than in other classes, and the idea of the Malagasy being jungle dwellers was markedly less present. For these pupils, the Malagasy farmers' backwardness was primarily revealed in their lack of environmental knowledge, and the focus of what exactly the Malagasy were considered to be lacking rested with knowledge rather than material possessions. Following from this point, these grammar school classes differed from other classes at the secondary education level in that they placed a pronounced emphasis on educating the farmers in Masoala as an act of moral duty. This is reminiscent of what we already encountered among many adult visitors at the exhibit at the zoo, a point I will return to in the conclusions to this chapter.

What is the reason for the difference between the grammar school classes who had had a project week and the other classes at the secondary education level? Although my evidence is not solid enough to make any strong claim, I tentatively contend, for two reasons, that the difference is due to the depth of engagement with the issues in question rather than the grammar school's higher academic level. First, two grammar school classes echoed, at times almost verbatim, the propositions voiced by academically lower secondary school classes. Second, it was precisely those grammar school classes whose curriculum had included several days engaging with questions surrounding rainforest conservation who produced a somewhat different discourse, albeit one which contained important features of the coconut schema.

This interpretation is supported by a comparison with the evidence from adult visitors to the zoo's Masoala exhibit. As briefly discussed in chapter 3, it is reasonable to assume that the socio-economic backgrounds and levels of education of zoo visitors are varied. At the same time, the present study revealed that the great majority of visitors to Little Masoala share a number of basic assumptions and ideas about Madagascar and the Malagasy people. The combination of these two points would suggest that the coconut schema is a widely shared, cultural schema, the essential features of which are not fundamentally influenced by educational background.

Consider the following example. One afternoon while interviewing visitors inside the Masoala greenhouse at the zoo, I first talked to a man in his late sixties. He told me he was the son of a farmer, worked as a butcher, and had only flown in an aircraft once in his life. A short while afterwards, I spoke to a couple in their late thirties. Both worked as teachers at a grammar school, one of them teaching Latin. Below the surface of different vocabulary – 'not yet civilised like us' in the words of the butcher, 'still caught in superstitions and mythical traditions' in those of the teachers – their core ideas struck me as almost identical. For example, both the butcher and the grammar school teachers clearly embraced the notion that the Malagasy people are somehow stuck in the past and are in need of help from such as the Zurich zoo in order to move forward. Despite the socio-economic and educational differences between them, they shared an imagination of the people of Madagascar as providing a window into humanity's past.

The Issue of Deforestation

In many classes at all levels from primary to grammar school the topic of deforestation was a key issue. Unlike the features discussed so far, however, there was, at least at the primary school level, a clear difference between those classes who had been to the zoo's Masoala exhibit and those who had not. In what follows, I will therefore differentiate along these lines.

Primary Education

In the 1st-, 2nd- and 3rd-grade primary school classes children never mentioned deforestation, regardless of whether or not they had visited Little Masoala together with their teachers or other adults. From the 4th grade onwards, however, deforestation was raised as a topic in *all* the classes by the pupils themselves, without any prompting on my part.

In those primary school classes who had *not* been to the zoo the children talked about deforestation primarily in connection with a book called *Stickermania – Adventure Rainforest*. In the spring of 2009, one of the two largest supermarket chains in Switzerland called Migros launched a campaign together with the WWF in support of the world's threatened rainforests. The campaign worked like this. For every twenty Swiss francs worth of shopping at Migros, one would get a pack of five stickers displaying various rainforest animals, and at every Migros counter one could purchase the above-mentioned book for the price of five Swiss francs, of which one franc was donated to the WWF. (It was later announced that the profit from the campaign, a total of 605,000 Swiss francs, would be used for Nature conservation projects in Borneo and Madagascar.[3]) The book is organised as a tour around the world's rainforests undertaken by fictional children's characters. Landing in various places along their way – in South America, Africa and Asia – they tell the reading child about many specificities of each rainforest (such as what it looks like, its climate, how old it is, which animals live there) as well as explaining that these rainforests are threatened. In Africa, the journey includes landing in the Congo and in Madagascar. Besides explanations concerning the properties of rainforests, the book contains two hundred empty spaces onto which the stickers obtained through purchases at Migros could be glued each in its intended place, and each accompanied by explanations about the behaviour of the displayed animal. The book ends with an image of a degraded rainforest which could be 'resurrected' by being covered with six stickers depicting lush rainforest. Below the degraded/resurrected forest it reads: 'The tropical rainforest is very valuable for animals and plants – but also for people because it contains many raw materials. People destroy large tracts of the rainforest because they log, or drill for oil. They for example build roads and fell many beautiful trees in order to gain pastures and to make plantations for palm oil and soya' (my translation from German). For about two-and-a-half months in the spring and early summer of 2009, probably tens of thousands of Swiss children were enthusiastically involved in this *Stickermania* campaign by Migros and the WWF. When it ended, a daily newspaper headlined: 'Mum, you can shop at Coop [Migros's main competitor] again'. When I asked the children in the primary school classes with whom I was working what they had learnt from the *Stickermania* book (these discussions also took place in 2009), they invariably talked about 'people cutting down the rainforest' and about the consequent extinction of animal species. Many recalled the last 'resurrect a rainforest' image vividly.

    The primary school classes who had been to the Masoala exhibit had either had a guided tour through it by zoo staff or had otherwise engaged extensively with the topic of rainforest conservation – for example, by watching a thirty-minute documentary film about the purpose of the Masoala partnership project and the creation of Little Masoala (produced by the Swiss television cooperation in 2004 within a series entitled '*School Television*'). Many of the children in these classes retained the received input to a very noticeable degree and were able to recount much of the information they had been provided with, even months after their visit to the zoo. As we saw above, children who had not been to the Masoala exhibit also talked about the loss of the rainforest in connection with Madagascar and without any prompting on my part, but after a visit to the zoo (and the accompanying consolidation of the issues in question) children's statements became much more detailed and specific. For instance, when I asked a 6th-grade primary school class seven months after their visit to Little Masoala whether they had learnt anything new about Madagascar other than with reference to animals and plants – they had already talked about these at length – and what came to mind when they heard the word 'Madagascar', they said:

> Boy 1: That large tracts of forests are cut down there.
> Boy 2: The guide explained that the rainforest on the right-hand side on the map [Madagascar's east coast] used to be much larger than it is now.
> Boy 3: Somewhere there was written that almost daily an area as large as the entire Masoala Hall is cut down. That it is about sixteen such fields every day.

When I enquired about the reasons for deforestation in Madagascar, they mentioned poverty, the construction of fishing boats, pastures for cattle and the cultivation of rice. Some children recounted how coral reefs in Masoala were being destroyed by local fishermen using harpoons, a matter that is talked about in the above-mentioned documentary. The conservationist input that the children had received proved to be extremely catchy, probably because it fitted into already established schemas and was therefore easy to store and to recall, even a long time after they had received it.

Secondary Education

Moving to the secondary school level, deforestation was a big issue indeed. It came up spontaneously in all the classes at all academic levels when I enquired about the pupils' thoughts in connection with Madagascar. All classes, both in *Sekundarschule* and in grammar school, had a strong awareness of the problem of deforestation. Taken together, the secondary school pupils echoed the adults' reflections about the causes of the loss of the rainforest on the Masoala peninsula that we have already encountered several times: unscrupulous logging by profit-oriented multinational companies, on the one hand, and local farmers' agricultural practices, on the other. These two explanations were equally present, competing for attention, as it were, with one or the other moving into the foreground at different times. Also, ignorance, poverty and traditionalism were seen as chief reasons leading farmers to cut down the forest.

At the secondary school level, my data does not allow any conclusions with regard to the possible effect of a visit to the zoo's exhibit. Of the fourteen classes I spoke with, eleven had visited Little Masoala together with their teachers – in six cases, I was present during these visits – while only three had not. Moreover, it became evident in the course of the conversations with the pupils of the latter three classes that many of them had been to Little Masoala in other contexts than a school visit and that, furthermore, some had seen documentaries like the one mentioned above on television.

In sum, the evidence from the twenty-seven school classes I worked with suggests the following with regard to the issue of deforestation. From the age of ten onwards, primary school children have an awareness of deforestation being an issue in Madagascar, although this awareness is somewhat vague. In those primary school classes who received specific input about this issue through a school visit to the zoo and other sources, in contrast, the information provided proved to stick, so that the children tended to have clear and detailed ideas concerning the problem of deforestation in Madagascar even several months after having received the information. At the secondary education level, the connection between Madagascar and deforestation was firmly established and was a key issue in all the classes. It is worth remembering in this context that since the opening of the Masoala exhibit at the zoo in 2003, Madagascar has featured extraordinarily prominently in the Swiss print and electronic media and that, almost always, the island's threatened biodiversity is the key topic of any public information about it. At the moment of writing, for example, two full-page articles – one concerning Madagascar, the other Masoala, and both highlighting the problem of deforestation – have appeared within one week in two different daily newspapers in the canton of Zurich. It seems likely that by the time children reach secondary school level they will have heard about the forest in Madagascar/Masoala being threatened by one or several such sources. Finally, with the increasing depth of engagement with the topic of forest conservation, primarily in the grammar school classes, the idea of environmental education as a moral duty is gaining prominence.

Conclusion

In chapter 4 we saw how the adults, teenagers and children I spoke with tend to think of the Malagasy people as representing a particular *kind* of humans thought to live in different parts of the non-Euro-American world. In this chapter, I have looked more closely at how children and teenagers imagine this kind, and which characteristics they attribute to it.

The various features that are very regularly mentioned and thus stand out as particularly prominent together form what I call the 'coconut schema'. At its core, assumptions about deficiency, poverty, corresponding clothing, and a life as hunters and gatherers prevail. Around these core representations, specific ideas about Malagasy houses and their inhabitants shine particularly brightly within the peripheral areas of the coconut schema. It is important to emphasise, however, that there is scope for much variety of just how closely the Malagasy are thought to represent the prototypical 'coconut person'. This is a matter of more or less, not of either/or.

Within the coconut schema, the idea of backwardness plays a crucial role, and it appears in various guises. On the one hand, in the statements of many primary and *Sekundarschule* pupils, and some grammar school pupils, the Malagasy people are explicitly described as primitive, uncivilised, backward and not modern. On the other hand, the pupils in those grammar school classes who spent several days engaging with the topic of rainforest loss in Madagascar emphasised the importance of educating the farmers in Masoala about sustainable agricultural practices. For these pupils, educating the Malagasy was a moral duty that would allow the latter to free themselves from self-destructive ignorance and traditionalism. It was a matter of enlightening them by making them understand the importance of Nature conservation. We find also in many adults' statements the same coexistence, and at times combination, of backwardness in the guise of primitivity and backwardness in the guise of lack of knowledge.

These ideas clearly echo the well-known evolutionist trajectory that academics in the nineteenth and early twentieth century considered to characterise the development of humanity and that seems to continue to play an important role, in various guises, for a majority of those children, teenagers and adults I spoke with. The frequent use of the word 'still' as in 'The Malagasy are still traditional' or 'yet' as in 'They are not yet civilised' are audible markers of an evolutionist gaze towards Madagascar that seems extremely prevalent. In other words: *if* the Malagasy are at all noticed, it is from an evolutionist perspective.

Moreover, and particularly importantly for the present discussion, these evolutionist ideas have lately been married to the prevalent Nature conservation paradigm. Through various channels of input and information that are available to adults and children in Switzerland – the zoo's Masoala exhibit, reports in the print and electronic media, documentary films shown on television, the *Stickermania* campaign, the Hollywood film, Globi's adventures – Madagascar has become closely associated with worries about the world's rainforests and the imperative of acting against their destruction. The Malagasy people's asserted lack of ecological knowledge and foresight, and the moral duty of those who know better to show them how to use their environment sustainably, are key notions within this discourse. Many of those I spoke with saw the embracing of Nature conservation, as understood within the contemporary global conservation paradigm, as a manifestation of evolutionary progress, and as a step on the way towards a modern, civilised society. In other words, to understand why one must not cut down the rainforest has become a sign of civilisational progress, and the opposite a mark of backwardness. Nature conservation has thus become a new, morally supported way of imagining people like the Malagasy as 'primitives'.

The idea of the alleged lack of ecological knowledge as a manifestation of backwardness is easily incorporated into the coconut schema because the schema already contains several elements through which those to whom it is applied are projected back in time. The lack of adherence to Nature conservation as an indicator of insufficient societal progress thus falls on the fertile ground of already existing evolutionist assumptions. Thus, alleged ecological ignorance has become a new component of the coconut schema.

A particularly striking example of this line of reasoning was provided by the 11-year-old Kim. Shortly after her class had visited the zoo's Masoala exhibit, the teacher had asked the children to write an essay about their visit and what they had learnt. Kim wrote: 'The Malagasy don't know that they must protect the rainforest. One has to explain this to them'. When I talked to the class five months later, Kim was a very active participant in the discussion and it became clear that she had absorbed a lot of information provided by the visit to the zoo, and especially by the aforementioned documentary film about the Masoala rainforest conservation project that the class had seen twice. It also became evident that *she* had understood the importance of not cutting down the rainforest. The combination of her text and her oral contributions suggested that, in her eyes, people like herself were in a position to teach the farmers in Masoala how to engage appropriately with their natural environment. What could possibly induce this 11-year-old girl to imagine herself in this way vis-à-vis a Malagasy farmer if not an evolutionist assumption about the world that she had already learnt to embrace at her young age?

In her contribution to *Finding Culture in Talk*, Strauss discusses ways through which ideas may gain power in people's minds. One of these is 'holistic mental schemas' that are 'so deeply internalized that people are hardly aware they hold these beliefs' (Strauss 2005: 203). Among the children, teenagers and adults I spoke with, the coconut schema was one such tacit, taken-for-granted anchor of thought. Secondly, ideas may gain power when they turn into a 'social discourse' (ibid.). In contrast to schemas, social discourses are *explicit* statements that are voiced in public so often that they attain the status of a paradigm in a given society and thus become surrounded by an unquestionable aura of truthfulness. The contemporary Nature conservation discourse is such a social discourse, an observation that is manifested in the fact that many zoo visitors voice as their own opinion quasi-verbatim reproductions of the public discourse. These two dynamics combine in the integration of the Nature conservation paradigm into an evolutionist trajectory of human development.

Notes

1. The presence of the 'coconut schema' confirms the continued force of colonial images in Euro-American public culture as discussed in postcolonial studies (for the Swiss context, in particular, see Purtschert, Lüthi and Falk 2012). However, what I wish to highlight is not so much the mechanism of 'othering' but the mechanism of *obliterating* the real people of Madagascar by processes of generification (chapter 4) and stereotypisation (this chapter). It could be argued that the obliteration of people from the picture is the most radical act of 'othering' them.
2. In her account of the European imagination of 'the tropics' (see chapter 4), Stepan (2001: 18) emphasises the importance of visual representations.
3. http://www.migros.ch/de/medieninformationen/medien/aktuelle-meldungen-2009/17-07-2009.html

Extract from 'Marrakech', written by George Orwell in 1939

All people who work with their hands are partly invisible, and the more important the work they do, the less visible they are. Still, a white skin is always fairly conspicuous. In northern Europe, when you see a labourer ploughing a field, you probably give him a second glance. In a hot country, anywhere south of Gibraltar and east of Suez, the chances are that you don't even see him. I have noticed this again and again. In a tropical landscape one's eye takes in everything except the human beings. It takes in the dried-up soil, the prickly pear, the palm tree and the distant mountain, but it always misses the peasant hoeing at his patch. He is the same colour as the earth, and a great deal less interesting to look at.

(...)

For several weeks, always at about the same time of day, the file of old women had hobbled past the house with their firewood, and though they had registered themselves on my eyeballs I cannot truly say that I had seen them. Firewood was passing – that was how I saw it. It was only that one day I happened to be walking behind them, and the curious up-and-down motion of a load of wood drew my attention to the human being beneath it. Then for the first time I noticed the poor old earth-coloured bodies, bodies reduced to bones and leathery skin, bent double under the crushing weight. Yet I suppose I had not been five minutes on Moroccan soil before I noticed the overloading of the donkeys and was infuriated by it.

(...)

This kind of thing makes one's blood boil, whereas – on the whole – the plight of the human beings does not. I am not commenting, merely pointing to a fact. People with brown skins are next door to invisible. Anyone can be sorry for the donkey with its galled back, but it is generally owing to some kind of accident if one even notices the old woman under her load of sticks.

(Orwell 1946: 183–86)

Part II

Chapter 6

Living with the Masoala National Park

This book tells two stories about how the Masoala partnership project between the park management in Madagascar and the zoo in Zurich is perceived by 'ordinary' people at both its ends, and what it entails in terms of these people's mutual imaginations of one another. The first part has examined what visitors to the zoo's Masoala exhibit reflect about when they look at the project as it is presented to them at the zoo. In this second part of the book we move to Masoala itself, investigating what it is that the people on the peninsula perceive when they look at the park. The two stories will be juxtaposed in the final conclusions.

Let me begin with a remark about the meaning of the word 'Masoala'. The zoo in Zurich and the Wildlife Conservation Society consistently proclaim that 'Masoala' means 'The eye of the forest' (e.g. Rübel et al. 2003), on the basis of *maso* meaning 'the eye' and *ala* meaning 'the forest'. This translation is, however, not confirmed by people who live on the Masoala peninsula, including residents in the village of Masoala at its southern tip. According to them, the origin of the name 'Masoala' has nothing to do with the forest. The southern tip of the peninsula is surrounded by coral reefs making it difficult for canoes to find their way in (dugout canoes are a frequent means of transport in the area). *Oala* refers to an opening within the reef that would allow passage, and *maso* (the eye) refers to the person standing at the front of a canoe looking out for an *oala* and pointing the way. *Masoala* can refer both to the opening itself or the person looking out for it. There is no written source for this information but it is consistently given by people living on the Masoala peninsula and is also supported by some etymological reflections. Malagasy belongs to the Austronesian language family (Madagascar has clear historical links to the Indonesian archipelago [e.g. Cox et al.: 2012]), and the explanation of the meaning of the word 'Masoala' given by local people corresponds with this origin. In Maanyan, which is spoken in Borneo and to which Malagasy is most closely related, *kuala* means 'embouchure' (Dahl 1951: 77) or in Malay, for example, *kuala* means 'river mouth/estuary' (as in Kuala Lumpur: 'muddy estuary').

The following account is based on a total of eleven months of fieldwork that I conducted in two villages on the Masoala peninsula between 2005 and 2012 (I have been conducting fieldwork in the district of Maroantsetra to which Masoala belongs since 1998 for a total of thirty-two months, including the eleven months dedicated to the present research). One of these villages, Ambanizana, where I spent most of the time, is located on the periphery of the Masoala National Park, a short walking distance from its boundary. The other, Marofototra, is an enclave inside the park and has the status of a Zone d'Occupation Contrôlée.

Ambanizana: A Village on the Park's Outskirts

Ambanizana is beautifully located between the forest and the sea. It is both the administrative centre of the municipality of the same name and, with roughly twelve hundred inhabitants of whom only half are over the age of eighteen (census of 2008), it is the largest village within the *Commune Rurale* of Ambanizana. The village can only be reached on foot or by boat or canoe. No track on which even a bicycle could travel leads to it. Some of the village's houses are made of wooden planks, some of more perishable materials, and all are raised from the ground due to the wet climate. The houses are placed along one main and several smaller roads, with numerous paths crisscrossing between different families' compounds. Except for one other village in close proximity on the other side of the river, all neighbouring villages lie at a walking distance of between two and four hours. Ambanizana has its own primary school. The nearby village also offers secondary education as well as a modest health centre run by a trained nurse and assistant staff.

Ambanizana is located at the mouth of a river and is surrounded by a fair amount of flat land suitable for wet rice cultivation. According to oral accounts, the village was founded at the end of the nineteenth century, before the advent of French colonial rule, by two women and their families who had migrated to the area in order to make a living from land that they had inherited from their father. Employing the labour of slaves, the land was transformed into wet rice fields. Over the decades, further migrant groups from different regions of Madagascar arrived in Ambanizana, many of them carrying with them the legacy of former slavery. Just how important this aspect of the village's history is in connection with the Masoala National Park will become fully apparent in chapter 10. Beyond the rice fields, the landscape is dominated by steep hills.

Photograph 6.1 Ambanizana

The people of Ambanizana make a living in a variety of ways, depending on wealth. The better-off families grow rice in the valley. During difficult times, the additional production of hill rice by shifting cultivation (slash-and-burn method; *jinja* in the local dialect, *tavy* in official Malagasy) provides food security. Tropical storms regularly hit the area and may lead to the destruction of the wet rice harvest. Poorer families who do not own enough or any fields in the valley entirely depend on growing rice on the hilly land beyond the village. All families grow supplementary crops such as manioc, tarot, maize, beans, bananas, pineapples and sugarcane on the hillsides on family-owned plots, mostly not exceeding a few hectares in size. Many also grow vanilla and cloves as cash crops. Depending on the world market prices, which often fluctuate dramatically (cf. Sodikoff 2012: 117, 123, 126), the money thus earned may or may not be sufficient to cover a family's needs for the next year. Beyond the cultivation of vanilla and cloves, there are very few other ways of earning cash.

Ambanizana has several village shops, locally referred to as *boutiques*, where necessities such as soap, washing powder, clothes pegs, pens, writing paper, envelopes, batteries and nails are sold, as well as foodstuff including rice, cooking oil, sugar, beans, lentils, onions, biscuits, and soft and alcoholic drinks. The shop owners are important people in Ambanizana. They own boats and regularly travel to the district's only town, Maroantsetra – a four- to six-hour boat journey across the Antongil Bay – to stock up on their supplies, thus providing the village's population with whatever they need. Because of the necessity to own a boat, becoming a shop owner, at least one of a shop of any size, requires a considerable amount of starting capital. In the absence of any government-run means of transport to town, the shop and boat owners take as many passengers as they possibly can on their journeys to and from town. The fee is not cheap but is affordable. The boat owners not only take people but also people's goods that the latter either wish to sell in town or bring back to the village (e.g. foam mattresses), again for a fee. At the time of the clove harvest, for example, the village's three or so boats travel back and forth very regularly, thus offering many possibilities to commute to town and back. During much of the year though, transport is more irregular, and when the sea is rough it is quite possible that there is no transport for a week or more.

The shop owners also own electric generators. In the evenings these power their personal television sets – in 2012, three households had television – at times attracting quite a crowd of children and teenagers peeking in through the window. The owners do not mind others watching with them, and they often place their television sets in such a way that the screen can also be seen by the outdoors viewers. Occasionally, owners of electric generators arrange a public film programme – usually an action film – that is announced in advance on boards on the veranda of their shops. On these occasions, a viewing area with bench seats is arranged, allowing those who have paid the small fee to watch the film. Such distractions from daily life are rare though. Besides this 'village cinema', once or twice a year there is a *spectacle* when a pop group from the district of Maroantsetra or beyond comes to Ambanizana to perform. These are very popular events, especially but not exclusively with the youth, involving immensely loud music blasting across almost the entire village, for at least one but often two consecutive nights, into the early morning hours. Other festivities are almost always connected to rituals for the ancestors, which I will return to in later chapters.

Ambanizana is a long way from any telephone line. However, since the introduction of mobile phones in the district in the late 2000s, some people in Ambanizana own a mobile phone, but they only work in certain spots along the beach and only under certain weather conditions.

The Masoala National Park

The Masoala National Park was established in 1997. Within a quickly growing nationwide network of various types of protected areas, it remains, in 2013, among the very biggest. Only one other conservation zone, which is adjacent to Masoala and has been operating under protected area status since 2005, is larger in size.[1] Extending over a surface area of 2,300 square kilometres, the Masoala National Park takes up half the peninsula.[2]

Defining the Park's Boundaries

During the preparatory years leading up to the park's creation, the Wildlife Conservation Society (WCS) was already playing a crucial role in the realisation of the park project (Hatchwell 2003; Ormsby 2003: 62–63). Scientists working for WCS were also highly influential in determining the park's exact size and boundary line. The proposal, drawn up by a team led by the zoologist Claire Kremen (Kremen et al. 1995, unpublished) who at the time worked for WCS, was subsequently implemented with only minor changes to it (Kremen et al. 1999: 1064).[3]

According to the team's published report which details the factors and criteria guiding the design of the Masoala National Park (Kremen et al. 1999), the team 'took care to develop the park proposal in consultation with people at local and national levels' (ibid.: 1065). The unpublished proposal (Kremen et al. 1995)[4] also makes it clear that the team undertook extensive analyses concerning a variety of issues including mapping the territories currently used by village populations for their subsistence needs, and that the aspired ideal was to design the park in such a way as to avoid conflict with villagers wherever possible. The crux of the matter, however, lies in the last two words: 'wherever possible'. The unpublished proposal, especially, shows the limitations of consultation. First, negotiations with villagers took place only within already determined parameters set by conservation targets (for a similar point, see Corson 2011b). Second, it is evident in both the published and the unpublished texts that when determining the park's size and shape, the top priority was habitat protection for endangered animal and plant species, and that local people's land uses were only considered as long as the latter did not interfere with conservation goals. Luckily, it was found that the more populated peripheral zones of the peninsula along its eastern shore did not need to be included within the park in order to achieve its conservation goals (all relevant species were also found within what became the park's 'hard core'). This considerably reduced potential conflict with local populations. In cases of conflict, especially on the west coast of the peninsula where my field sites are located, 'special negotiations' (Kremen et al. 1999: 1064) with villagers were required. A third limitation concerns the question of who, on the local level, the team worked with. The published report states: 'Village territories were mapped (by the ground-truthing procedure) as defined by village participants rather than by legal tenure, and included both farmlands and areas for collecting forest products. Socioeconomic and agricultural data were obtained through focus-group interviews in 25 villages' (Kremen et al. 1999: 1058). Although the team was at pains to stress their intention to respect traditional land rights, neither the published nor the unpublished texts give any details as to who represented the villagers in such negotiations. The not unlikely possibility that those representing the village were members of local elites is supported by the following description of the procedure in cases of conflict over territories between conservation goals and claims by villagers:

> Villagers were never evicted from lands they had settled, despite their lack of legal tenure, *unless social norms permitted eviction*. For example, social norms dictated that the communities illegally established near the corridors [narrow forested strips joining up larger forest areas] should not be evicted because these communities had invested heavily in developing irrigated rice paddies over a long period of time. We knowingly increased the park's management burden to respect these norms and gain local support. In contrast, other villagers (47 households) were practicing slash-and-burn farming illegally out of temporary settlements near the headwaters of several watersheds. Here, social norms encouraged the reintegration of these people into permanent villages because they had made no investment in permanent agriculture and their activities potentially threatened the water supply of downstream communities. (Kremen et al. 1999: 1065; emphasis added)

In all likelihood, it would be the already better-off families who own irrigated paddy fields and who would therefore benefit from the above 'social norms', while those practising hill rice cultivation out of temporary settlements far away from villages – that is those to be evicted and resettled – would be the poorest of all. Thus it seems extremely likely that the social norms referred to in the report were determined by members of the village elite who, because they are elite members, would be the most likely to represent their village in such a committee (cf. Evers 2013: 130–31).

The unpublished park proposal (Kremen et al.: 1995) details the points the villagers are said to have agreed to, including the following: Isolated pieces of land far away from permanent villages would not be taken into consideration; and all new deforestation would be heavily punished, including the possibility of expelling culprits from villages and even expelling entire villages in case of failure to cooperate with the authorities. The proposal further states that there was no opposition to these points on the part of the villagers who, however, expressed anxiety about the future of their children unless they would be assisted in the cultivation of their existing fields. It is also mentioned that the farmers were clearly aware of their weak legal position – none of them having any official land title – and that they therefore entered the negotiations in a 'consensual' manner. Moreover, it is not impossible that when interviewed by Kremen and her team, who would be associated with the state authorities, their respondents produced what is locally referred to as *récitation*. In French, *récitation* refers to the reproduction of matter one has learnt by heart. I have many times heard people in the villages make statements like 'When they (people connected with the park) come along, we produce *récitation*' (*mañano récitation zahay*), meaning 'we say what we know they want to hear but this is not necessarily what we really feel and think'. The reasons leading people not to speak their mind in such situations are complex, but they likely have to do with a pan-Malagasy cultural tendency to avoid conflict, especially with people considered powerful, out of fear and for fear of repercussions as well as wanting to keep the door open for possible benefits that might come their way in the future (see also chapter 9).

It would take another study to analyse in detail how the proposal of the Masoala National Park that Kremen and her team designed was actually implemented on the ground,[5] and which processes have led to the present situation as it manifested itself in the villages of Ambanizana and Marofototra. However, if it was true that the proposal of how the park should be designed and implemented 'won the approval of local residents' (Kremen et al. 1999: 1055), something must have gone seriously amiss since. Between 2005 and 2012 when I conducted fieldwork for the present study, local people in Ambanizana and Marofototra almost universally perceived the Masoala National Park as a threat to their livelihood, and only in the rarest of circumstances did anybody voice any opinion in favour of the park.

While at the beginning an international development NGO (CARE) was involved in the park project, since the year 2000 the Masoala National Park has been co-managed by the WCS and ANGAP (Association Nationale pour la Gestion des Aires Protégées), the Malagasy National Protected Areas Agency[6] (see Wohlhauser and Kistler 2002: 54–55). In 2011, ANGAP was renamed 'Madagascar National Parks', in English. Because most of the research on which the present account is based was conducted before the renaming and because only a handful of local people have received news of the change of name, in what follows I will refer to the park's agency by its old name of ANGAP.

Various funding bodies (including USAID, the WWF and the MacArthur Foundation) have been involved in the course of the park's seventeen years of existence.[7] One of the most permanent and reliable partners has been the zoo in Zurich, which has been a major ideological supporter and donor since even before the park's inauguration. As already mentioned in the introduction to this book, the zoo has committed itself to contribute at least $100,000 (U.S.) annually, that is between a quarter and a third of the park's annual operating costs, via its partner organisation, the WCS. In

June 2007, ten years after its inauguration, the Masoala National Park was declared a UNESCO World Heritage Site, with the Zurich zoo having been a major lobbyist for this move.

The Park's Zones

The Masoala National Park consists of three types of zone, in each of which different regulations apply concerning access and the exploitation of natural resources, as well as different penalties for violation of these regulations. Almost the entire surface area of the park is designated the 'Noyau Dur', or Hard Core. Access to the Hard Core is only open to park staff, paying guided tourists and researchers (also paying), but not to the local population except when, on special occasions, authorised by ANGAP. The exploitation of natural resources within the Hard Core is punishable by fines and/or imprisonment. The present national legislation pertaining to protected areas in Madagascar, called Code de Gestion des Aires Protégées (COAP) and which came into force in 2005,[8] distinguishes between crimes (*crimes*) and offences (*délits*) depending on the severity of a transgression. The deliberate felling of trees inside the Hard Core would, for example, count as a crime, whereas accidentally losing control of a fire would be considered an offence. The stated penalty for a crime is forced labour (*travaux forcés*)[9] for a period of between five and twenty years, plus an immense fine equivalent to the value of between two and four hundred head of cattle. The penalty envisaged for an offence is a fine (a tenth of the amount of fines for crimes) and/or six months to two years in prison.[10] In the political district of Maroantsetra, in which my research sites are located, these incredibly harsh punishments are mostly not enforced to the degree stated in the law's text (but see below on prison sentences). Nevertheless, the existence of this legislation certainly does not fail to frighten the population, even if the great majority only half knows and half understands what COAP is and what it contains.

The second type of zone within the Masoala National Park is the 'Zone Tampon' or Buffer Zone. Along the park's edges, comparatively narrow (roughly 1–2 km wide) strips of land have been designated Buffer Zones, inside which the population living adjacent to the park is allowed to make limited use of the available natural resources – uses that are considered sustainable by the park authorities. The cultivation of hill rice in particular is prohibited also in Buffer Zones, as it necessitates the use of fire.

The third type of zone consists of inhabited enclaves inside the park called 'Zones d'Occupation Contrôlée', or ZOCs.[11] Although, according to Kremen's published report (Kremen et al. 1999) and personal communications with park staff, the border of the Masoala National Park

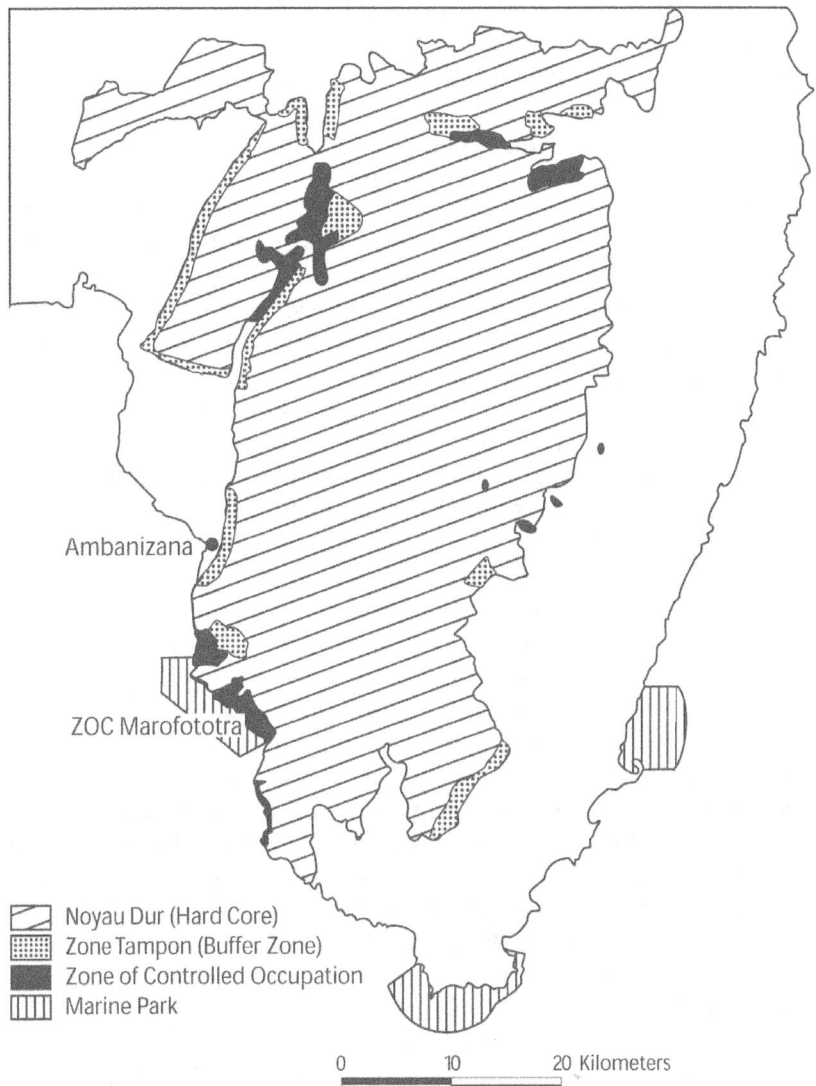

Image 6.2. Masoala National Park. Map provided by ANGAP in Maroantsetra in 2005, modified by Eva Keller

was drawn, whenever possible, to exclude human settlements, some villages and hamlets have come to fall inside its boundaries. These places, plus a relatively small area around them including most of people's cultivated land, now form enclaves within the park. The inhabitants of such enclaves are allowed to continue to live there and to use (most of) their already cultivated land. However, all their activities are only allowed within the parameters specified in the relevant regulations and are supposed to be monitored by park staff. The use of fire as an agricultural technique is categorically prohibited inside any ZOC. Importantly, this makes the cultivation of hill rice impossible. Given the landscape of the Masoala peninsula which does not offer many opportunities for wet rice cultivation, certain villages have been very short of rice since the establishment of the park, even more so than before. Remaining forest inside a ZOC may only be exploited in limited ways (for house building, for example) and its transformation into agricultural land is explicitly ruled out. The village of Marofototra, which I will introduce below, is such a Zone d'Occupation Contrôlée. Although the much larger village of Ambanizana does not lie inside the park but on its periphery, the people are much affected by the park, too, as it takes less than an hour to walk to its boundary. Visually speaking, the park begins halfway up the hills surrounding Ambanizana, and it is considered by the villagers to lie right on their doorstep. Theoretically, and on the map, there is a Buffer Zone between the outskirts of Ambanizana and the Hard Core of the Masoala National Park. This represents a stretch of land roughly ten kilometres long and one kilometre wide for the purpose of sustainable use by villagers. In reality, however, for reasons that park staff were unable to explain to me, this particular Buffer Zone does not exist. What should be a Buffer Zone accessible for sustainable use is, in fact, part of the park's Hard Core. Seen from Ambanizana, then, there is only 'inside' or 'outside' the park, the boundary between the two being marked by red paint on trees and stones.

Particularly difficult for the local population is the fact that the park's *de facto* boundary has changed several times over the years, always moving further down the hills in the direction of the village. When the boundary was first marked in the late 1990s, men from Ambanizana in fact helped with designating it (by red marks on trees, plastic ribbons and a two-metre wide corridor), and they received an appropriate salary for their work. At that time, the park was not considered a problem because it was much further removed from the village than nowadays, and the villagers had been previously informed about the proceedings. Between 2002 and 2006, however, ANGAP staff brought the marks further down in numerous places, this time without properly informing the local people about the park's new course, let alone consulting them. A later change was affected in 2008 in an area where many families from Ambanizana have land, now bringing the park's boundary right down to the sea.

Park staff do not deny these changes but challenge the villagers' interpretations. According to the director of the Masoala National Park (personal communication, 6 October 2008), the first demarcation was but a *proposition* (local people counter this explanation by asking why they were asked to cut a corridor to mark it if it was not a proper boundary yet, and by asserting that nobody had made it clear to them that this was not yet the definite boundary). This proposition was, however, later rejected by higher ANGAP authorities beyond the district because it did not conform to the park's official boundary as it had been determined. Subsequently, the latter was implemented over the course of several years from 2002 onwards. In 2008, the (thus far) last changes were effected so as to render identical the park's boundary on the map and on the ground.

Locally, the repeated de facto alterations of the park's boundary were experienced as a continual increase of the out-of-bounds area of the park. The changes, as well as the lack of consultation or even information, have caused a sense of great uncertainty among the population of Ambanizana and they fear further encroachments in the future. The fact that the alterations of the boundary were unpredictable for local people has also destroyed any trust in the park administration that they might previously have had.

The Loss of Land

Not all of the land that the people of Ambanizana are already cultivating is affected by the creation of the Masoala National Park, as many fields continue to lie outside the park's boundary even after the latest shift. The use of the land outside the park is, however, also subject to certain restrictions due to nationwide regulations concerning the exploitation of natural resources. All cultivation of hill rice, for example, needs to be authorised, and its authorisation is subject to a number of criteria such as the steepness of the land in question lest cultivation leads to soil erosion.

A household survey in the village of Ambanizana which I conducted together with my research assistant Harimalala Paul Clément in September and October of 2008 (that is after the latest boundary change) revealed that at least fifty-seven households representing about a quarter of the village's population have had substantial parts or all of the land on which they rely for their subsistence included within the park's boundary. What exactly does this mean for the concerned families?

Customary and State Land Rights

Customary land tenure in Masoala (as elsewhere in Madagascar) grants land ownership to the person who first clears a particular plot for cultivation. In Masoala, this right is inherited by the original owner's descendants, both male and female. A person intent on acquiring a new piece of land looks for *tany malalaka* (land where there is space), that is land that nobody else presently cultivates or claims as theirs. Elders of already established kin groups may be approached on such matters, but many other people as well have impressive knowledge concerning which land belongs to whom and which has no owner yet, and this in a hilly, almost entirely forested and complicated landscape. When a suitable piece of land has been found, its new owner embarks on marking the boundaries. Streams running down the hills often serve the purpose of delimiting someone's plot on two sides. In order to mark the upper limit and if necessary other important points of reference, the new owner plants a few banana or papaya trees or other fast-growing plants in the relevant spots, clearing just enough forest around them to make them visible as land-ownership markers. Only a part, mostly at the lower end of the new possession, is usually cultivated at first, leaving the rest untouched for one's descendants. Thus if, for example, a couple has acquired a piece of land of ten hectares (e.g. 200 x 500 m), they themselves may only cultivate two or three hectares; their sons and daughters and perhaps their grandchildren will cultivate the rest in the future. This system of customary land rights is universally respected in the village of Ambanizana including with regard to the forested, uncultivated land. Historically, different kin groups have through this process of acquiring land ownership established themselves as the landowners in particular areas in Ambanizana with descendants branching out until they reach someone else's land. Newcomers must find a slot somewhere on the margins with the consent of the already established landowners. But land is also bought and sold, in the latter case often because of some hardship hitting a family who have no other means to cover whatever expenses incur.

State law follows another logic. Christian Kull summarises contemporary forest regulations in Madagascar thus:

> Land tenure in rural zones is based on a mix of customary and state-sanctioned rules. While most permanent crop fields are private property (either officially titled or through customary tenure agreements), claims to upland zones are complex. Tradition gives land ownership to the descendants of those who originally clear plots; legislation upholds this practice but requires permanent cultivation for official title. . . . In most areas, de facto land rights in fallow-field zones and adjacent pasture or forest are under lineage-based control, unless a richer villager or outsider has obtained a government-sanctioned land title. All untitled, uncultivated land is also technically state domain, and the state claims most remaining natural forest areas as classified forests, reserved forests, or protected areas. (Kull 2004: 32)

The area on the west coast of the Masoala peninsula where Ambanizana is located is part of what Kull refers to as 'upland zones', with the hills starting directly at the shore or not far beyond. Next to nobody in Ambanizana has an official title to their upland zone land, partly because people did not consider it necessary to register their land with the state before the Masoala National Park was created and partly because the procedure is extremely lengthy and costly. 'We don't have any papers (*Tsisy taratasy mazava*)', people would explain, summarising in one expression the difficulties resulting from a situation of legal pluralism. Whatever the official legislation granting a certain weight also to customary law, the upland zone around Ambanizana was clearly not considered as being subject to any negotiations between the customary owners and the designers of the park (see also Kremen et al. 1999). The Masoala forest is clearly state domain, not only technically.[12]

The Convention

Fortunately for those households in Ambanizana who had substantial parts of the land on which they depend for their livelihood included in the park area, the present park director recognises the severity of the situation for many families and that it is untenable to simply stop them from further using their land without offering them an equivalent alternative of some kind, either in the form of land elsewhere or in the form of money, neither of which, according to him, ANGAP has been able to do. In 2005, he therefore drafted a convention between the park management and the people of Ambanizana which was intended as a temporary solution to the situation. This handwritten convention, however, is not a legally valid document, the park director told me, and he therefore asked me not to actually reproduce it in any publications but agreed to its main points being summarised (personal communication, 6 October 2008). The convention contains nine articles written in Malagasy, and it was signed by the park director, six further representatives of the park, three political leaders of the village of Ambanizana and thirty-six farmers. The key points of the convention state that the present boundary of the park shall not be changed (an assertion that was later violated by further de facto changes) and that the local people may continue to use already productive, cultivated plots. Land referred to as *savoka* – bush land without any current crops that has regrown after clearing – must, however, not be touched anymore. As the cultivation of hill rice in Masoala necessitates the previous burning of such *savoka* vegetation, the convention excludes the possibility of producing rice on the land in question. As mentioned earlier, many families have no other option to grow rice, a crop that is not only the main staple food but that is also heavy with cultural meaning (see next chapter).

Although the convention is a relief for many families and has meant that they have been able to continue to actually plant certain crops on the land that is now inside the park, they are but temporarily tolerated on their own land and the future is uncertain. The sense of uncertainty is heightened by the repeated changes of the park's boundary, and people's trust in the park authorities has dropped to virtually nil. Many farmers have given up hope that they will once again become the recognised owners of their land, others still hope. 'I am really sad (*malahelo*) about what the park is doing to us', one young man remarked.[13]

Fifty-Seven Households

What has the inclusion of (some of) their subsistence land meant for the concerned families? Of the fifty-seven affected households in Ambanizana, I present thirteen examples chosen to represent the variety of situations people find themselves in (reporting the situation as of October 2008). For many of those whose situation we recorded in the household survey that my research assistant and I carried out, it was difficult to estimate the size of the land in question, as people in rural areas in Madagascar are not used to thinking in European forms of measuring land. One woman, for example, described the size of her land inside the park thus: 'It reaches from the sea to where you cannot hear the waves of the sea anymore'. People's loss in the following examples is therefore mainly rendered in terms of the crops that were previously grown on the land, as well as the estimated percentage that loss represents with regard to their overall subsistence activities.

Because many of the issues discussed below are sensitive, all the names of the individuals referred to hereafter are pseudonyms chosen completely arbitrarily from among names commonly used in the area. For the sake of clarity, I have largely avoided teknonyms though they are very often used in Masoala. Also, in a few places in the course of the following chapters, though not in the thirteen situations described below, I have changed certain details concerning particular individuals or their stories (such as changing someone's gender or moving a story from one village to another) when I felt this was necessary to render a person unrecognisable. None of these changes, however, affect the particular points made.

Koto is about forty and has five children, the oldest of whom is twenty. He and his wife have lost all the fields available to them to cultivate rice. Not owning any wet rice fields in the valley, they used almost all of their land on the hills surrounding the village to grow rice and, rotating between different plots, were able to produce a sufficient amount for their own consumption throughout the year. Now they have to buy all the rice they eat. Their land that now lies within the park's boundary has become overgrown (*dobo*) because Koto does not dare to use it any longer for fear of being imprisoned. The family now makes a meagre living from the little land that they have left outside the park, cultivating cash and food crops other than rice.

The 50-year-old Patrice and his family, too, used to grow enough rice to last them through the year. Now that about three-quarters of their land has come to lie inside the park, they lease some wet rice fields in the valley which provide rice for three months of the year. The rest, they have to buy.

The family of Maman' and Papan' i Ramena comprises six people. They own wet rice fields outside the park which feed them for nine months of the year. They also used to cultivate hill rice to cover for the remaining three months. This they are no longer allowed to do since about a third of their land was included within the park's boundary at the latest change in 2008. They now have to buy rice for three months of the year.

Jao's family already had to buy rice during nine months of the year before the park was created. Now they have no rice of their own at all.

Tody is about fifty, and he and his wife have six children. On the hill land that they inherited from their forebears they grow numerous crops including cloves, vanilla and coffee for cash, as well as food crops like manioc and other roots, sugarcane and fruit. All of this land is now within the park's boundary.

Beby and Jean-Paul are in a similar situation. For thirty years they had put all their efforts and resources in a piece of land perhaps four hectares in size that was included within the park's extension at the latest change of the boundary. Thanks to the convention described above, they can continue to grow vanilla and to herd their four head of cattle on the land in question, but the production of rice is ruled out.

Josephine lives in a tiny house together with her only daughter, providing for the two of them by herself. She inherited a small piece of land from her parents on which she cultivates various crops which are the basis of their livelihood. Her inheritance now lies within the park's boundary. She leases a tiny wet rice field outside but has to buy rice for eleven months of the year. Outside the park, she only owns four clove trees.

The land of Leva, a man of about thirty-five, was not yet included within the boundary when the latter was changed for the first time. He and his family continued cultivating coffee, bananas and other fruit, various roots and raffia, and in 2007 they also planted vanilla which takes about four years before yielding any beans. But their entire land came to lie inside the park in 2008.

Arivelo and his family used to cultivate twice as much rice as they needed for their own consumption, selling the surplus of their annual harvest. But when the boundary of the park was changed the first time, they lost half their rice fields. They can now produce no more than what they eat themselves.

Four adults and three children live in the household of Solo. Together with kinsmen he invested much time and effort in clearing a piece of forest which he estimates to be about one hectare large. The plan was to turn the land into a wet rice field. When this land was included in the park, it had already been cleared but was not productive yet. Solo's family now rents some rice fields which provide food for three months of the year.

As a young man about thirty years ago, Be Toto bought some land, on part of which the previous owner had already planted fruit and cash crop trees, while the rest was still forested. Be Toto's parents lent him the money for the purchase which he then paid back over many years. He extended the size of the cultivated parts of the land by clearing some more forest, but leaving most untouched for his own children and grandchildren to cultivate in the future. Later on, he also began executing a plan of turning a small, suitable piece of land into a wet rice field by constructing a water canal leading from a nearby stream to the future field. But in 2005, a quarter of his land came to lie inside the park, before the wet rice field could be used.

Another family lost already productive wet rice fields which had yielded a harvest of approximately seventy baskets of paddy rice a year.

Benoit and his wife are a couple at the beginning of their joint adult life, and do not as yet have any children. Benoit's father gave them land to cultivate on which they had begun growing vanilla, coffee and cloves, as well as various food crops. Although their inheritance was included in the park in 2006, they do not have to buy rice at the moment as they are still eating in Benoit's parents' house.

A few families have given up their land in the park despite the convention allowing them to continue to use already productive plots for the time being. Among these is Dolphin, a man of about thirty years of age whose two-and-a-half hectares of land were included in the park in 2005. He and his wife have three children and they used to grow rice, coffee, vanilla, tarot, bananas, pineapples, sugarcane and other edible roots and fruit on their land. Rather than continuing to cultivate it, they decided to leave it and to make a new start by buying new land a relatively long way from the present park boundary. 'What sense does it make to cultivate things on land that isn't ours any longer? If I continued and then later they came back to take the land away from us completely', Dolphin told us, 'that would be like my artery was cut', implying that this would be both emotionally unbearable and economically disastrous. In the past, Dolphin used to employ agricultural day labourers, whereas today he is, besides cultivating crops on his new piece of land, employed by others. 'I saw what happened in Ambodiforaha (a nearby village): first they told the people there "Go and work your land", but then they took the land away from these same people. Therefore we decided to make a completely new start now rather than in five or ten years.' Dolphin clearly does not have any trust in promises made or conventions signed. Most families, however, continue to plant manioc and other permitted crops on the land referred to in the convention, and hope for the best, largely for the lack of any other option. Many, however, are disinclined to make any long-term investments, as the threat of losing their land entirely and definitely hangs over the farmers' heads like the sword of Damocles.

The shrinking of the land area on which people are allowed to grow rice has at certain times led to a shortage of rice in Ambanizana. Some families were forced to cultivate their land outside the park twice a year, even if this reduces soil fertility. Some families who in the past had relied entirely on their wet rice fields now also began to practise slash-and-burn rice cultivation on plots outside the park. My host family, for example, despite being among the richer in the village, grew hill rice for the first time in 2008. This was because they had to share their rice with kin who did not have enough due to the restrictions set by park rules, so they themselves ended up not having enough stock to survive in the not unlikely event of a cyclone or other unpredictable incident. Such shortages of rice in the village also increased its price, which set those households who were able to engage in rice trade, especially the owners of *boutiques*, at an even greater advantage than they already were.

Land for Future Generations

Perhaps even more far-reaching and more worrying than these restrictions on the present uses of the land is its loss for future generations. Recall the customary process of acquiring and marking land ownership. As explained above, only a part of it is normally cultivated by the generation who acquire it either through inheritance, purchase or the clearing of forest. The rest is left untouched for future generations. The convention between the concerned families in Ambanizana and the park director, which grants local families certain de facto (though not legal) usage rights for an indeterminate length of time, exclusively concerns land that was already cultivated before it was included within the park's boundary. It does not concern forested land that people had left untouched for their children and grandchildren. Therefore, precisely because such land has remained forested, it has become, literally, no-go. Commenting on their lack of an alternative to living from the land, one elderly woman said bitterly:

> We have no diploma (*diplôme*) to . . . get us anywhere, other than farming. We have no *diplôme*, our *diplôme* is here. And some of our children don't have any *diplôme* either [cannot read or write]. We lack *diplômes*, our *diplôme* is there (pointing to the hills).

In fact, a lot of forested land in the vicinity of the village of Ambanizana was, according to many local residents, cleared between the early and the mid-1990s when people first got wind of the creation of something called a *parc* which would mean that the customary owners of still forested land would lose it. The news of the possible loss of forested land, which was received locally as something between a rumour and a threat, made those who believed it to be true and who had the necessary labour force rush out and clear as much of their land as possible in order to mark it as owned.[14]

The majority of the households briefly presented above also suffered, besides the loss of productive land, the *complete* loss of the forested land that they had kept in reserve for their descendants. In the cases of Jao and Leva for instance, the great majority of the land they owned was still uncultivated. Consider two final examples from the village of Ambanizana. Of an estimated fifteen hectares of land, Faliarivo had cleared two pieces of forest of about 50 × 50 m each for growing hill rice. The rest he intended for his children. All of this land is now inside the Masoala National Park. The 25-year-old George owns a piece of land of about three hectares of which about a quarter to a third he had cleared by the time the park reached it. He now has to feed his four children from the fruits of a piece of land of about one hectare in size.

The economic aspects of all these restrictions and losses are obvious. The sense of loss that the people concerned experience and feel is, however, far greater and much more profound than a mere economic calculation would suggest. I will discuss this sense of loss in the next chapter.

The Question of Compensations

For a long time, only people who had been physically evicted from their land or homes were internationally recognised as displaced persons. Due to voluminous amounts of evidence presented in social scientific studies which showed that not only physical but also economic dislocation leads to the impoverishment of rural people,[15] the World Bank in 2002 changed its policy. From then on, it has recognised as 'displaced' and hence entitled to proper compensation also those who are economically impoverished by their access to the natural resources on which they depend becoming restricted. Many such cases concern Nature conservation projects. Several other large institutions followed the World Bank's lead but Nature conservation organisations have been much slower in this respect (Cernea 2006). Certainly those working in Masoala, and Madagascar in general, have not followed suit.[16]

Nobody in Ambanizana has been offered compensation either in cash or kind for the losses described above, except for in the following four cases. In 2003, four people in Ambanizana received an amount of cash from ANGAP to compensate for loss of land. One person received the equivalent of the value of two 50 kilo bags of white rice and a mosquito net to compensate for approximately one hectare of productive wet rice fields plus a large piece of pasture. In comparison to the loss, the amount is too small to count as compensation. The second person received an even tinier amount. For a piece of land which yielded up to seventy baskets of unhusked hill rice, he was given a symbolic amount of 50,000 Malagasy francs,[17] the value of a single metal cooking pot. According to the narratives of several people in Ambanizana and beyond, the calculation of these amounts of cash has to do with the fact that ANGAP only evaluated the value of productive wet rice fields and cash crops (vanilla, cloves, coffee) but not of any other land such as pasture, current fallows or land on which people grow subsistence crops such as manioc or maize. The third person (Jao, already mentioned above) received the substantial amount of 1.9 million Malagasy francs. With this money, he invested 1.5 million in buying a new piece of land outside the then boundary of the park, and the remainder he used to buy a few household items (a foam mattress, for example, at the time cost about 400,000 Malagasy francs). But two years later, in 2005, when the de facto boundary unexpectedly moved further down the hills, half of this new piece of land also came to lie within the park, and after the latest change in 2008 only a small piece of the newly acquired land remains outside of it. Miriam, the fourth person who received cash from ANGAP in 2003, was given 9 million Malagasy francs, at the time the equivalent of three head of cattle. With this money she bought a new piece of land for 3 million which, as in the above case, was incorporated into the park a year later. The rest of the money Miriam had invested in buying wooden planks for a 4 × 3 m house. The money was sufficient to cover half the expenses of the house she intended to build. In 2008, her house was still unfinished. In sum, the overall net benefit obtained from ANGAP in the entire village of Ambanizana amounts to the value of half a 4 × 3 m house, plus a few household items.

The cash payments to these four people are recorded in a written document produced by ANGAP stating individuals' identity card number, their place of residence and the amount of money received. The payments are signed by the recipients and a representative of ANGAP. One of the four people signed with a thumbprint, another's signature looks extremely shaky. Except in one case, the amount stated in the document is higher than the amount the recipients claim to have actually received. I have no reason to believe that the latter intentionally lied or could not remember the exact amounts of money they were given. People in the village, although many of them illiterate, are very precise at remembering monetary values, but for those who are illiterate written numbers do not make much sense. Additionally, many villagers are not at ease with the form of written documents. Thus it is a fair guess that the people concerned did not realise that they had received less than what they signed as having received. Where the rest of the money went is an open question. In the one case where the amount stated on the document is identical to the amount the recipient claims to have received, the cash was received (for reasons that need not concern us here) in the headquarters of the Masoala National Park in town, in the presence of the park director rather than in the village. Since these payments in 2003, nobody in Ambanizana has received any money as compensation for the losses resulting from the park's present de facto boundary. In 2004, ANGAP evaluated the value of the land (counting cash crops and wet rice fields) of certain people but the promise of monetary compensation never materialised. This was confirmed to me by the park director. But even if it had, it could never substitute for land, because as one woman put it: 'The land never rots. No matter how many children, grandchildren and great-grandchildren you have, the land doesn't rot. But money will one day be gone'.

Prison Sentences

In 2006 and 2007, eight men from Ambanizana received prison sentences for violations of regulations concerning the use of natural resources. Consider the following examples.

At the time he told me his story, Roger was in his mid-twenties. He had two small children. When the park was demarcated the first time, Roger was one of those villagers who helped in cutting a narrow corridor into the thick vegetation, about the size of a door, and in applying red paint on trees and stones in order to mark the boundary. At that time, his land was a long way from the park's limits but it later came to lie inside. He and his wife do not own any wet rice fields in the valley. In 2006, Roger cleared a small piece of land in order to plant subsistence crops. 'I know that the forest is important and that the water supply depends on it, but I have no choice. I don't have any diploma or know-how, I depend on farming; people here in the countryside have nothing but their land.' Roger is convinced that someone from the village blew the whistle on him, perhaps under the influence of alcohol and for a fair amount of cash, he speculates. When one day he came back from his fields, the village's park employees were already waiting for him and immediately arrested him. He spent two days at their office in the village with his hands tied behind his back 'like a real criminal', he recalled. He was arrested together with another man from the village who had cleared a piece of forest outside the park. After two days, they were brought to town and put in a tiny windowless room for two weeks while waiting for the court session. At the tribunal, they each received a one-month prison sentence which they served in the prison in town. As this is the only prison in the district, everyone serves their sentence there, from thieves to murderers, to people like Roger. Having served their sentence, the two men were then allowed to cultivate the land they had cleared.

After the early death of his mother, Rakoto and his two younger siblings grew up with their grandmother (the father did not care for the children). In order to help her with the agricultural work, he left school at the age of twelve. In 2007, when he was eighteen, he cleared a piece of forest of approximately 20 × 20 m, bordering on already cultivated land of theirs. The land in question lay outside the park's boundary and there were no large trees left on it due to a cyclone which had hit the area. This is why Rakoto chose this particular piece for clearing. He did not ask for permission with the relevant authorities as he feared not to receive it. He was sentenced to one year and eight months in prison. But Rakoto was 'lucky'. After being in prison for just five weeks, a wealthy person from town who owns fields near Ambanizana arranged for Rakoto to work for him instead of being imprisoned. Henceforth he had to present himself at the prison twice a month as evidence that he had not run away, and he had to work on his patron's fields rather than his own during the length of his sentence. That was the price for his freedom.

Philippe had begun clearing the bushes on a piece of his land of less than a hectare that he was sure was outside the park's boundary. 'I saw the red marks – they were a long way further north, at least a kilometre or so.' Although he had not yet felled any large trees, he was sentenced to fifteen days in prison – plus three days under arrest at the village's ANGAP office and another three days at the police station in town for the interrogation – and he also had to pay a substantial fine. He has not touched the land in question since.

The prison sentences that the eight men from Ambanizana received in 2006 and 2007 ranged from two weeks to eighteen months, and in one case five years. In the last case, the culprit had felled a small number of trees (he said five) which shaded his banana trees. Moreover, the land in question lay outside the park. It is difficult to know why this one man received such an extraordinary punishment but it seems to have been due to a combination of his inability to pay a bribe, his difficulty in expressing himself in court and of understanding the judge speaking official Malagasy, and of the judge wanting to make an example of his case for other potential culprits. Some of the eight men could reduce their prison sentence to the ones stated above through 'payments'. Two of them had to pay a substantial fine additionally to their prison sentence. The sentences given for specific violations do not follow any logic that is recognisable to either the local population or indeed to an outside observer like myself. Their apparent arbitrariness further adds to a sense among local people of being at the mercy of forces beyond their control.

As Time Moves On

Between 2005 and 2012, I spent a total of eleven months mainly in Ambanizana and partly in the enclave of Marofototra that I will introduce shortly. In these seven years, things did not remain static. The period between 2005 and 2008 was very much informed by a strong and omnipresent sense among the local people of the Masoala National Park approaching the village like an enemy lurking in the background and watching the villagers, an enemy whose next move was as uncertain as it was feared. The park was felt to be an immediate threat. In the spring of 2009, after months of intense political turmoil, a new national government called Haute Autorité de la Transition, or HAT – and which eventually remained in place until the end of 2013 – took power in Madagascar. The new situation led to many kinds of difficulties all over the country. In Masoala it meant, among other things, that the control over the villagers' use of the natural resources became less pronounced for reasons that need not concern us here, and anyway are not in my competence to comment on. When I returned to Ambanizana in 2010, the same people who had bitterly complained about the imminent threat the park posed to their livelihoods reported that ANGAP had become 'a little softer' (*malemy hely*), less harsh, and that the park was not too much of a problem for them at the moment. The park employees that are stationed in the village (see below) had apparently stopped going on patrols up the hills, allegedly because they had failed to receive their salaries. They were often absent for long periods and their office in the village simply closed, and so the cultivation of hill rice, even inside the park, had become considerably less risky. A couple reported:

> They don't come up the hills anymore as they used to in the past; we don't have to reckon with a patrol at all times and anywhere. Nowadays, they only walk along the path along the shore. At the moment it's even possible to grow hill rice. Quite a few people have gone back to cultivating hill rice but we haven't, we wouldn't dare.

Furthermore, concerning land that lies *outside* the park, a new system of getting authorisation for the use of natural resources was introduced in 2009. Since then, the farmers in Ambanizana have no longer needed to deposit demands with ANGAP or the district's Ministry of Water and Forests, but do so with a new institution called V.O.I., or Comité de Base.[18] The new system transfers the right to grant or to reject authorisation for cultivating hill rice outside the park or cutting a tree for building a house, for example, to the members of the V.O.I. The following information was provided by Ambanizana's V.O.I. president. Each village of the *Commune* must name eight V.O.I. members. One turn of office lasts three years. In Ambanizana, the selected people did not volunteer as members but the village president was asked to suggest candidates. The V.O.I.'s president, for example, used to work for the American Peregrine Fund for three years, making him an obvious candidate both because of his knowledge of the terrain and his ability to deal with paperwork. The V.O.I. members are not paid even though they have a number of duties. In particular, it is their job to examine all demands concerning the cultivation of hill rice, the use of certain leaves for roofing, the felling of a tree to make a dugout canoe, and any other demand that involves the use of natural resources outside the park's boundary. The demands have to be examined on the basis of a fifteen-page document which specifies what is and what is not allowed. For example, authorisation for the cultivation of hill rice must not be given if a territory is too steep lest it should lead to erosion, or if the land is too close to the mouth of a river or stream. This documentation was produced by ANGAP and WCS, the two bodies that co-manage the park. The local V.O.I. members are required to go *sur terrain* several times a year in order to inspect local people's activities and make sure that they all have the required authorisations. The territory that Ambanizana's V.O.I. members are supposed to control in this way stretches across an area of approximately 1.5 × 10 km. First-time and minor violations of the rules are dealt with in the village (fines are supposed to go to communal projects), and only repeated or drastic violations are brought to the attention of the relevant authorities in town. Good news for the farmers, the V.O.I.

president said, but bad news for the members because it means a lot of work for no money. This situation has led to only two of the eight V.O.I. members in Ambanizana being actually active, the president himself and one other man. A further problem complicating the V.O.I. members' situation is that as they are local people they have to check on their kin and co-villagers; the implications are obvious. ANGAP still goes on patrol, the V.O.I. president told me, but only if they have a concrete suspicion about someone doing something illegal – for example, if someone is seen with a new canoe but the V.O.I. cannot produce an authorisation for the felled tree. Such cases then fall back on the V.O.I. members as they are accused of not having done their job. Although the new system at first looks like more participation and self-government by local communities, the V.O.I. members are put in charge of monitoring others' rules and are forced into a pseudo-cooperation with the park management.

Concerning land *inside* the park, there has been no official change of the situation. People's land still lies inside the park and they continue not to be recognised as its rightful owners; they are merely granted right of limited use for an undetermined length of time on the basis of a legally invalid handwritten document, the aforementioned convention. Importantly, although in Ambanizana the situation is presently felt to be 'softer', the threat, from the point of view of local farmers, of it deteriorating again at any time remains. Moreover, people hear stories from other villages that enhance distrust. In a village a three-hour walk away from Ambanizana, and connected with Ambanizana by numerous kinship ties, the Masoala National Park begins only about two hundred metres beyond the village. In early 2011, a devastating cyclone ravaged the area, destroying many crops including much of the wet rice planted in the valley's fields. Additionally, the same year, it did not rain enough and so the remaining rice fields yielded much less than usual. In such a situation, planting hill rice is an emergency strategy. Two men from the village in question who had grown hill rice for consumption were imprisoned in April 2012 and held until their trial which eventually took place in October of the same year. They each received a five-year prison sentence. However, at the time of writing (December 2013), the sentence of one of them has been suspended on probation and subject to monthly payments, and the other man is allowed to leave the prison during daytime but has to return each evening.

Their case is well-known in Ambanizana and surely beyond, and does not fail to trigger new fears of a harsh wave coming along. One of the most difficult aspects of the situation in Masoala is the permanent and prevalent sense of uncertainty among the local population as one never knows what might happen next, and the question concerning trust in the park authorities is usually answered with one French word: *zéro*. The situation keeps changing for reasons that remain opaque to the families concerned. As a result, people live with a permanent sense of not knowing what their situation will be like in one, two, five, ten years from now: whether they will still be allowed to at least cultivate certain crops on their land in the park, whether they will lose their land completely, whether the boundary will change again, whether the park management will introduce new rules, and many other 'whethers' of this kind. But as they have no option to do anything other than farming and nowhere else to go, they have no alternative but to keep their noses to the grindstone and hope for the best.

During certain periods since 2009, illegal logging of precious wood has taken place from deep inside the Masoala National Park, especially rosewood and ebony, at times on a very large scale, in which young men from the Masoala peninsula were involved as day labourers (Randriamalala and Liu 2010). From some local people's point of view, such business provided a welcome and rare opportunity to earn good money. The labourers' wages were good but not extraordinary by local standards, but if one stayed inside the forest for a few weeks or longer, one could save up a considerable amount of money. The following example that I chanced to witness illustrates what involvement in such trades means from the perspective of those who work at the bottom of the ladder.

The case I recount here involved a young man from a village in Masoala who had spent three months away from his wife and young child doing the difficult and dangerous job of cutting trees and dragging them along to the next river from where they were floated to their next destination. Upon his return, he bought a foam mattress and built a proper kitchen for his family, replacing the previous simple shed. In order to celebrate his achievement, he gave a party inviting kin and neighbours to drinks. On arrival, each guest briefly went into the young couple's house and performed a kind of step dance in front of the new mattress, thus expressing joy. Having seized the opportunity to make extra money quickly, although risky and dangerous from a number of perspectives not least in terms of potential injury, the money thus earned made the difference between having and not having a mattress, and gave this young man the chance, in his own eyes and those of many others, 'to become someone'.

Marofototra: An Enclave inside the Park

In some cases, new villages have been created by the park authorities to bring together in one location those who formerly lived in separate hamlets inside the forest. Marofototra, the second of my research sites, is one such village that was created as part of a resettlement programme instigated by the park authorities. It is a Zone d'Occupation Contrôlée or ZOC.

The village of Marofototra lies within an area that underwent extensive logging activities during the colonial era. Tens of thousands of tons of rosewood, ebony, and other precious woods were cut and then shipped from nearby ports to destinations such as Mauritius and La Réunion (Petit and Jacob 1965: 51–53; see also Fremigacci 1998, 2009).[19] After the end of French colonial rule in 1960, most of those who had worked as lumberjacks for the *colons* moved back to their homes, leaving the area almost completely uninhabited. A relatively short time after this, however, beginning in the mid-1970s, people (mostly from nearby villages where agricultural land had become sparse, and sometimes the same people who had formerly worked for the colonial logging businesses) started to return to the densely forested area in the environs of today's village of Marofototra to embark on creating a livelihood there. In many cases, single men came first, spending many months by themselves transforming forest into agricultural land for their future families. Once established in the area, people cultivated rice, manioc, and other tubers for subsistence, and vanilla to obtain cash. Additional income might occasionally have come from selling a piece of rosewood or ebony. These new settlers lived dispersed within the forest either in individual households or small hamlets on the land that they had cleared for themselves, often only a short distance from other families' residences. All of the families of Marofototra, except one, are first- or second-generation migrants.

With the arrival of the Masoala National Park a couple of decades after many of these people had begun creating a livelihood in the area of Marofototra, life took a dramatic turn for them. Because the particular stretch of the rainforest they had chosen as their home is considered to be of outstanding importance for conservation goals, it was included within the boundary of the park (see Kremen et al. 1999). In 2001, the area's inhabitants were relocated from their hamlets to the new village. Each household was allocated a courtyard of exactly the same size: 20 × 30 m. About ten families left, returning to where they had come from in the first place. By 2006, almost four hundred people lived in Marofototra. The new village forms the centre of the Zone d'Occupation Contrôlée of Marofototra and is surrounded by an area of land of approximately 7 × 2 km. This is the space that the inhabitants of Marofototra are allowed to use for their livelihood. What lies beyond forms part of the Hard Core of the Masoala National Park into which local residents have no access rights. Most of people's land that was already productive at the time of the new village's creation lies within the usable area – as do the old hamlets which are now in the process of decay – but some fields, including wet rice fields, have come to lie inside the park's Hard Core. According to local people's narratives, the already productive land of eight families was included. In contrast to the situation in Ambanizana, the families in Marofototra who lost productive wet rice fields and cash crops received pecuniary compensation from ANGAP. In some cases, the money received was sufficient for the concerned people to buy new land elsewhere. In other cases the amount ridiculed the actual loss. One family who decided to leave when Marofototra became a ZOC received sufficient money to buy new land as well as a house. In another case, the compensation amounted to a mere 100,000 Malagasy francs (less than 10 euros at the time) for a field which had yielded enough rice for three months' consumption.

The Dina

As mentioned, inside the enclave's extension, Marofototra's inhabitants are allowed to continue to cultivate the arable land already in use but only in ways considered sustainable by the park authorities. A document specifying the legislation pertaining to the ZOC of Marofototra was signed in 2002 by various representatives of the relevant political and juridical bodies, along with the Masoala National Park authorities and representatives of the local community. The latter claim that they had no real voice in the consultation process and that they either had to accept this agreement, called a *Dina*,[20] or else leave the area and give up their land. According to local residents, they had only a minimal say concerning the *Dina*'s final content, despite lengthy negotiations between themselves and ANGAP. The *Dina* of Marofototra specifies which activities are prohibited inside the ZOC and details the penalties for flouting the regulations. Its twelve paragraphs concern residence, forestry, agriculture, fishing, hunting, and commercial activities. Of particular importance for local people is the prohibition on new residents settling in the village (with the exception of spouses), the permanent fixing of the ZOC's extent to its present size, and the prohibition on selling material derived from natural resources found within the ZOC (especially wood) to outsiders. Also significant is the prohibition on selling one's land if one permanently moves away from the ZOC; in such cases, the land in question reverts to the park without any compensation being given. In other words, the people's land has become the property of the park which makes it available for cultivation to farmers as long as they or their direct descendants cultivate it themselves. Moreover, three paragraphs of the *Dina* foresee the possible permanent eviction of all the residents of the village of Marofototra for failure to adhere to the *Dina* or failure to report to the park authorities individual residents who violate it. To make sure that wrongdoers are reported, a Comité de Surveillance was installed in Marofototra. In 2007, it consisted of eight residents whose duty was to keep under surveillance, as the name suggests, the observance of the *Dina*, thereby instigating an internal policing system among the villagers themselves.

From the point of view of biodiversity conservationists, the biggest problem in Masoala is the local practice of slash-and-burn rice cultivation on hillsides, a practice on which the population in the forested area of Marofototra depends even more than the people in Ambanizana. There is very little land in the vicinity of Marofototra that is suitable for wet rice cultivation; only two kin groups own wet rice fields of significant size. In acknowledgment of people's dependence on this agricultural practice, the *Dina* signed in 2002 allows the authorised and controlled practice of a limited amount of slash-and-burn rice cultivation inside the ZOC of Marofototra. However, in the event of a legal conflict between the *Dina*, which is a local law, and the national legislation pertaining to all protected areas in Madagascar (the Code des Aires Protégées mentioned earlier), the latter overrules the former. The national legislation categorically rules out the use of fire within protected areas in Madagascar, including ZOCs such as Marofototra. In the agricultural season of 2006–7, farmers in Marofototra did not receive the necessary authorisation to cultivate rice on hill slopes and nobody in the village dared to disobey. As only few people either had, or were able to buy, enough rice to last them through the year, this situation inevitably extended, by as much as three or four months for some, the 'period of scarcity' (*silôño*), during which people largely have to live off manioc and other tubers to fill their stomachs. Whether the sudden curtailment of allowing a certain amount of hill rice cultivation was due to the Code des Aires Protégées is unclear. The timing certainly made it look like that at first. The year after, however, a limited amount of rice on hill slopes in the ZOC of Marofototra was authorised again – why, and why not the year before, the farmers did not know. I tried to establish the reasons behind these changes by enquiring both with the local park staff and with the park director in town. I received different explanations, which were neither consistent nor even always compatible, and nor were they known to the people in Marofototra. As in Ambanizana, the uncertainty resulting from such a situation is a key worry for the people who live in the Zone d'Occupation Contrôlée of Marofototra.

As in Ambanizana, changes of the park's boundary occurred subsequent to what the local people had understood to be the determination of its definite size. In December 2010, I met Jacques, a former president of the village. He was clearly upset and told me why:

This year, ANGAP changed the boundary twice. The old limit was marked with red paint on trees as well as a narrow corridor cleared to mark its course. This year, the boundary was moved, in two steps in quick succession. ANGAP said that the old marks had not been 'according to the law' (*ara-dalàna*) and that the new boundary was the correct one. 'Why did you mark the old boundary in the first place if it wasn't correct?' I asked them. 'Moreover, paragraph 4 of the *Dina* states that the boundary of the park cannot be changed unless all the signatory parties agree.' That is what I said to them. We only signed it in the first place because the park director at the time [not the present one] offered us no choice other than to either accept it or to leave. But the *Dina* states that in Marofototra the boundary cannot be changed unless we, the *fokonolona* (the village community), agrees, and we do not agree with this latest change.

The additional land that in 2010 came to lie within the park included productive hill slopes as well as wet rice fields. 'They told us that we are allowed to continue to work our already productive fields within the new boundary but I don't believe anymore what they tell us', Jacques continued. He also told me that the village had filed a complaint about this issue with the authorities in town. By October of 2012, when I last met Jacques, their complaint had not had any effect. On the contrary, in one place near the village the boundary has once again been moved in the direction of the village. 'Our space is becoming ever smaller' (*Mahay tery fô*), a man from Ambanizana commented on these latest events in Marofototra.

The Marine Park

The enclave of Marofototra is surrounded on three sides by the Hard Core of the terrestrial Masoala National Park; on the fourth side, it faces a stretch of the sea that has been designated a marine park. A second *Dina* pertaining to fishing prohibitions inside this marine park and to penalties in case of rule breaking was signed in 2005. This second *Dina* specifies permitted and prohibited fishing methods and equipment, as well as the species that may not be taken at all, or only during particular times of the year, or of a specified minimum size. Within these parameters, the population is allowed to fish for consumption and sale.

Of particular significance for the local population is the prohibition on catching sea cucumbers. Because selling dried sea cucumbers represents, along with the cultivation of vanilla, one of the few possible sources of cash income for Marofototra's inhabitants, in 2006 and 2007 it was not uncommon for sea cucumbers to be sold secretly, although engaging in this activity always carried the risk of a fine and, in the case of repeated offences, imprisonment.

Photograph 6.3. Women in Marofototra catching fish

Surveillance

In both Ambanizana and in Marofototra, ANGAP has an office normally staffed by two or three men, their *Agents*, who live permanently in the villages. Their main duties are to keep the park boundary properly marked, to regularly go on patrol (*manao patrouille*) in the forest in order to check on illicit activities and report infractions to their superiors in town, as well as to sensitise the villagers to the importance of forest conservation. ANGAP staff never work in their own home villages because it is understood that if they had to keep watch on and possibly report on their own relatives, this would never happen, but most agents originate from the area and are thus not considered 'foreign'. They are replaced relatively frequently (normally every three to four years) which also makes it clear that theirs is primarily a surveillance role; the development of close ties with local people is avoided by means of this frequent rotation, a practice that is also common in Madagascar in the police force, for example.

Although park staff often stay in their offices doing rather little that is recognisable as work to the local people, they may turn up anywhere and anytime, attempting to catch villagers red-handed in possession of sea cucumbers, for example, or felling a trees without authorisation. For the people of Ambanizana and Marofototra, the continual presence of ANGAP staff within their living space creates a strong sense of being under surveillance, although, as discussed earlier, the de facto level of control has varied over the years. When I asked people in Marofototra why they thought that ANGAP had made them move to the new village, many responded: 'So that they can watch us'. Some emphasised these words with mimes of their hands or arms being tied together. Not all ANGAP staff act their role as surveillants in the same way. Some seem to be accepted by most villagers, others are almost hated. One member of ANGAP once sent a letter to the *Gendarmes* in town alerting the latter to his life being in danger due to his job. I have also heard several people express their view that the agents do not dare to go on patrol alone, for fear of being attacked or worse.[21]

From Everyone's Perspective?

The description of the situation the people in Ambanizana and Marofototra find themselves in might give the impression that not a single person has gained anything from the park. This is not true, however. There are those who have taken opportunities to work for the park or its forerunner called *Projet Masoala*. There are those who have a seasonal job in the tiny tourist industry connected with the park. Although there is no tourist infrastructure in either Ambanizana or Marofototra, there are three lodges for eco-tourists halfway between the two villages a three-hour walk from each – they are all owned or run by white foreigners (see chapter 10) – and some women work there as cooks or chambermaids while a handful of men are employed as gardeners or porters. However, not only are these jobs few and far between, but they are restricted to a short tourist season which, unfortunately, coincides precisely with the time when there is most agricultural work to be done.

The park has also led to a small number of 'micro projects' that are partly financed by the zoo in Zurich. As we saw in Part I of this book, these projects are presented in the zoo's information centre, and many a visitor referred to such 'development projects' as an important aspect of biodiversity conservation. In Ambanizana and in Marofototra, some water canals made of cement have been built, replacing traditional ones made of split bamboo, in an attempt to improve the yield of wet rice fields. However, such projects often come to a standstill, for a number of reasons, before they are finished, or fail to be reconstructed when destroyed by a cyclone. Moreover and more importantly, water canals for wet rice fields support those families who own such fields, and these are already the best off. The poor in both villages quite simply do not own any wet rice fields to be irrigated. Without intending to negate either the good intentions behind such projects or their benefits to some, it would be a gross misrepresentation to suggest that they in any way provide an alternative to the immense losses that the creation of the Masoala National Park has entailed for so many.

I am aware that it is unfashionable to present 'the people of Ambanizana' or 'the population of Marofototra' in what some readers might perceive as unduly homogenising terms. To talk about their views of the park as if they were all speaking with one voice may give the impression of glossing over the inevitable differences within a village's population and the ways in which the more powerful, better schooled or better connected individuals or families will be able to grasp the benefits that might come along with a biodiversity conservation project such as the Masoala National Park. Other researchers have pointed to such internal differentiation in connection with Madagascar's numerous protected areas which may enable a small minority of locals to monopolise assets (Pollini 2007: chapter 11). In her analysis of a protected area in Madagascar's north, Gezon (2006), for example, focuses on local people's agency in the face of allegedly overpowering global forces discussing how local actors of varying social status bring to bear their influence in order to turn things to their advantage. I am not dismissing the validity of such a point, and in Ambanizana and Marofototra, too, not everyone is exactly in the same position vis-à-vis the park, as this chapter has made clear. However, emphasising the power of local farmers or fishermen to turn the kind of situation as prevails in Ambanizana and Marofototra to their advantage carries the risk of masking the drastic global power inequalities inherent in such situations and the extremely high level of external control over local people they entail (see Duffy 2006; Corson 2010, 2011a). I agree with Tsing when she writes that, on the one hand, one must 'avoid the idea that new forms of empire spring fully formed and armed from the heads of Euro-American fathers'. On the other hand, one must also avoid 'too eager a celebration of a southern cultural autonomy capable of absorbing and transforming every imperial mandate' (Tsing 2005: 5).[22]

In the case of Ambanizana and Marofototra, it would quite simply be ethnographically incorrect to say that different people have very different views of the Masoala National Park depending on what position they hold in the villages or what interest group or family they belong to. Take the example of Jaozoky. Jaozoky is a very influential local person holding an important political position. He owns many wet rice fields, and he is the direct descendant of the group who, using the labour of their slaves, created these very rice fields a good hundred years ago and founded

Ambanizana. He personally has not lost any land to the park, though his parents-in-law have. His views of the park as a threat to people's livelihood and as a manifestation of great injustice towards the local population are identical to those of Roger who ended up in prison for cultivating subsistence crops inside the park. If local people had any say, they would reset the park's boundaries to where they originally thought they were going to be, beyond the living space of the present and the next few generations. Even many park employees sympathise with local farmers' views when one catches them off duty. In the seven years when I repeatedly spent considerable amounts of time in the two villages, I never came across anyone who was happy with the situation as it was, even if they themselves were not directly affected by the park's extension. With the exception of a handful of people such as schoolteachers and park employees who had, but only to a certain extent, embraced the conservationist perspective promoted by the park management and its partners, everyone I ever talked to shared the view that the Masoala National Park has taken away land from people that is rightfully theirs. Not everyone wanted the park to disappear altogether, though many did, but close to everyone wanted its boundary to retreat so that people have enough space to live decently and in dignity. The most sympathetic view of the park was that the development projects offered by the park were utterly insufficient to make up for the losses and that the way forward was to enhance and multiply such projects. Besides a deeply felt sense of injustice, the omnipresent sense of uncertainty may further encourage a negative view of the park, because even those who do not materially suffer from its existence at present feel that they cannot be sure that they will not suffer from it in the future.[23]

The problems that the Masoala National Park entails for the people in Ambanizana and Marofototra are not unique in Madagascar. Similar situations have been shown to occur in connection with other protected areas as well. The large, well-funded parks in particular tend to involve practices that are highly problematic for local populations and are therefore received with considerable hostility (see Ghimire 1994; Harper 2002; Kaufmann 2008; Ferguson 2010b: 54–64; Sodikoff 2012: 6, 142). At times, the lack of concern on the part of conservation staff for local people's well-being is disturbing (see Harper 2002: chapter 7).

The quasi-universal dislike of the Masoala National Park among the people of Ambanizana and Marofototra is not only due to the fact that in these particular villages the benefits in connection with the park are extremely meagre and that many a family has experienced real losses as a result of the park's creation. The sense of loss goes way beyond present-day economic constraints. Perhaps the most important reason why there is so much agreement about the Masoala National Park being a really big problem is people's sense that it threatens local families' ability to be in control of the land upon which their future and the futures of their children and grandchildren depend. In both villages, uncleared forest that parents and grandparents have been keeping in reserve for their children and grandchildren can no longer be transformed into agricultural land as people are only allowed to continue to cultivate already productive land. What exactly this means to the people in Ambanizana and Marofototra I discuss in the next chapter.

Notes

1. There (Makira), too, the WCS is the key player (see Wildlife Conservation Society 2012 and 2013).
2. Statistics on how many people live on the Masoala peninsula are hard to come by and appear not too reliable, and it is not always clear whether or not the towns of Maroantsetra and Antalaha are included. In the mid-to-late 1990s, the population without the two towns was estimated at 39,000–45,000, and 80,000 if including the towns (Kremen et al. 1999: 1057; Wohlhauser and Kistler 2002: 37; Ormsby and Mannle 2006: 275). In 2009, the Zurich zoo stated that 117,000 inhabitants were living 'in 180 villages in the park's peripheral zones' (Masoala National Park 2009: 2); a zoo publication in 2013 speaks of 120,000 inhabitants 'around the Masoala National Park' (Zurich Zoo 2013a: 10). The source of this information is not revealed, and it is unclear whether the numbers include the towns or not.
3. This is a good example of the collaborations between science, government policy and non-governmental organisations that Fairhead and Leach analyse in their book *Science, Society and Power* (2003). Kremen, a scientifically trained biologist and zoologist, worked as a scientific expert for WCS and in this capacity was entrusted with designing a national park, thereby exerting a direct influence on Malagasy national policy.
4. I thank Claire Kremen for having shared with me upon request her team's unpublished proposal of 1995.
5. For instance, the restrictions in access to land on the peninsula were envisaged to be counterbalanced by the export of sustainably produced timber. Kremen and her team calculated that local communities would end up with an annual net benefit of $130 (U.S.) per household (Kremen et al.: 1999: 1063) if they engaged in marketing 'eco-timber' instead of continuing slash-and-burn rice cultivation. However, to the best of my knowledge, no such programme has ever been realised in Masoala – quite apart from other issues surrounding the proposed transformation of subsistence farmers into timber producers for the global market.
6. ANGAP is a semi-private or parastatal association that was created in 1990 in the wake of the National Environmental Action Plan (for details, see Mercier

2006). ANGAP was commissioned by the Malagasy government to manage the country's protected areas and is 'run and funded by a group of international NGOs and donors in conjunction with Malagasy state agencies' (Duffy 2006: 737). In 2007 the management of protected areas was reorganised and now involves other bodies besides ANGAP (Pollini 2007: 100; Corson 2011a), but at the time of writing, the Masoala National Park was still co-managed by ANGAP and the Wildlife Conservation Society (WCS).
7. Personal communication with the current director of the Masoala National Park, 30 December 2006. See also Wohlhauser and Kistler 2002: 59.
8. Code de Gestion des Aires Protégées: Law N° 2001–05, 11 February 2003; application decree No 2005–013, 11 January 2005.
9. For a discussion of colonial forced labour, see Fremigacci 2009 (concerning the district of Maroantsetra) and Sodikoff 2005; for perceived continuities with contemporary conservation practices, see Sodikoff 2004.
10. Code de Gestion des Aires Protégées, Loi No 2001–05: Articles 44, 45, 61. The meaning of COAP's various paragraphs was explained to the concerned population in a meeting organised by ANGAP in 2005 in the town of Maroantsetra, where the headquarters of the Masoala National Park are located. The meeting was attended by the leaders of numerous political communities from the Masoala peninsula who were then entrusted to convey the information to the rural population.
11. In Malagasy, these zones are called 'Faritra ivelomana araha-maso' or 'Faritra vaohara-maso'.
12. Since 2004, a national land tenure reform has been underway in Madagascar (see Evers 2013; Middleton 2013). At the time of writing, however, no discernible effect of this reform had reached the Masoala peninsula.
13. In a completely different context, Jennifer Cole reports on the expression *malahelo* being used by urban Malagasy people to express feelings of 'bitterness and resentment' at being 'mistreated' and humiliated (2010: 47, 66, 113).
14. A similar process is reported by Karen Middleton (2013: 157) concerning an area in southern Madagascar.
15. The situation in Madagascar is far from unique, especially in sub-Saharan Africa where Nature conservation measures have often been implemented in a particularly crude way, insensitive to the rights and concerns of local people (see West, Igoe and Brockington 2006; Brockington, Duffy and Igoe 2008; Agrawal and Redford 2009).
16. Corson (2011a: 716) notes that the dispossession of peasants particularly consists in the fact of having been deprived of the authority to decide what is going to happen with their land and of having been marginalised in the negotiations over land use.
17. In the course of Malagasy history, two currencies have been in use at different times, the Franc Malgache and the Ariary. The Ariary is worth a fifth of the Franc Malgache, i.e. 2,000 Ariary are equivalent to 10,000 Francs Malgaches, for example. The Ariary was reintroduced after independence but coexisted with the Franc Malgache – banknotes had both values printed on them – until

2005 when the Ariary became the only official currency. In the area where I work, people still count in both currencies depending on context and the amount involved. The amounts stated in the ANGAP documents at issue here are in Francs Malgaches.

18. For a critical evaluation of such Comités de Base, see Pollini 2007: chapter 11. For critical reflections on the rise of 'community-based' forest governance across the globe, see Fairhead and Leach 2003: 226–28.
19. Colonial extraction of precious wood from the area is documented as early as 1900 (Centre des archives d'outre-mer, Aix-en-Provence: 2D 153, 2D/154). For a comparison of pre-colonial and colonial forest exploitation, see Petit and Jacob 1965.
20. A *Dina* is a traditional juridical institution present in many parts of Madagascar, typically used for dealing with theft and other such problems in a local context (cf. Woolley 2002). In Madagascar, the appropriation of locally based juridical and political systems for the purposes of government administration and control goes back to the early nineteenth century (Bloch 1994a: 19). In the district of Maroantsetra, the colonial administration introduced the political entity of the *fokonolona* (village community) at the beginning of the twentieth century in the context of forced labour and the forced resettlement of people living in dispersed hamlets into villages of at least 'thirty roofs' (Fremigacci 2009: 72–3).
21. For an insightful account of the situation of park employees at Mananara Nord Biosphere Reserve, which lies on the other side of Antongil Bay, see Sodikoff 2007.
22. A number of authors have discussed how far Nature conservation represents a new form of hegemony and how far it offers leeway for agency, among them Escobar 1998; Campbell 2005; and Carrier and West 2009.
23. In her Ph.D. thesis in Environmental Studies and in her subsequent publications (Ormsby 2003, 2008; Ormsby and Kaplin 2005; Ormsby and Mannle 2006), Alison Ormsby discusses the relations between staff of the Masoala National Park and residents of two villages, one which lies 5 km beyond the park boundary, the other 15 km, at an early stage of the park's existence. Her analysis is primarily based on interviews (using an interview guide), focus group discussions and environmental education workshops that she carried out with the help of a translator. Her key finding is that people's views of the Masoala National Park are influenced by the following factors: the history of the park, local people's awareness of the park's existence, their personal interactions and experiences with park staff, and a rural community's direct benefit from it (through eco-tourism, for example). Marcus (2001) has compared local people's acceptance of three national parks in Madagascar, among these the Masoala National Park. He found that although people consider Nature conservation a valuable goal, they cannot afford it because the at-the-time popular ICDPs (Integrated Conservation and Development Projects) failed to provide sufficient livelihood alternatives.

Chapter 7

The Banana Plant and the Moon

In an article about the nature of Malagasy kinship (and kinship theory, more generally), Rita Astuti introduces readers to Dadilahy, an old man coming to the end of a long life. In Dadilahy's view of kinship, he has contributed to the generation of a great many descendants. This makes him happy and gives him a sense of having led a successful life. In his vision of who his children are, Dadilahy includes not only his own sons and daughters, their children and grandchildren, and so on, but also the descendants of his brothers and sisters as well as of other kin of his generation. It is as if Dadilahy has extended himself outward in the course of his long life, like a conically shaped fishing net expanding from its apex into ever-larger circles of mesh loops. It is as if Dadilahy's many children are the catch in the vast net of kinship that he has produced in his life (Astuti 2000).

The desire to have many descendants – in Dadilahy's inclusive sense – is, I believe, almost universal in rural Madagascar. At the end of a long conversation that my research assistant Harimalala Paul Clément and I had with an older woman and two of her sons in Marofototra, we came to talk about the joy the Malagasy feel when they have produced many descendants. Rounding off the conversation, Paul recounted the following myth:

> Zanahary (the Creator) asked the Malagasy whether they preferred to die the way a banana plant dies or the way the moon dies. The Malagasy chose the banana plant, because when it dies, many new banana plants will grow from its base. But when the moon dies, it leaves no children behind.

The banana tree, although it only lives for a short period of time, produces many new shoots that grow out of their parent plant, sprouting around it while it is still alive and continuing to grow after it has died. The moon, in contrast, although it is eternal and never truly dies, does not produce new life. 'The moon of February is still exactly the same in March, in April and in May, it is still just one single moon', Paul added. 'The moon has no children, or', looking at his audience with a smile on his face, he ended, 'has anyone ever heard of a child of the moon, or of its brother?', a question which the old woman and her two sons answered with an equally telling smile. It is because a successful life is one that leads to the birth of many descendants who will continue to prosper and to produce new human life that the Malagasy chose the fate of the banana plant and not the moon's static eternity.

The Process of Growth

Malagasy societies are fundamentally dynamic and forward moving, although this in no way implies a lack of attachment to land. This forward movement, that is, migration to 'land where there is space' (*tany malalaka*) is likely to be triggered by the shortage of land resulting from the growth of a kin group, but other factors may also play a role. Once such a move is undertaken, during a process of anchorage that may take several generations to mature and to become definitive, people progressively root themselves in the new land from which they have chosen to make a living for themselves and their descendants. This, however, does not mean that they become detached from the place they previously occupied; the contrary is, in fact, the case. Anchorage in the *tanindrazana*, the 'land of the ancestors', continues to be marked and constituted by people taking their dead back to be buried there. The Malagasy concept of the 'land of the ancestors' is not comparable to the European notion of a 'homeland' with its emphasis on eternal emotional attachment to the static territory of a nation. Rather, *tanindrazana* is the land where one's ancestors are buried. Thus, a place where people live but where they have no ancestral burial ground is, by definition, not their *tanindrazana*, irrespective of how long they might have lived there. Eventually, however, after perhaps two or three generations, the land in which people have become increasingly rooted over the course of time acquires a quality that makes it possible for them to imagine or envisage it as their new *tanindrazana*. What exactly makes a particular home area imaginable as 'land of the ancestors' is difficult to say and may depend on a variety of factors, but the length of time of having made a living in a place is certainly crucial. However, it is not simply the number of years that have elapsed since one's ancestors first arrived in one's present home that affects this issue. Rather, it is the depth of the 'roots' that have grown in the land over a long period of time – through agriculture and through social-emotional attachment – and especially the success of having produced children who, in turn, have produced more children, that makes a place imaginable as one's *tanindrazana*. When that depth has been achieved, a burial ground is created close to one's present home, which, precisely through this event, becomes one's new 'land of the ancestors', although links to the old *tanindrazana* may persist for a long time. This dynamic process of migrating to a new place, growing roots there, and eventually making it into *tanindrazana* by establishing tombs is widely documented for Malagasy societies all across the island and may, indeed, be pan-Malagasy (see, for instance, Deschamps 1959; Feeley-Harnik 1991: part 1; Bloch 1994a; Thomas 1997; Cole 2001: 155; Evers 2002; Woolley 2002: 11–35; Keller 2005: 31–36).

The process of creating *tanindrazana* may involve, as it does in Masoala (but also elsewhere; see Bloch 1994a: 206–15; Graeber 2007: 107, 109), the transfer of ancestral bones from the existing *tanindrazana* to the one to be newly created. In such cases, the reason for 'moving house' is explained to the ancestors during the ritual of transferring their mortal remains to the new location – their descendants might explain, for example, that 'We are taking you to a new home, so that we can all be together and because it has become too difficult for us to care for you properly if you are so far away' – and the ancestors' blessing for this move is sought.

Thus, through a long process of becoming anchored to new land, Malagasy people progressively turn neutral soil into *tanindrazana*. This, however, does not mean that Malagasy kin groups continuously move from one place to another without becoming firmly rooted anywhere. Indeed, the importance, in all Malagasy societies, of having a strong link to one's *tanindrazana* can hardly be exaggerated; arguably, it is the single most important attachment for people in Madagascar, both in rural and urban contexts. At the same time, the concept of *tanindrazana* is a dynamic one because it is part of an overall process of growth. Thus, migration from one's *tanindrazana* onto new land and the eventual creation of a *tanindrazana* in that new place should not be understood as a withdrawal from the old *tanindrazana* but as forward movement. The new *tanindrazana* is not perceived as a substitute for the old – although a *tanindrazana* from long ago will begin to fade from memory – but, rather, represents the branching out of a kin group. The creation of a new burial ground marks such a success story.[1] Moreover, the time during which people might live away from their 'land of the ancestors' is not a time of rootlessness but a time during which people become ever more anchored in their new land, which, because of the growing depth of their roots in it, becomes increasingly imaginable as a *tanindrazana*. The growth of a kin group over the course of generations may be thought of, to use another botanical metaphor, as comparable to the growth of those plants that send out creeping runners over the soil, like the periwinkle or couch grass; the runners become rooted in new places, but, for a long time, they remain attached to their parent plant.[2] Indeed, both the banana plant and couch grass are used in certain rituals in Madagascar as key symbols of growth and fertility (see Bloch 1986).

What I refer to as 'the process of growth' is a fundamental concept, an ethos, for people living in Masoala as in other rural Malagasy contexts. However, they hardly ever explicitly express it as such, perhaps precisely because it is so fundamental. 'Growth' refers to a whole network of aspects, especially to generating descendants and being able to give them land; to sowing, harvesting, and eating rice; and to obtaining one's ancestors' blessing, to which, indeed, the growth of one's kin group testifies.[3] I suggest that this process be thought of as a process of *growth*, because it is future oriented. When Dadilahy, the old man I introduced at the beginning of this chapter, looks, with satisfaction and pride, at all his children around him, he not only sees his achievement in the course of his own life, which is approaching its end. He also envisages the future growth of his kin, growth that he helped to generate and that, once he becomes an ancestor, he will continue to generate by blessing his descendants. Thus, people's relationship with their ancestors is both past and future oriented. It is not only concerned with showing respect to one's forebears – for example, by abiding by ancestral taboos – but also with properly caring for them in the hope that they will bless and make it possible for one's descendants to continue to prosper in the future. Without the ancestors' blessing, growth and forward movement – quite literally: 'pro-gress' – is not possible. Moreover, in some contexts, the ancestors themselves physically move forward with their kin when a new burial ground is created. In some ways, just as the ancestors create future growth through their blessing, the growth of their living kin constitutes the ancestors: 'Ancestors emerge in the birth of children' (Feeley-Harnik 1991: 52). This is why, as more children are born in a place to where a family or kin group has migrated, that place becomes increasingly imaginable as *tanindrazana*, as 'land of the ancestors'. The birth of children, the interaction with the land and the communication with one's ancestors are all different aspects of a single process of the continuation and growth of human life. I refer to this process as the *Malagasy* ethos of growth (rather than as specific to the Masoala region or to the people usually named Betsimisaraka who live along Madagascar's east coast), because, as numerous ethnographies demonstrate (see above), not only is it widely shared among groups of Malagasy people all across the island, it is also absolutely fundamental to (at least rural) Malagasy people's outlook on life. Dadilahy could have been an old man in any region of the island, and the myth about the banana plant and the moon could have been told anywhere.

In many ways, the process described here is reminiscent of Kopytoff's analysis of the African frontier dynamic (Kopytoff 1987; on the frontier

Photograph 7.1 A woman with two of her grandchildren

concept, see also Geiger 2009). Kopytoff argues that most sub-Saharan societies emerged as a result of small groups of people leaving their present home, for a variety of reasons, including the shortage of good land within reach, in search of a new place within Africa's vast frontier areas, that is land beyond the control of any established political centre.

In the course of time, some of these small-scale frontier settlements would grow, either by attracting further migrants or by subjugating other populations, and some would eventually mature into new established polities of varying size from where, once again, 'frontiersmen' would leave to found new settlements elsewhere. Kopytoff argues that African socio-political systems owe much to this continually ongoing migration dynamic *away from* political centres, rather than being determined by the latter. In Madagascar, the 'process of growth' is in tune with the general dynamic described by Kopytoff for continental Africa. However, there is also an important difference. In contrast to Kopytoff's analysis, the Malagasy 'process of growth' is, essentially, not about numerical growth, the purpose of which is to become dominant vis-à-vis others in a given region. Rather, the process of a kin group growing over the generations makes possible the fulfilment of a deeply rooted understanding of what is, ultimately, the purpose of life. The Malagasy 'process of growth' is not a strategy, it is an ethos.

Kinship and Continuity

As Dadilahy's vision exemplifies, the concept of descendants in Madagascar includes not only one's own children, grandchildren, great-grandchildren and so on but also those of one's relatives of the same generation. All these people, together with all those who have generated them and those who will come after them, constitute a kin group. A kin group thus includes ancestors, their presently living and their future descendants. It is the relations between these different generations of kin that in Masoala primarily constitute a person's identity and place in society. Thus kinship (*fihavanana*) – a notion that involves much more than genealogy: in particular, moral ties and obligations – is at the core of what it means to be a human being.[4] Therefore, the purpose of life is to continue, to strengthen and to make grow the relations between the different generations of people who together constitute a kin group. These relations are maintained and created in many ways in daily and in ritual life, but become particularly evident in the generation of children. The birth of a healthy child is a sign that the ancestors are satisfied and that they have therefore blessed their descendants with a new life; when ancestors are angry they may (besides other manifestations of their displeasure) deprive their descendants of children. The success of the relationships among kin does not necessarily depend on every couple having lots of children, and it is indeed not the case that all families have or even want many. In Ambanizana and Marofototra, many women and many men had only two or three children, and some only had one or none, while others had eight or more. People's desire to have many descendants is not measurable or quantifiable, and it does not follow a simple logic of 'the more, the better' (cf. Feeley-Harnik 1995). However, within the parameters of an ethos that is oriented towards the fruitful continuation of the relations between kin of different generations, every new human life is a positive event that strengthens these ties and, therefore, growth is good.

In Ambanizana and Marofototra, the main stem of a banana plant is called 'the mother' (*reny*) that is said to 'give birth to children' (*mamaitry, manaranaka*), to 'children who will replace it' (*zanany mandimby azy*). The concept of *mandimby* is crucial to the way the people in Masoala conceptualise the relationship between the different generations of kin. *Mandimby* is usually translated as: to replace, succeed, substitute, take the place of (Abinal and Malzac 1993; Rajaonarimanana 1995). The relationship between ancestors (long and recently deceased), parents, children, grandchildren and great-grandchildren is a relationship of one generation taking the place of the one before it, a relationship of descendants continuing to 'pro-gress' by walking in the footsteps of their predecessors and, at the same time, preparing the way for those to come after them. The concept of *mandimby* creates an endless chain of interconnected persons and generations that allows the dead to continue to exist in the lives of their descendants and allows the descendants to build their lives on the achievements of those who paved the way for them.

I once observed a wonderful illustration of the continuity between the different generations of kin in Ambanizana. Around 1st January each year, the different kin groups of the village go to their respective burial grounds – they lie on the margins of the village, hidden among bushes and trees – in order to bring the ancestors new clothing. In 2011, I went to the burial ground with relatives of my host family. We all knelt down by the tombs,[5] and the ritual leader of the concerned ancestry, kneeling by the side of the oldest ancestor with his hat removed and his head bent, addressed the ancestors explaining to them why we had come. Then, the lids of several of the sarcophagi in which the ancestors rest[6] were lifted so that those who had brought some money or clothing were able to put it inside. Individual ancestors were spoken to briefly but loudly as if speaking to people who are a little deaf. Things were said like: 'Today we are celebrating the New Year, and we have brought you new clothes. Make us all healthy and strong'.

Bringing new clothes to the ancestors at the burial ground is part of extended New Year's activities in Ambanizana that continue for several days and that also include endless visits to one's senior kin as well as others to whom one stands in a relationship of respect. The day after visiting the ancestors at the burial ground, my host family had such a New Year's

Photographs 7.2 and 7.3 New clothes for the ancestors and elders

gathering in the house of its oldest members, a couple in their eighties. As every year, all their children, grandchildren and great-grandchildren came; lots of people of all ages were gathered in the old couple's house. This year, however, there was an innovation to the annual ritual: not only the ancestors would get new clothes, so a spokesperson of the family

Photograph 7.3

explained, but also the living elders (*ray aman-dreny*). This announcement having been made, two of the old couple's great-grandchildren stood up and wrapped exactly the same type of cloth around their great-grandparents' shoulders as the ancestors had received the previous day (a kind of Malagasy sarong that is used for different purposes and that is obligatory for women to wear at all ritual occasions; many men wear it, too). The youngest generation wrapped ritual clothing around their elders who would, probably in a few years time, join the ancestors in their tombs. Together, they would ensure the kin group's future, the young by continuing to work the fields and to care for their dead kin, the latter by giving the former their blessing thus making growth possible.

Friction between the Moon and the Banana Plant

Unlike in certain animistic societies,[7] in Madagascar, animals and plants are not conceptualised as being members of society. Animals are thought to live in a world distinct from the world of humans, and the people in Ambanizana and Marofototra spend little time pondering about the former. But neither do they share with those who embrace and promote Nature conservation a notion of a transcendental entity of intrinsic, universal worth that exists disconnected from human life referred to as 'Nature'; the people in Masoala do not embrace, in other words, a 'naturalist ontology' (Descola 1996, 2005). For them, the land is inseparable from their endeavour of creating a livelihood and of making human life grow. The land turned fertile for human growth is an essential part of what makes kinship and thus society possible, and different generations of kin are connected with one another through their common link to their *tanindrazana* in which their ancestors are buried.

In contrast to the Malagasy ethos of growth, the conservationist ethos, which provides the rationale and justification for establishing protected areas like the Masoala National Park, grants no privilege to the human over any other species. Instead it is founded on the ideal of a perfect, but static, equilibrium among the different species present on the planet.[8] One might call it the 'moon ethos', in contrast to the Malagasy 'banana plant ethos'. Within the moon ethos, the growth of human life is seen as a critical threat to the aspired equilibrium amongst all species and is therefore termed 'over'-population. While for the farmers in Masoala, growth of human life is *progress* – 'pro-gress': forward movement, –, the moon ethos aspires toward the stagnation, and preferably decline, of the numbers of people present on the peninsula as a means of restoring an ecological equilibrium that is seen to have fallen out of balance.[9] While from one perspective growth is reckoned in numerical terms, from the other perspective growth represents an ethos of life.

The encounter of the banana plant and the moon ethos is, indeed, an instance of friction (Tsing 2005), an awkward interconnection across geographical and cultural distance brought about by the global agenda of

Nature conservation. In the context of the Masoala National Park and its mini-replica in Zurich, the one ethos meets the other at several conjunctures. Their encounter triggers friction in people's imaginations when, for the visitors to the Zurich zoo, one's moral responsibility lies primarily with protecting endangered animal and plant species from human activities that might impinge on their undisturbed living space, while for the farmers in Masoala, to act morally is to contribute to one's kin group's growth. The friction between the banana plant and the moon ethos also manifests itself in material terms when farmers in Masoala find themselves losing their land to the park.

Those who support and finance the Masoala National Park justify its existence on two grounds. First, they point to the global importance of the Masoala peninsula for biodiversity conservation. Second, combining the notion of 'conservation' with that of 'development', they argue that there will not be any future for local people if they continue to destroy the forest, especially through slash-and-burn cultivation, in other words, if they cut the very branch on which they sit: without forest, no rain; without rain, no rice; without rice, starvation – a people on an ecological suicide track. The necessity to protect the area's lemurs is explained to people in Masoala in similar terms: lemurs support the dispersal of trees by eating and excreting seeds and therefore they are crucial to the maintenance of the forest. This line of argument is regularly put forward in contexts of 'educating' local farmers about the value of the forest. Such activities, which are referred to in Masoala as *sensibilisation* (in French), sometimes, as during a 'lemur festival' in the Masoala area partly organised by Peace Corps volunteers in 2005, culminate in statements such as: 'To kill lemurs is to kill one's descendants'.

The argument that the park is beneficial to their future, however, makes no sense at all to the farmers in Ambanizana and Marofototra, and is indeed absurd to them, because in their experience the effect of the park is exactly the opposite of safeguarding their future. Take the example of Jean. In 1985, at the age of thirty, he set up his own household together with his wife Marianne. To the south of Ambanizana, they found forested land that suited their plans. They created wet rice fields and began to cultivate coffee, cloves and vanilla. Like most other people in their situation, they failed to register their land with the state authorities, seeing no need to do so at the time. 'The land didn't belong to anyone! The land was still "totally dark" (untouched, uncultivated)[10] at that time!' Jean explained. When the boundary of the Masoala National Park was demarcated for the first time in 1997, Jean and Marianne's land was not included within the park. When, in 2004, the park authorities altered the boundary, however, all of their land – productive wet rice fields as well as cash-crop plantations – came to lie inside the Hard Core, that is the area of the park that is off-limits for any purpose other than scientific research and tourism (unless specifically authorised for a limited purpose). They lost everything that they had created over the course of twenty years. In December of the same year, ANGAP evaluated the value of their loss and promised them compensation of ten million Malagasy francs – roughly equivalent to the value of two years of their cash crops – but, at the time of writing, nine years later, this still remains an empty promise. By 2006, Jean and Marianne were working as sharecroppers on other people's land. It is evident to people like Jean and Marianne that the creation of the Masoala National Park does not safeguard the future of their descendants by protecting the forest; on the contrary, it threatens their future by taking away the land on which that future should have been built.

As we saw in the last chapter, many people in Ambanizana and Marofototra have lost already-cultivated land; Jean and Marianne's case is one among many. And even more people have lost forested land that, according to customary law, does belong to them but which they had not yet begun to cultivate because it was intended as the reserve for their children and grandchildren. It is in particular the loss of such land that represents a threat to local kin groups' ability to provide their descendants with a basis for their future. A kin group's successful growth not only depends on the birth of children but also, equally importantly, on its ability to provide these children with land on which to create a livelihood together with their partners, and to thus continue the productive process of life. Therefore, by taking away land from local people that was intended as the basis of future livelihoods, the Masoala National Park represents a direct and deeply felt threat to the ethos of growth.

The situation in Masoala also mirrors a fundamentally different concern with boundaries by those embracing the moon ethos, on the one hand, and those embracing the banana plant ethos, on the other. The key concern of the designers of the Masoala National Park was to establish permanently fixed boundaries between off-limits, semi-restricted and right of usufruct zones. 'Mistakes' with regard to the implementation of the park's official delimitations were corrected in the course of several waves of re-marking its limits in various places around the peninsula, leading to tremendous confusion and trepidation among local farmers. Article 4 of the *Dina* of Marofototra defining permissible and forbidden activities within the Zone d'Occupation Contrôlée of the same name states: 'No future events will change the limits of the zones which have been determined by the government' (my translation from the Malagasy original). In perfect contrast to this ideal of the staticness of set boundaries, from the perspective of the people in Masoala, all landscape boundaries represent a temporary situation within the continual movement of people, and boundaries are endlessly changing as part of what is considered the self-evident process of producing life – like the periwinkle extending its overground roots in all directions as it grows. However, since the creation of the park and especially since the farmers in Ambanizana and Marofototra have experienced several completely unpredictable de facto shifts of the park's limits – in every instance I know of to their disadvantage – they, too, have become very much concerned with what is locally referred to as the *limite*. Forced to play by the rules of the more powerful, the local population have joined conservation managers in demanding the reliability of the park's boundaries in order to prevent any further encroachment on the land available for growth.

Defeated in the Purpose of Life

In juxtaposing the Malagasy ethos of growth and the moon ethos embraced by conservation agents in Masoala and also by visitors to the zoo in Zurich, my aim is not to assess who is right or wrong, and my argument does not depend on any such judgment. Rather, I wish to draw attention to how fundamentally different these two views and these two visions of a desirable future are. This fact is rarely recognised but it is crucial for understanding the full significance, beyond economic loss or gain, of the establishment of the Masoala National Park which enjoys so much Swiss support, for directly affected farmers in Madagascar. I argue that, by defining most of the forest land on the peninsula as off-limits, the park has come to be seen by the people in Ambanizana and Marofototra as something depriving them of the possibility of continuing their efforts to 'pro-gress' and to grow over the generations. Therefore, the encounter between the Malagasy ethos of life and the politically immensely more powerful moon ethos leaves local people with a sense, as they often say, of having been 'defeated' (*resy*) in the purpose of life.

When the people in the two villages talked about their situation vis-à-vis the Masoala National Park, two notions, linked to one another, were omnipresent: the loss of their *tany fivelômana* and the experience of having been defeated. *Tany fivelômana* may be translated in a variety of ways, including 'land for subsistence' or 'land where people create a livelihood'. The sense of what the park is locally perceived and experienced to take away from farmers, however, is best captured by translating *tany fivelômana* as 'land that enables life' (see Abinal and Malzac 1993: 824).[11] Land referred to as *tany fivelômana* is the agricultural land that people either already cultivate or forested land that will be available to future generations. *Tany fivelômana* is land that enables life in more than one sense. Being agricultural land, it provides nourishment for people. But also, and equally importantly, *tany fivelômana* is land that enables life in the sense discussed above: it enables kin groups to grow, to branch out, and to increasingly root themselves in new land. This is why the loss of land means much more than the mere loss of economically valuable soil. 'We never agreed, we have been defeated' (*Zahay tsy nañeky fô raha resy è!*), one man in Marofototra, talking about the incorporation of much of his land into the Hard Core of the park, complained in a highly representative statement. If leading a successful life is to engage in the process of growth, then losing one's *tany fivelômana* is to be defeated in the very purpose of life.[12]

Defeat is particularly strongly felt in the Zone d'Occupation Contrôlée of Marofototra. The at times complete ban on slash-and-burn cultivation, combined with the shortage of suitable wet rice land and the prohibition of trading in forest and marine products other than fish, is making life in Marofototra increasingly difficult. The permanent limitation on the extension of cultivable land at the park's boundary threatens not only people's present livelihoods but also their descendants' ability to move on and to create more 'land that enables life'. 'We can't move, not even a little bit' (*Tsy afaka mietsiketsika zahay na mba hely*), local people would often say. Or, using a particularly forceful metaphor that captures their situation of living inside a territory bounded by the terrestrial and marine parks, they would repeatedly say, 'We are just like inside a chicken coop' (*Añanty rôva zahay*), in a tone of voice that expressed acknowledgment of defeat. Such statements refer not only to the ban on physically entering the Hard Core of the park that surrounds people's living space but also to their inability, and especially that of future generations, to move their lives forward and to create new *tany fivelômana*. Most of today's residents of the newly created village of Marofototra came to the area twenty or thirty years ago and spent the strength of their youth making the land productive. (This is a village where Kopytoff's frontier dynamic can be literally watched in its initial stage.) They had barely embarked on the long process of turning neutral soil into 'land that enables life' (and, eventually, into 'land of the ancestors') when they were abruptly stopped in their endeavour by the arrival of the Masoala National Park, which fixed the point beyond which there is now no entry. It is as if they had been stopped by a sign in the middle of their path saying, 'Up to here and no further!' Their inability to move on and to create new *tany fivelômana* is the key reason why Marofototra's residents see no long-term future for themselves or their kin in the village. Even if the current population succeeds, just about, in making a living in the village, the *tany fivelômana* for their children and grandchildren remains closed off beyond the boundary of the enclave.

In Ambanizana, the situation is different because Ambanizana lies not inside but on the periphery of the park, and there is a considerable amount of cultivable land outside its boundaries. However, in Ambanizana too, the park begins just a couple of kilometres from the village, and it is within sight of people's houses. 'Beyond there', people would explain, pointing halfway up the nearby hills, 'it's all theirs, it is only what is below that line which is still ours'. Although it is considerably more immediate in Marofototra, defeat is also felt in Ambanizana because, there too, the park sets a clear limit as to how far people can move on in their aspiration to grow like the banana plant. Whereas in Marofototra the process of becoming rooted in the land was stopped almost immediately after it began, in Ambanizana, a village with a history of at least one hundred years, the continuation of 'pro-gress' is now threatened.

Giving Up

In Marofototra, where the marine and terrestrial parks surrounding the enclave have had a dramatic effect on people's livelihoods, many residents seem to be in the process of giving up the aspiration of making a living as subsistence and cash-crop farmers and of investing their strength and their resources in the long-term future of cultivation. This seemed to me to be the case in at least three respects. First, living with farmers in both Ambanizana and Marofototra, I observed a marked difference between the two villages with regard to people's motivation for doing agricultural work. Whereas, in Ambanizana, my hosts and other families I knew well would work in the pouring rain or the blazing heat for hours on end, if necessary, people in Marofototra seemed to be considerably more inclined to neglect the agricultural work waiting for them if the circumstances were not the most desirable ones. 'I can't be bothered today', people would sometimes say, explaining their failure to go to the fields. Second, I gained the distinct impression that many people in Marofototra have begun to think of themselves as the passive recipients of money or goods that ought to be given to them by those responsible for the park, or by others. The reality is, though, that they end up mostly waiting in vain. 'There is no work to be done, we just sit around' (*Ehè, tsisy tabà, mantôtry fô anteña*) they would remark, and at the same time they would applaud the few tourists who came to Marofototra and who distributed pens or T-shirts to the children. And, third, Marofototra's residents have begun to turn towards means of income other than those related to farming, although these pursuits are utterly unreliable and provide no security for the future. Some residents expressed their hope that their children might get paid jobs in town or at one of the tourist lodges at a few hours walking distance. Others have begun to engage in small-scale commercial activities – some of them legal, some not. It is, of course, a common feature of Malagasy villages that some people engage in activities other than farming and fishing; after all, most villages have shopkeepers, traders and craftsmen. However, the point here is that, in Marofototra, this is now happening as a direct result of people losing faith in a future based on cultivation and at the cost of cultivation. In other words, many people in Marofototra seem to be in the process of giving up the perception of themselves as people involved in attending to and creating *tany fivelômana*, a perception they certainly held when they came to the area in search of land to cultivate. Consider Solo's story.

Solo, who was in his late forties when I lived with him and his second wife, came to Marofototra as a young man to create a livelihood here with his first wife and their children. He is a first-generation migrant to the region, who came from a town to the west of the Masoala peninsula, where his 'land of the ancestors' lies and where he will be buried one day. When Solo was a young man, his family's land had become insufficient to provide for him and his five siblings. Solo, thus, began to work on a ship taking passengers around the Masoala peninsula, a job he held for several years. During his many voyages along the coast, he noticed the existence of much unclaimed forest land on the peninsula's western shore. He asked leave of his *patron* and enquired among the appropriate political leaders and elders about the possibility of cultivating in Masoala. Having obtained the necessary permissions, he began cultivating in 1986, setting all his hopes, as did others in the area, on the cultivation of vanilla. Solo at first spent many months by himself, clearing forest to turn it into arable land. 'I didn't have my own rice or any other food at that time', he told me. 'In order to feed myself, I worked for a few days for other people who were already cultivating in the area, then I lived off what I had earned – rice, manioc, potatoes – until I ran out of food, then I went back to work for food.' It was very hard, but Solo continued in his efforts to turn 'dark', forested land into *tany fivelômana* that he would be able to cultivate, even after he suffered serious injury when he was hit by a falling tree. When I met him and his second wife, twenty years after he initially came to the area, they had a sizeable vanilla plantation, pastures (but only one head of cattle), and a small wet rice field; they rented a second field. During good years, the income from the vanilla covered most of their expenses, including the purchase of rice, but during bad years, when the harvest was either meagre or the retail price for vanilla low, slash-and-burn rice cultivation on a hillside in the past provided an alternative means of feeding the family for about three months of the year. 'We were still free then' (*Mbôla libre anteña*), Solo commented, thinking back to their life before they were incorporated into the Zone d'Occupation Contrôlée of Marofototra. They had been free to do the work they wanted and needed to do and to make their *tany fivelômana* grow; they were not yet trapped 'inside a chicken coop'. In the agricultural season of 2006–7, when there was a complete ban on slash-and-burn cultivation inside the ZOC, instead of buying rice for six months of the year, Solo and his wife had to buy for nine. 'If we had known what would happen, we would not have come here to create an existence', Solo ended his story.

Solo, however, was lucky in one respect. Even when he and his wife were still living in their hamlet in the forest prior to their move to the new village, they had a tiny shop in their house in which they sold daily necessities such as salt and petrol to neighbouring settlers. Thanks to this activity, Solo had a *patron*, a rich trader in another village who supplied him with such goods. When I lived with him and his wife, they increasingly relied on this sort of small-scale commerce, at the cost of cultivation, selling rum, cigarettes, petrol, sugar, biscuits, and other things, and around New Year, they turned their house into a store selling European second-hand clothes that Solo had bought in town. Solo's main activity, however, for which he travelled long distances along the peninsula's coast, often not returning home for a week or more at a time, was the sale of dried sea cucumbers, which he bought in places outside the marine park, where it is legal to catch them, and which he then sold to his *patron*. At the time, this was the most lucrative local business. Eventually, after having passed through the hands of various middlemen, the sea cucumbers are said to end up in a Chinese cooking pot somewhere in Madagascar's cities or beyond.

Solo came to Masoala in search of land to cultivate. He spent all his strength, as he put it, clearing the forest and turning it into *tany fivelômana*. He intended this land to become the home of his children, who would likely themselves branch out further and create more *tany fivelômana*. Eventually, after several generations perhaps, his *tany fivelômana* might become the 'land of the ancestors' of his descendants. However, this process of becoming rooted in the land around Marofototra has been abruptly stopped by the creation of the Masoala National Park. A long-term future in farming now looked increasingly unlikely in Marofototra, so much so that Solo began to turn away from farming and towards a kind of small-scale commerce, which made him totally dependent on his *patron* as well as on the flows of the local and supra-local market over which he had no control. For the people in Ambanizana and in Marofototra, the Masoala peninsula once looked like a place that would provide *tany fivelômana* for many generations. With the park appropriating most of the forest, however, that vision has become seriously threatened, and for the inhabitants of Marofototra it has all but disappeared.

The people in Marofototra seemed not only to be giving up a sense of themselves as being in the business of creating *tany fivelômana*. The park also wiped out any intention, however distant in the future, of moving one's ancestral tombs to the area. It wiped out the idea of Marofototra ever becoming one's descendants' *tanindrazana*. The majority of the inhabitants of Marofototra are first or second generation migrants while a handful of families have lived there for three generations, and one family for four. Only the latter has a burial ground close to the village, a burial ground that already existed prior to the creation of the park. All the other families continue to bring their dead home to where they or their forebears migrated from, in most cases to Ambanizana or other nearby villages. With the arrival of the park, the very idea of perhaps some day in the future creating a burial ground in Marofototra has completely vanished, and none of the families are currently even contemplating any such move.

Conclusion

For the people of Ambanizana and Marofototra, the core of a successful life is the continuation of the process of becoming evermore rooted in the land, a process started by their ancestors in the past when they first arrived on the Masoala peninsula. The generation of a growing number of descendants who will continue this process is, therefore, perhaps the local people's most important aspiration in life. Access to land that has not yet been claimed by anyone and that can be transformed into a source of life – in the sense of both producing food and continuing life through one's descendants – is an essential aspect of this process.

With the establishment of the Masoala National Park, the local people have been confronted with an ethos that stands in stark contrast to their own. Their aspirations have been challenged by an ethos that is fundamentally opposed to the growth of the population and the leaving of human marks on the landscape. The encounter of the banana plant ethos and the moon ethos reveals two completely different visions of a desirable future. For those promoting Nature conservation – among them the visitors to the Zurich zoo's Masoala exhibit – to create a future is to protect the forest and to work towards an equilibrium among the different species present on the Masoala peninsula, including but not privileging the human species. But for the farmers, to create a future is to generate children and grandchildren and to create *tany fivelômana* for them so that they will be able to continue the productive process of life. Whereas the moon ethos is understood by those advocating Nature conservation as guaranteeing the continuation not only of animal and plant but also human life – recall, for instance, those zoo visitors and pupils who talked of Malagasy farming practices as being self-destructive (chapter 3) –, for the farmers, the moon ethos implies exactly the opposite of safeguarding the continuation of life: it leads to policies that 'kill' people (*mamono*) by taking away from them the basis of their future lives.

The difference between the conservationist vision and the local farmers' vision of the relationship between people and the land is not a matter of degree but a matter of kind. In its essential premises, the conservationist ethos is categorically in conflict with the Malagasy farmers' vision of what the purpose of human life is. Therefore, to ask the latter to stop turning forested land into 'land that enables life' and, eventually, 'land of the ancestors' represents an assault on one of their most fundamental values – the value of the growth of life through kinship and through roots in the land. Therefore, to expect the farmers to approve of the park in its present size is to ask them to embrace an ethos that is fundamentally opposed to what they value most; friction indeed.

Notes

Substantial parts of this chapter were first published in 2008 in the *American Ethnologist* 38(4): 650–64.

1. Because of the importance of forward movement in Malagasy societies and because land becomes *tanindrazana* through the presence of ancestral remains (which can be moved from one place to another), the Malagasy concept of the 'land of the ancestors' is fundamentally dynamic and fluid. Despite this fluidity, however, the location of one's *tanindrazana* and people's anchorage in it are, especially in ritual contexts, often represented as unchanging and fixed in time (Bloch 1994a, 1996). Thus, out of movement is created an image of permanence.
2. I thank Maurice Bloch for suggesting this metaphor.
3. Although, as several ethnographies have pointed out (esp. Graeber 1995; Cole 2001), the *road* to obtaining the ancestors' blessing may not always be smooth but can be difficult and fraught with constraints imposed by the dead on the living, ancestral blessing remains the *goal* towards which the living direct their efforts.
4. For a beautiful ethnography of similar ideas among the Ohafia in Nigeria, see McCall 1995 (especially p. 258–59).
5. On the funerary practices in this region, see Keller 2005: 170–71.
6. Most sarcophagi contain the bones of several ancestors, normally between two and four put on top of one another. Women and men are never placed inside the same sarcophagus. The sarcophagi used in Ambanizana are made

of cement or wood, depending on the financial resources available, and are mostly small with a length of about one metre and a height of perhaps 60 cm including the lid (cf. Cole 2001: 313n16).
7. For an excellent ethnographic example, see Descola 1994.
8. I am aware of new trends in ecological studies that are no longer based on equilibrium theory (Fairhead and Leach 2003: 42–43; Campbell 2005: 301). This, however, has so far not affected the canonical discourse (see Introduction) that informs conservation policy in Madagascar.
9. I do not want this to be read as implying that the growth of kin groups in Masoala necessarily and inevitably leads to environmental degradation. These issues are hotly debated concerning Madagascar (e.g. Kull 2004; Pollini 2007) and elsewhere (e.g. Boserup 1993 [1965]). In Masoala, no scientific study has been conducted that would allow any assertion one way or another.
10. See Bloch 1995 for a discussion of the importance of the notion of clarity in Madagascar.
11. *Fivelomana*: 'L'entretien, la subsistence, le métier qui nourrit, la vie' (Abinal and Malzac 1993: 824). See Tucker et al. 2011 for a discussion of the similar concept of *velomanpò* among the Mikea in south-western Madagascar.
12. In her examination of '*jeunes*' – young people who behave in such a way as to be recognisable as modern, fashionable and in touch with the world – in the port town of Toamasina, Cole (2001: 51–59) discusses these *jeunes*' behaviour as a manifestation of what it means to be socially mature in rural Madagascar: to have the ability to contribute one's share within a system of exchange between kin across different generations, including the ancestors, that is, the ability to 'make others living' (*mahamelona*). As in *tany fivelômana*, the notion of *velona* (to be alive) is crucial here.

Chapter 8
The Island of the Wanderer

The Island of the Wanderer, Nosin-dRendra, is a tiny islet offshore a small village that lies between Ambanizana and Marofototra, a few hours' walk from each. If there were a path, one could walk around it in ten minutes. The trees and thicket covering it hide from the gaze of those who have no business coming here a small clearing on which there is a burial site containing the post-mortem homes of several dozen ancestors belonging to different kin groups. As Nosin-dRendra is all rock, nobody has ever lived there – except for 'the wanderer'.

Photograph 8.1 The Island of the Wanderer

A long time ago, local people used to come to the islet for seasonal fishing, camping overnight. One day, so the story goes,[1] a stranger turned up in the area – a man who was no one's kin and whose identity or real name nobody knew. He settled on the islet, finding shelter from the wind and rain underneath an overhanging rock. He became known as 'i Rendra', the wanderer.[2] After living on the islet for many years, he died. People put his body into a wooden sarcophagus and laid him to rest underneath the rock, and from then on, the islet was known as the Island of the Wanderer, Nosin-dRendra.

[In parentheses: It is not clear at which point in history it became a local practice in the area to first bury the deceased inside wooden coffins in the soil, then to exhume their bones some years later when the flesh had decomposed, and to finally put them to rest in a sarcophagus, together with kin, as is done today. I have been told that prior to the colonial period it was not a local custom to first bury the dead; instead the deceased would be placed directly above ground. This practice was, however, considered unhygienic by the French who therefore forced local people to bury their dead in the ground. In this new situation, local people resorted to exhuming their ancestors once their bones were dry and clean, because it was and still is considered utterly uncivilised and immoral to just leave the ancestors' bones to rot in the soil without caring for them, 'as if throwing people away like dogs', as local people expressed it.[3] Nowadays, exhumation and a cattle sacrifice for each ancestor a couple of years later are the most important 'works for the ancestors' (*asan-drazana*). If these rituals are not performed, a kin group's well-being and future prosperity is in danger from ancestral resentment.]

With the wanderer having been laid to rest on the islet, people began to recognise the advantage of Nosin-dRendra as a burial place. Because it is an island – though only a short distance through shallow water from the shore – the ancestors would be safe from both roaming pigs and witches eager to dance on the tombs at night. At the same time, the ancestors, dwelling in a place separated by water from people's settlements, might perhaps be less likely to bother their living descendants with demands and constraints. For whenever ancestors are brought to a burial place, their kin emphasise, when addressing them during the ritual proceedings, that they are now living *here*, that their new house is a good house and that they should please stay in their new home rather than wandering into the village and interfering with their descendants' lives at unexpected moments. Offering these advantages, Nosin-dRendra turned into a burial site as several kin groups began to bring their ancestors there once they had been exhumed (there is not enough soil for burying a coffin). Up until the creation of the Masoala National Park, new ancestors continued to be brought to the Island of the Wanderer despite the existence of other, newer burial grounds on the outskirts of villages. In Ambanizana, the decision of whether or not to bring an ancestor to Nosin-dRendra did not follow any strict rules but was made in each individual case on the basis of a variety of criteria, in particular reflections about who the newly deceased would like, or ought, to be close to.

Losing Control

With the creation of the Masoala National Park, the future of the Island of the Wanderer became an issue. In 2002, a few years after the inauguration of the terrestrial park, three marine parks around the lower part of the peninsula were added to the extension of the protected area (see map on p. 125). One of these incorporates Nosin-dRendra. Of its surface area of 36 sq km, 2 sq km have been classified as Hard Core – that is, off-limits to local people unless specifically authorised by the park authorities (the rest is a Zone d'Utilisation Contrôlée). The Island of the Wanderer came to lie right in the middle of the Hard Core and, as a result, it became increasingly difficult for people in the nearby villages to engage in ritual practices for their ancestors on the islet. The park management, being aware of the sensitivity of the issue, made sure not to categorically deny permission to hold rituals on Nosin-dRendra, and ANGAP staff I spoke to were at pains to emphasise that the carrying out of such rituals was not at risk. The park management as well as individual employees clearly did not want to appear to be disregarding local culture in such a crude way as to disrespect the significance of a burial ground.[4] However, so many conditions were attached to carrying out rituals on Nosin-dRendra that local people felt they had lost control over their burial place, and that the park had become the owner of, and master over, their *tanindrazana* (land of the ancestors).

Firstly, prior to carrying out any ritual activity, local families now needed to request permission to do so from the park authority in town. Secondly, because Nosin-dRendra had become a part of the Hard Core of the marine park, no one was allowed to effect any change to the vegetation on the islet, even if the impact would not be long term. For example, it was no longer permitted to cut bamboo for building shelters for the guests during the night-long festivities preceding the central ritual act. In fact, these festivities were no longer allowed to take place on Nosin-dRendra itself, as they ought to according to custom, because this would have necessitated the clearing of an area of vegetation for the shelter for the guests. A number of prohibitions of this kind, which were confirmed by ANGAP staff, formed the parameters within which the park authorities allowed local families to continue to perform rituals on Nosin-dRendra. Also, at least one member of park staff was supposed to be present during rituals in order to supervise the activities and prevent possible breaches of the above conditions. Moreover, the forested area opposite Nosin-dRendra is part of the terrestrial park's Hard Core so that certain plant material needed in connection with such rituals could not be taken from there either. These various restrictions made the carrying out of people's duties towards their ancestors not only a practical nuisance, but it also created a strong sense among the local population – not only the directly concerned families – that the point of classifying the Island of the Wanderer as part of the Hard Core was to appropriate even more land from its rightful owners. The inclusion of this tiny islet on which nobody ever set foot other than in connection with ancestral rituals was felt to be a demonstration of power by the park authorities and a matter of recommitting the local people to the place befitting their status vis-à-vis the park. The inclusion of Nosin-dRendra into the Hard Core was locally seen as chicanery for a number of reasons: because rituals on the Island of the Wanderer were by no means frequent; because there already existed an ancestral taboo against removing anything from Nosin-dRendra (thus there was no danger of people cutting down trees); because nobody has any interest in exposing the tombs, which are always sheltered from view by vegetation; and because, as one person put it, one can almost watch bamboo regrow, so 'why not let us at least cut bamboo to construct shelters for the guests?' It was quite beyond local people how the occasional ritual performed on Nosin-dRendra could reasonably be considered a threat to the island's vegetation. The park authorities for their part emphasised that it was the marine life in particular that they intended to protect through the measures they were taking.

As we saw in the last chapter, land is the sine qua non for the process of growth to occur. While it may take generations for a kin group to anchor itself sufficiently in new land for it to become imaginable as *tanindrazana*, 'land of the ancestors', the creation of a burial ground within one's present living space marks the successful culmination of the process of growth and anchorage. The actual land which holds the tombs of one's ancestors is the key place where living and dead kin communicate with one another, where people care for their ancestors and where ancestral blessing, which will manifest itself in prosperity and growth, is asked for and received. The loss of control over a burial ground, therefore, represents a particularly painful and significant threat.

Becoming Anxious

After Nosin-dRendra had become part of the Hard Core of the marine park, it was unclear to local people what exactly the park authorities planned to do with it, yet it was perceived as obvious that they must have some kind of plan. Speculations abounded. Many people in Ambanizana and Marofototra thought that the government planned to build a lighthouse on the islet to guide the ships in the bay, as apparently some years ago, a number of government representatives and foreigners had come to the area to inspect such a possibility. Others believed that ANGAP planned to turn the Island of the Wanderer into a tourist attraction. Perhaps they would keep lemurs and other wildlife there, thus establishing a kind of zoo on it so that the tourists would not have to go far into the forest anymore to look at these creatures? 'Perhaps it will be like *Masoala Kely*' (Little Masoala at the zoo in Zurich), commented one of the very few people I met who had a clear idea about what kind of thing and where 'Little Masoala' was.

The inclusion of Nosin-dRendra within the Hard Core of the park not only produced speculations about its future but also anxiety. A few years ago, people recalled, a group of tourists staying in one of the nearby eco-lodges canoed to Nosin-dRendra in their kayaks, disembarked, walked up the path leading to the burial site and subsequently disappeared from sight (as anyone would because the islet is completely forested). Some time later, they reappeared and left. There is absolutely nothing on Nosin-dRendra but the burial ground, and for the Malagasy it is unthinkable to go to burial grounds unless in connection with duties towards the ancestors. Therefore local people who observed this, and many more who later heard about the event, wondered what on earth these white foreigners were doing on Nosin-dRendra. Were they perhaps planning to steal the bones? Theft of bones from tombs is a horror scenario for the Malagasy, and such theft is regularly reported on the radio to have occurred in various parts of Madagascar. It is said that the bones are sold to Chinese merchants for the production of dubious medicine.[5]

In fact, the kayaking tourists were likely to have been Swiss – perhaps having been inspired to travel to Masoala by a visit to the zoo's exhibit – because the eco-lodge where they stayed and which had organised the excursion was at the time owned and run by a Swiss woman and a

Photograph 8.2 The sacrificial stone amongst the tombs

white South African man, and the majority of their guests came from Switzerland. Whoever they were, ever since they had been observed on Nosin-dRendra without the purpose of their visit being clear to local people – although it was likely to have been no more than a stroll or picnic in a nice place – it was feared by some that the ancestors might be in danger. It was feared in particular that Nosin-dRendra might come under the control of foreigners, the memory of colonial rule and the present vicinity of the foreign-run tourist lodges rendering such a scenario not entirely unlikely. If this should happen, people worried, what would become of their ancestors' bones? 'It's not as if our bones had any value for these foreigners', one man remarked. If Nosin-dRendra was turned into a tourist site, would the visitors step or sit on the sacrificial stone where the sacrificed cattle is presented to the ancestors? They probably would, as the flat stone on the ground is hardly discernable as a sacred spot to the untrained eye (see photograph 8.2). Would they urinate, or worse, close to the tombs? A number of such fears circulated. Not only would such acts desecrate the place, they would also carry great potential to evoke the anger of the ancestors, bringing misfortune on those who depend on their blessing. Whatever else might happen on Nosin-dRendra and to the tombs on it, people contemplated, one thing was clear: with the islet now under the authority of the park management, they had lost control over the burial site.

Moving the Tombs

In December 2006, elders and others from the three kin groups in Ambanizana who had ancestors on Nosin-dRendra met to discuss what was to be done, as did other kin groups in other villages who found themselves in the same situation. The decision was reached that the best way forward was to move the tombs away to a safer location. The ancestors on the Island of the Wanderer were to be moved to the burial site on the outskirts of the village, where they would join all the other ancestors. 'The foreigners have taken over Nosin-dRendra'; 'Nosin-dRendra now belongs to ANGAP', many people commented bitterly. One man said to me: 'It is those who are defeated who must go' (*ny resy fô handeha*). The decision having been reached, the event had to be organised. It was agreed that all three kin groups from Ambanizana who had ancestors on Nosin-dRendra would move them in February in a joint ritual. Once the date had been fixed, preparations began, including the search for appropriate sacrificial animals. The transferral of the ancestors was to be a costly enterprise because it necessitated, for each kin group, the sacrifice of two head of cattle in order to ask the ancestors for their blessing of the move. Each kin group was to sacrifice one head of cattle on Nosin-dRendra when explaining to its ancestors that and why they were going to move house, and another upon arrival at the burial site in Ambanizana when introducing the ancestors to their new residence. This was especially important as it had been decided that the ancestors from Nosin-dRendra were going to remain together rather than being placed with their respective kin. The burial site in Ambanizana consists of several compounds, one for each kin group, with the different compounds being separated by bushes and trees. The descendants of the ancestors from Nosin-dRendra felt, however, that the latter had been together for so long on the island that it would be wrong to separate them now. Thus, in preparation for their arrival, a new compound within the village's burial grounds was cleared. It was named 'Nosin-dRendra having changed place' (*Nosin-dRendra nifindra*).

Preparations in Ambanizana also included the sewing of clothes to be given to the ancestors, the collective pounding and sifting of the rice to be consumed, the purchase of some new sarcophagi to replace the very old wooden ones that were in the process of decay, as well as the organisation of the transport. Nosin-dRendra lies many kilometres to the south of Ambanizana, and because a dozen or so heavy cement sarcophagi were going to be moved in one go, the two strongest motorised boats available in the village were hired for the occasion.

Apart from these financial costs, the transferral of tombs is always risky because ancestral anger at the move cannot be entirely ruled out, though every effort was made to win the ancestors' consent. Before anything was actually done, a specialist for such matters, an *ombiasy*, was consulted; *ombiasy* are considered to have the ability to communicate with the ancestors via dreams. The *ombiasy* gave the concerned kin groups the green light. Furthermore, the ancestors were directly addressed and their blessing sought in a ritual of invocation by their kin, and they were asked to let their descendants know, through dreams, if they should not agree. As this did not happen, it was concluded that the endeavour could go ahead.

On 3 February 2007, the tombs were moved. All rituals were carried out correctly, both on Nosin-dRendra and at the new compound in Ambanizana. On Nosin-dRendra the ancestors were taken out of their sarcophagi; old, rotten cloth was removed and the ancestors' bones were wrapped in new fabric. When everything had been done following protocol, the ancestors were placed into travel bags or other suitable containers for the duration of their journey.

Photograph 8.3 An empty sarcophagus is being carried to the boats

Hundreds of people had joined the event, and the two boats carrying the ancestors to their new home were heavy with the sarcophagi and accompanying kin. The fact that the sea was calm confirmed the ancestors' consent. Upon arrival in Ambanizana, the ancestors were welcomed by the loud and cheerful singing and clapping of the women who had stayed behind to help with the preparations and who had rushed down to the beach as soon as the boats had come into sight. After the second two head of cattle had been killed, ritually offered to the ancestors and consumed by the living, the ancestors were put back into their sarcophagi that had in the meantime been placed, heads facing east, on the soil of the new burial compound.

Moving individual ancestors from one burial site to another is not, as such, an out-of-the-ordinary event. Especially when relatives die far away from home, they are often buried where they died, for example, if there is insufficient time for a kin group to organise the necessary finances for the transport, or if the weather does not permit it. But once the bones are dry and clean and can thus be exhumed, it is vitally important to take them to the *tanindrazana* (land of the ancestors) of the concerned kin group. Moving a whole group of ancestors from one location to another is not unknown either, though much rarer. As discussed in connection with 'the process of growth', it occurs when a kin group decides that the land they live on and that their forebears had migrated to in the past has become their true ancestral homeland.[6]

The event of moving ancestors individually or collectively from one burial site to another is thus not unheard of. What makes the example of Nosin-dRendra different is the fact that it in no way marked the successful transformation of neutral soil into 'land of the ancestors' – on the contrary. Moving the tombs away from Nosin-dRendra and placing them in a safer place out of the reach of the park meant 're-gress' rather than 'pro-gress'. 'It is those who are defeated who must go'.

Regaining Control

In the speeches to the ancestors during the ritual, when it was explained to them why they were being transferred from Nosin-dRendra to a new burial compound in Ambanizana, no reference was made to either the park authority or to possible interference by foreigners as a reason for the move. Instead, another rationale was put forward. The ancestors were told that Nosin-dRendra was too far away from Ambanizana (the journey takes a couple of hours by dugout canoe), and it was difficult for people to carry out the rituals (*mijaly zahay*) and so it would be easier for them to care for their ancestors if they were closer to home. This explanation had also been voiced by many people prior to the day of the actual transferral of the ancestors, but it was always put forward as a second, less important reason for the move. The main reason given for the move of the tombs prior to the ritual was always that Nosin-dRendra had been lost to ANGAP or to the foreigners, that the Malagasy had been defeated and that the ancestors on Nosin-dRendra were in danger. But on the day of the ritual itself, neither the ritual speechmaker nor any of the guests I heard talking among themselves or to whom I spoke indicated that it was because of the park that the event was taking place. On the contrary, everyone emphasised that it had been their free will (*sitraponay*) to bring the ancestors to Ambanizana, and that the sole reason was the practical difficulties implied by the distance between Ambanizana and Nosin-dRendra. People even quite emphatically denied any other suggestion on my part reminding them of what they had previously said. At the end of the ritual proceedings, one man remarked to me: 'Now, the ancestors are happy, because they have come home', while during the preceding weeks and months, the same person had repeatedly expressed his distaste at ANGAP and the foreigners for having appropriated Nosin-dRendra for their own purposes.

Arguably, while the distance between the village and the island had never been a major problem before, it actually did become a nuisance precisely because of the various new conditions attached to carrying out the rituals on Nosin-dRendra such as not being permitted to cut any bamboo on the islet. However, something else seemed to be going on as well. The actual movement of the ancestors away from the reach of the park authorities meant that their descendants had in fact regained full control over their ancestors' remains. As already mentioned, the *physical remains* of the dead play a crucial role in all of Madagascar. The rhetorical shift in explaining the reason why the tombs on Nosin-dRendra had to be moved indicates that the point of the move was to regain control. By turning the involuntary loss of, and the retreat from, the burial ground into an act of free will, and by emphasising how happy the ancestors were to 'come home' (*mody*), the people in Ambanizana effectively reversed the logic. Instead of having been pushed out, they were once again in charge.

When I returned to Ambanizana one-and-a-half years later, I enquired about how people now felt regarding the move of the tombs. Most people I spoke to reported that both they themselves and the ancestors were happy; it was much more convenient to have the ancestors on the outskirts of the village than miles away on Nosin-dRendra, and it was thus easier to properly care for them. 'If they need new clothes, we can bring them easily. But in the old days, when they were on Nosin-dRendra, we didn't manage to go there sometimes for two years on end.' The ancestors were obviously happy, too, as manifested in the lack of any unusual misfortune in the village since the move. Again, my query as to whether or not the park-related regulations had pushed them towards the move, as lots of people previously had consistently claimed, was emphatically denied by most. Not everybody agreed, however. One woman with whom I discussed this issue, who is both a renowned spirit medium and an equally renowned midwife in the village, expressed her continued disagreement: 'I don't like it. The burial ground on Nosin-dRendra is so old that nobody knows when it actually began. It was the really old ancestors (*ny razam-be talôha, ny kazana*) who chose it as a burial ground and therefore it ought not to have been moved'.

In this and the previous two chapters we have encountered three kinds of perceived threats caused by the creation of the Masoala National Park. First, the park has resulted in the loss of substantial parts of the land that the people in Ambanizana and Marofototra already cultivated, and in far-reaching restrictions concerning agricultural practices. Second, by not recognising local farmers' ownership of still-forested land and strictly prohibiting any future transformation of forest into cultivated land, the park poses a serious and strongly felt threat to the process of growth, thereby attacking one of the most fundamental values of rural Malagasy people. And third, as the history of the tombs on Nosin-dRendra reveals, the park may even pose a threat to that most fundamental of relationships on which Malagasy societies are built: the mutual dependency of ancestors and their living kin in caring for one another and thereby jointly securing the prosperity of the kin group. But who is responsible for these various threats that the people in Ambanizana and Marofototra feel are facing them? Who is behind 'the park'? What exactly *is* 'the park'? This is far from clear.

Notes

1. I have heard several slightly different versions of the story of Nosin-dRendra. The following account is a synthesis focusing on the least controversial parts.
2. These days, the word *rendra* is used to refer to young people who never stay put at home but instead are always out and about looking for fun.
3. The account of exhumation being a relatively new practice would be confirmed by a short article written by Decary in 1939. In it, he cites a writer called Lastelle whose description from 1797 of the burial of a chief does not involve interment and subsequent exhumation but instead recounts that the body was placed in a wooden coffin which was then put on the ground and left without ever being touched again. 'On le met sur la terre et on le laisse ensuite sans jamais le déranger. Cette grande confiance vient de ce

qu'ils n'ont à craindre aucune bête féroce' (Lastelle 1797, cited in Decary 1939: 50). By 1939, local burial custom seems to have been almost identical to contemporary burial practices involving interment and subsequent exhumation, with Decary remarking that: 'Ces practiques ne sont, en somme, pas contraires à l'hygiène, la désincarnation du cadavre étant toujours complétement terminée lorsque le squelette est placé définitivement dans le cercueil' (1939: 49).
4. Compare Evers and Seagle 2012: 102 in this respect, reporting on the destruction of tombs by Rio Tinto for the sake of its mining project in south-east Madagascar.
5. For news reports about such theft see, for example: http://news.bbc.co.uk/2/hi/africa/3039513.stm
6. This happened, for example, in another village in the district where I previously conducted fieldwork. Several generations after the first people had settled there, all the ancestors were brought from a faraway location to a newly created burial site nearby the village (see Keller 2005: 30–35).

CHAPTER 9

Who Are 'They'?

There is an overwhelming sense among the population in both Ambanizana and Marofototra that those who represent the park (*ny parc*) have come to Masoala in order to appropriate the peninsula's vast tracts of forested land, thereby taking away from the local people the basis of their livelihood. Some people phrase it even more harshly, stating that the sole purpose of the park was to render local people poor. The intentions, in other words, of those behind *ny parc* are fairly clear in the eyes of the farmers who live in its vicinity.

At the same time, it is far from clear to most local people *who* is involved in running the park and what names of entities known to be working with ANGAP, the park authority, might stand for.[1] A jumble of words including ONG (Non-governmental organisation), WCS (the Wildlife Conservation Society), Zoo de Zurich, Banque Mondial and Missouri Botanical Garden made their way to Ambanizana and Marofototra where they led to considerable confusion about what and who they referred to. It was far from clear to most people in these two villages (and I am sure in other villages too) whether such names referred to some kind of organisation – and, if so, what exactly was 'an organisation'? – or perhaps to places abroad or to individuals? For instance, I sometimes heard the words 'Zoo de Zurich' being pronounced by local people in such a way as to make them sound like 'Zezeric', which might as well be a person's name. During the years leading up to the park's creation, what was to become the Masoala National Park was called the 'Projet Masoala'. One man in another village in the district once asked me during that time who the wife of 'Monsieur Projet' was. Having heard of something, or someone rather, called *Projet*, in French, he had apparently concluded that Monsieur Projet was one of the French men living in the district's only town who are married to Malagasy women.

For most people in Ambanizana and Marofototra, the forces behind the creation and repeated de facto expansion of the park represented a shadowy consortium of some kind of outsiders who, jointly, acted like an approaching enemy. One knew 'they' (*zare*) were out there and wanted to claim one's land, one knew 'they' were much more powerful than oneself, but one did not know who exactly 'they' were, what 'their' next move would be and how fast 'they' would approach. 'They have come to take our land', or 'They have thrown us out', were phrases that I heard very often indeed. There was a clear sense among the villages' population that they were being invaded by a new form of outside power – but who these outsiders were, who 'they' were, was far from clear.

Who Will Own Masoala?

One morning in Ambanizana in 2006, the village leaders called the population to come and listen to a public speech to be delivered by a group of government representatives who had arrived from town. The group included two *gendarmes*, the district's new head representative for the Ministry of Water and Forests, as well as Roland, a high-ranking ANGAP staff member reputed to be a tough conservationist (and therefore disliked by many people). As was customary at this sort of occasion, the villagers, about two hundred this time, gathered in a wide circle around the *Commune*'s vice-mayor's house from whose veranda the speeches were to be delivered. Roland was the first to speak. In addressing the crowd, he made, in roughly these translated words, the following points.

> Don't be afraid of us, don't be shy; talk to us about the things that bother you! We are all from the district of Maroantsetra, and we all speak the same language. None of us here is from Tananarive [Madagascar's capital city]! The forest is the source of our development (*fampandrosoana*). If we don't have the forest anymore, we are lost. Without the forest, we won't have any development, because the protection of the environment (*ny tontol-iainana*[2]) brings money to Madagascar – dollars and euros, and eco-tourism. The Malagasy government knows that we need the forest and it therefore protects the forest, for the sake of the people. The government does not kill people (*ny fanjakana tsy mamono ôlo*)[3] but it cares for the population, it protects people. In the past, Madagascar used to be all green (*maitso*), but nowadays it has become red earth (*tany mena*; [i.e. eroded]). Also here in Masoala part of the land has already become red earth. Those who deny this are not telling the truth! The President of the Republic [Ravalomanana, in office from 2002 to 2009] has announced that in the course of the next ten years, the surface area of all the protected areas of Madagascar will be extended from the present 1.7 million hectares to 6 million hectares.

After Roland's speech, one of the gendarmes took the floor, encouraging people not to be afraid of the gendarmes and not to run away from them (*aza matahotra, aza milefa izahay*) as they tended to, because, he said, it was the role of the police to protect them. He then went on to emphasise the importance of everyone having both a birth certificate and an identity card. The next speaker, the head of the district's Ministry of Water and Forests, addressed the necessity for people to always obtain authorisation before planting hill rice, on their land outside the park, and explained how this was to be done.

At the end of the speeches the audience was invited to ask questions. One of the six questions that were posed to the speakers concerned the announcement of the massive extension of the country's protected areas which, combined with people's experience of a repeatedly shifting park boundary, had caused many of those present that day to look worried. Would this mean, the questioner enquired, that the Masoala National Park was yet again to grow (as it subsequently in fact did)? Would the population of Ambanizana eventually have to settle elsewhere? But where would they go? The answer was evasive and failed to shed clarity on the issue (people afterwards referred to it as '*tsy mazava*': not clear). Another question was posed by Malaza, a well-educated man, who, just the night before, had heard on the radio that eight of Madagascar's national parks, including the one in Masoala which at that time had existed for almost ten years, were soon to be declared a *patrimoine mondial*. Did this mean, he wanted to know, that the land inside the park would no longer belong to Madagascar? The question was answered by Roland in the following way:

> I have not heard this yet, but a park becoming a *patrimoine mondial* does not mean that it will belong to the countries abroad (*tsy ho lasa andafy*). It means that the forest here is the wealth not only of Madagascar but of the whole world (*harenan' ny izao tontolo izao*). We are very lucky, because the population around the park will, therefore, not be forgotten, but will be cared for by the world and the government.

This was the first time that the term *patrimoine mondial* had been widely heard in the village, and the news was received by those listening with a mixture of worry and uncertainty as to what exactly this would imply. Again, Roland's answer had failed to make things clear. Although many surely could make sense of the word *mondial*, associating it with the world beyond Madagascar, it is likely that *patrimoine* meant nothing to almost everyone present. As a result, in the course of the next days and weeks, the expression was transformed in local parlance into *parc mondial*. This made more sense. Everyone knew what a *parc* was – a space which local people can no longer freely enter, a piece of forest from where they cannot now take any resources – and *mondial* was to do with the outside world. In the course of the following year, during which the Masoala National Park was indeed declared a UNESCO World Heritage Site, local people voiced a number of interpretations as to what the park being turned into a *parc mondial* really meant and would entail. These interpretations, though diverse in terms of their nuances, carried one clear message: the land would no longer belong to Madagascar but to the world beyond, and especially to the *vazaha*. *Vazaha* is a word used throughout Madagascar to refer to any foreigner (and sometimes even certain Malagasy; see below and chapter 10) but is typically used to denote white Europeans and North Americans. The *vazaha*, the people from 'beyond the sea' (*andafy*), would manage, and possibly own, the peninsula's immense areas of forested land. Perhaps they would buy Masoala from the central Malagasy government or share the exploitation of the forest's riches, especially its precious woods, with it? Some even feared the possible eviction of the local people from certain areas of Masoala. The whole discourse was coloured by a combination of anxiety and uncertainty – uncertainty as to who was behind this latest move and what would happen next. It was the same fear and uncertainty that we already encountered in connection with the Island of the Wanderer and local people's anxieties over its future which led, eventually, to the transferral of the tombs to a safe location.

For those who instigated and promoted the declaration of the Masoala National Park as an UNESCO World Heritage Site, prominently among them the Zurich zoo (Zurich Zoo 2007), such a site is a manifestation of a shared vision and of people from around the world acting jointly to protect a place of global interest. For the people in Masoala, however, the concept of *mondial* was far from incorporating all of humanity. On the contrary, it was understood as an expression of a power relationship through which nations from beyond Madagascar, and in particular the French as the former colonisers, would once again gain control over Masoala. *Mondial* referred to a concept implying the annexation of a part of Madagascar by the outside world – a concept that marked the separation between 'them' and 'us'.

From the perspective of the people who live their lives in Ambanizana and Marofototra, there is no clear answer to the question of who 'they' are, of who it actually is they are confronted with. If one were to paraphrase local people's perception of what is going on, they would say something like this:

> ANGAP, the park authority, whose staff are all Malagasy, are watching us, and they work together with the gendarmes and the tribunal in town in punishing those who engage in what they call illegal activities. At the same time, we believe it is the *vazaha* (white foreigners) who pay for the park and that it is therefore they who make the real decisions. But we do not know who these *vazaha* are, nor what they are truly planning to do. The one thing we do know for sure is that the park takes away our land, and that without it we not only lose our livelihood but we also cannot prepare a future for our children and grandchildren.

A Nebulous Coalition of Outside Forces

In people's discourses about the park, the expression 'they' (*zare*) represents a nebulous and ominous coalition of powerful outsiders, both state-related and foreign. I will discuss these two aspects in turn, beginning with the Malagasy state.

The Resurfacing of the State

Masoala is a very remote area that can only be reached on foot or by boat. As in other similarly isolated regions of the country, the state has been all but absent since the end of French colonial rule (Covell 1987: 88; Cole 2001: 234–35). Although in every *Commune Rurale* and in each village a handful of people are elected as government representatives (mayors, vice-mayors, village presidents, etc.), people's daily lives and affairs, prior to the creation of the Masoala National Park, were only subject to government control to a very limited extent.[4] By the same token, communities on the Masoala peninsula have rarely benefited from government services or programmes intended to advance economic opportunities for local populations, often simply because the villages cannot be comfortably reached by car or motorcycle. In the *Commune Rurale* of Ambanizana with a population of several thousand people living in far-flung villages, one single *dokitera* (doctor) – in fact, he is only trained as a nurse – is responsible for attending to all medical needs. For the sick farthest away from the *hôpitaly* which he runs together with a small team of assistants, reaching medical help involves many hours of travelling on water, walking or being carried by others.

With the creation of the park, people have experienced a sudden resurfacing of the state in their lives. First, by declaring the bulk of the Masoala peninsula as out of bounds for local people, the central Malagasy state has set tight limits on people's ability to create agricultural land. Second, the state has marked its presence by permanently stationing park staff in those villages where it considers that people's activities need to be monitored, among them Ambanizana and Marofototra. Third, the state has issued new legal codes aimed at the protection of the forest. One of these is a national law, the already mentioned Code de Gestion des Aires Protégées, which contains draconian measures for infractions such as the deliberate felling of trees or the cultivation of hill rice inside any protected area of the country. Many people in Ambanizana and Marofototra have vaguely heard about this law's existence, and are aware that it is incredibly harsh without knowing what it actually says. Its effects, however, have been felt dramatically; the prison sentences referred to in chapter 6 were all received in the course of the two years following the Code coming into force. In the enclave of Marofototra, the two *Dina*s (local legally binding regulations) which were drafted in the wake of the park's creation regulate the use of all terrestrial and marine natural resources within the Zone d'Occupation Contrôlée. A further decree was issued in 2006 by the national Ministry of Agriculture, Animal Husbandry and Fishery banning the use of fine-meshed fishing nets on the shores of Antongil Bay, where Ambanizana and Marofototra are located. 'En raison de l'urgence', the decree came into immediate effect as soon as it had received sufficient publicity.[5] This latest decree was targeted at a local fishing method that is practised in Ambanizana, for example, whereby (mostly) women catch fish by jointly holding and directing a large fishing net while standing in a large circle a few metres off the shore. The fishing net's owner receives half the catch, the rest is divided equally among all the participants in the joint enterprise. The criticism of this method is that the nets used (*ramikaoko*) are so fine-meshed as to catch tiny fish before they have a chance to reproduce, thereby damaging the bay's fauna.

The Return of the Vazaha

While the establishment of the park has led to a resurfacing of state control, it has simultaneously implied the return of the *vazaha* who once ruled Madagascar and who, many local people fear, have now come back to appropriate Malagasy soil once again. As an extraordinarily interesting region in terms of biodiversity, Masoala has in recent years attracted many different types of *vazaha*. People, young and old, ranging from biologists and zoologists, to tourists, representatives of funding bodies, and Peace Corps volunteers, as well as WCS-employees and personnel of the zoo in Zurich, have all made an appearance. Mostly, however, these *vazaha* do not venture into 'normal' villages, although some, including the director of the Zurich zoo, have in the past paid brief visits to Ambanizana and Marofototra, and some have given speeches about the importance of forest conservation.

Being a *vazaha* myself, I must, in parentheses, add a few words about my own case. I believe, and I have been told so many times, that the people living in Ambanizana and Marofototra clearly realise that I am not connected with the Masoala National Park. This is so for a number of reasons. First, I have worked in the area for many years, and I always stay with the same families, spending my days with the people in the villages and speaking with them in the local dialect. Other *vazaha* invariably stay with the park staff in the ANGAP offices (in Ambanizana it is the only building built of cement except for the school) or in one of the tourist lodges, and rare are those who come to the area more than once. Second, I do not socialise with the ANGAP staff in the two villages where I am based. I am polite to them as everyone else is, and I pay them the occasional visit as an act of courtesy or in order to speak to them about a particular topic, but no more. Even more importantly, I have never ventured into the Hard Core of the park, something I could easily do as a paying foreigner, thereby showing the local people that I have not come to watch the lemurs like all the other *vazaha*. In terms of acceptance and trust-based relationships, this is crucial.[6]

Many *vazaha* have turned up in the area since the Masoala National Park was instigated in the early 1990s and eventually created in 1997. However, during the years that I regularly conducted fieldwork in Masoala it was, to various degrees of confusion, far from clear to the great majority of the people I knew and talked with who the various *vazaha* were and what, exactly, the nature of their obvious interest in going into the forest was. With reference to another protected area in Madagascar, the Ankarana Special Reserve, Andrew Walsh has discussed how local people find it very hard to believe that anybody would go to such lengths as to travel a very long way and to spend a lot of money 'just to look at things' and take photographs. Surely, the *vazaha* who make such an effort to visit the reserve must be searching for something in there, while keeping it a secret what, exactly, that something is.

Similarly, different speculations circulated in the villages of Ambanizana and Marofototra as to what it really was the *vazaha* were after inside the Masoala National Park because, as in the case discussed by Walsh, their alleged interest in 'just looking' was bewildering. Were they perhaps searching for gold or precious stones? And why would some of them refuse to let the local porters carry their rucksacks? Was that not because the porters would feel the difference in weight once the rucksacks were holding these treasures? It had apparently occurred, at least once, that tourists had asked the porters of their luggage to stay behind in the camp while they went off into the forest by themselves. And what about these books with maps (travel guides) that all *vazaha* carried with them? Were the maps perhaps indicating the location of the precious stones and the gold inside the forest? And what exactly were those called *serser* (*chercheurs* / researchers) doing, who regularly come and stay at Andranobe (a research station located in an isolated spot along the coast) for weeks or months on end? Were they really just studying animals and plants as they claimed?

In 2001, a gigantic, colourful hot air balloon with an air raft in the shape of a pretzel attached to it, descended on the area. Local people recall the event as 'the time of the balloon'.

Photograph 9.1 The balloon over Masoala (copyright Océan Vert)
Retrieved 8 July 2014 from http://www.radeau-des-cimes.org/radeau/expe%20mada_fr.pdf

For two months, a crew of some forty interchanging *vazaha* spent days, and at times entire nights, as local people recall, hovering above the forest canopy on the air raft and snipping off leaves which were then conserved in bottles filled with alcohol. They camped near the *vazaha*-run tourist lodges located between Ambanizana and Marofototra. Some local men worked as porters for the crew, but when I spoke to them a few years later about this event, even they did not really know what the purpose of this enterprise had been. 'They wouldn't let us carry their luggage, only the cooking utensils', one man recalled. 'I don't know what they had in their rucksacks or what they intended to do with all the leaves they collected. They collected leaves of every kind, even the tiniest ones; and even ants!' Some people in Ambanizana suggested that the balloon crew was making European-type medicine (*fanafodin' ny dokitera*) out of the leaves. Some who had worked for them used the expression 'botanist', without being clear as to what a botanist was. According to the detailed online reports of the expedition at the time,[7] the Masoala expedition was a commercial-cum-scientific exploration led by the Swiss flagrance and flavour company Givaudan, a world-leader in its field, in cooperation with the non-profit organisation Pro Natura International and another partner. The Wildlife Conservation

Society, the Zurich zoo's collaborator in Masoala, was among the organisations involved as scientific partner in situ. The expedition was aimed at gathering botanical data as well as searching for new exotic flagrances in the rainforest's canopy to be used commercially, for example, in perfumes. In its annual report of 2001, Givaudan stated that the expedition had provided them with '80 interesting scents from flowers, fruits, woods, leaves and resins which since have been evaluated. Many of them have been reconstituted and are now a great source of stimulation and motivation for the creation of different types of fragrances and flavours' (Givaudan 2001: 31). The great majority of the local people in Masoala who had observed this enterprise, both from close up and from far below, were left wondering why the *vazaha* would go to such efforts merely to collect leaves and ants.

Joint Forces

Who are 'they', then, and what exactly is the true nature of their interest in Masoala? Why do foreigners go deep into the forest apparently scrutinising everything they find, while local people are kept out? There is no clear answer. It is generally feared that in connection with the Masoala National Park, Madagascar will lose, or has lost, sovereignty over part of its territory to the *vazaha*. At the same time, Nature conservation is not directly enforced by the *vazaha* but by Malagasy ANGAP staff and the state. Thus the government appears to have joined forces with the *vazaha* in taking control over the Masoala peninsula at the expense of local people's livelihood and ownership rights. The creation of the park, the subsequent opening of the *vazaha*-run tourist lodges, the repeated presence of various *vazaha* and government representatives in connection with the park, the *vazaha*'s alleged interest in taking control of the Island of the Wanderer, and the news that Masoala had become a *patrimoine/parc mondial* all added up, for the people living in Ambanizana and Marofototra, to a general sense of uncertainty about the future.

Indeed, it is not surprising that '*ny parc*' has come to represent both the state and foreign rule from the perspective of those who are at the receiving end of conservation policy. If one thinks back on that morning in Ambanizana during which the issue of the park becoming a *patrimoine mondial* was discussed, it was noticeable that ANGAP staff from town had turned up together with representatives of the government and the police force. Moreover, the group's speeches to the assembled villagers had covered topics relating to forest conservation and the involvement of the foreign countries in this, as well as to state control, in particular the necessity for everyone to obtain both a birth certificate and an identity card. Also, in answering the question as to the consequences of the park becoming a *patrimoine mondial*, Roland, the ANGAP employee, highlighted the care that would be provided for the local population, jointly by the government and 'the world', which, as we have seen, is locally perceived to mean the non-Malagasy world.

It is, in fact, questionable whether for the people in Ambanizana and Marofototra there is much difference between the power of the central Malagasy government and that of the *vazaha*. Both represent the 'outside' and are felt to be alien to life in the villages. In many rural places in Madagascar, including in Masoala, the main feeling associated with the government (*fanjakana*) is distrust and fear. The state is often perceived as an unwanted body of control and, at times, coercion – as 'something essentially alien, predatory' (Graeber 2007: 21; see also Cole 2001: 63; Horning 2012: 118). At the same time, the inhabitants of Ambanizana and Marofototra do not often dare to openly resist state orders. The usual comportment vis-à-vis state authorities is avoidance or polite consent to whatever they might say, regardless of whether or not one actually intends to follow their instructions. Therefore the filing of a complaint by some of the inhabitants of Marofototra concerning the renewed de facto expansion of the park's boundary, which I briefly reported in chapter 6, represented a highly unusual step.

Moreover, in the island's coastal regions people's largely negative view of the central government is enhanced because the latter is associated with the pre-colonial Merina empire (Cole 2001: 40–43, 293–95). The Merina are an 'ethnic group' (see Larson 1996) who live around the capital city in the central highlands of the country. They controlled most of Madagascar, including the area around Masoala, during most of the nineteenth century. The antagonism between the Merina and the *côtiers* (people from the coasts) has been used as a key political tool by both French and Malagasy political leaders since independence, thus keeping it alive and real for many Malagasy citizens. In local discourses in Masoala, the era of the pre-colonial Merina kingdom is represented as a time of exploitation and great brutality, equal to that of colonial times. The central government, with its seat in the old Merina capital in the highlands, is considered a continuation of Merina power, and for this reason people in Ambanizana and Marofototra expect little of the government except the exploitation of the coastal regions. Local people's experiences with the Masoala National Park have strengthened these pre-existing distrustful and negative feelings. In fact, the notion of 'foreignness' does not only apply to Europeans and North Americans, but the word *vazaha* is sometimes also used locally to refer to people from the central highlands (or other Malagasy perceived to be very unconnected and different to oneself).[8]

In many ways, local people's merging of the various kinds of Malagasy and non-Malagasy actors involved in the park into a group referred to as 'they' directly reflects what Duffy (2006), following Harrison (2004), calls 'global environmental governance'. It reflects a situation in which the Malagasy government enforces, through its body in charge of protected areas and other parts of the apparatus of the state, a foreign-determined conservation agenda, in the case at hand through the mediation of the Wildlife Conservation Society that co-manages the Masoala National Park together with the parastatal Protected Areas agency ANGAP and that is heavily financed in this endeavour by the zoo in Zurich. It reflects a situation, in other words, in which the state's role in conservation-targeted areas like Masoala is simultaneously strengthened and weakened. In such a situation, the respective roles of the Malagasy government and of globally active conservation bodies are difficult to disentangle. Thus, perhaps, the farmers of Ambanizana and Marofototra are confused because the situation is, indeed, confusing (cf. Fairhead and Leach 2003).

When the people in Ambanizana and Marofototra reflect about the park and the question of who is actually behind and responsible for it, they perceive a nebulous consortium of governmental and non-Malagasy outside powers. Indeed, it is precisely the Merina, with whom the central Malagasy government is still associated, and the *vazaha*, the foreigners from 'beyond the sea', who, in local people's understanding of the region's history, brought hardship to Masoala in the past. These two groups have now jointly returned to Masoala, and their respective intentions are thought to be identical, so much so that they merge into one, hostile, 'other' – into 'they'.

Notes

Substantial parts of this chapter were first published in 2009 in *Tsantsa* 14: 11– 20.

1. Exceptions would be those few individuals who have, at some time in the past, worked for either the *Projet Masoala* (an ICDP project [Integrated Conservation and Development Project] between 1992 and 1997; see Ormsby and Mannle 2006: 275) or the Masoala National Park or who, for other reasons, have acquired an understanding of its organisational structure. One man in Ambanizana, for example, worked as a lemur observer for eight years, both during the time of the *Projet* and thereafter.
2. In the course of the international conservation efforts in many parts of Madagascar, a special term for 'the environment', *ny tontol-iainana*, has been coined in the Malagasy language (see Sodikoff 2012: 87–89, 99; Seagle 2013: 196). This term has also become established in the district of Maroantsetra,

including on the Masoala peninsula, and is now widely used both by the park authorities and the local people when speaking about park-related issues.
3. Roland was obviously aware that local people sometimes talked of the park as 'killing people'.
4. Even during colonisation, the administration in Maroantsetra struggled to implement its policies due to a number of reasons, including the shortage of French staff (Fremigacci 2009).
5. Arrêté no. 18680/2006, issued by the Ministère de l'Agriculture de l'Elevage et de la Pêche on 30 October 2006.
6. In her account of fieldwork in a village close to another national park in Madagascar (Ranomafana), Janice Harper offers a disturbing account of how project staff, among them the American project director, hindered her research and attempted to intimidate her into not including critical reflections of the park in any publications (Harper 2002: 15, 160, 235–40). I must emphasise that I was never subject to any such obstructions. On the contrary, the Malagasy park staff, including the park director, have always been very friendly to me and willing to talk and offer information.
7. For the detailed *Journal de bord*, see http://www.tela-botanica.org/page: recit_mission_madagascar. For a summary presentation of the overall programme, see Pro Natura and Océan Vert n.d.
8. Local people who have the role of a *patron*, such as the owners of the boats in Ambanizana, are at times also addressed as *vazaha*.

CHAPTER 10

Historical Reflections

History continues

The perception of the Masoala National Park as a threat to local people's present and future livelihoods is quasi-universally shared in the villages of Ambanizana and Marofototra. Some people, however, express an even more drastic fear of what the park might entail.

The Narrative of an Old Man

Papan' i Lucien was a very old and frail man. His ID-card states that he was born *'vers* 1922'. When he was young, he had to carry out forced labour duties under the supervision of Senegalese soldiers of the French colonial army.[1] They were constructing a road connecting two administrative centres. Large stones had to be extracted from a quarry, cut into slabs, transported by canoe to where they were needed and then laid down one next to the other.

> People had to dig up the soil. *'Un! Deux! Trois!'* That was how they commanded.... *'Un!'* one shovelful was thrown to the side, *'Deux!',* another shovelful. 'Enough. *Repos. Repos! En avant!* Hurry up!' People had to work really fast! *'Repos!'* That's how it was.

Having difficulties walking and being more or less housebound, Papan' i Lucien was keen to spend time talking. When I asked him, on two occasions just a few days apart, to tell me about the history of Ambanizana, a narrative connecting events throughout the twentieth century unfolded.

His story began with an account of how, in the past, many families lived in hamlets dispersed in the forest and how the colonial government had forced them to settle in permanent villages so that 'they would be safer' and 'it would be easier for the government to visit the villagers', as the colonial officers had said. During the first decades of the century, numerous colonial enterprises were present on the Masoala peninsula. They were engaged in the logging of precious woods, caoutchouc production, and the cultivation of coffee, cloves and vanilla. These enterprises were directed by white *colons* (colonial settlers) from Europe, Mauritius and La Réunion (see Petit and Jacob 1965) who relied on the labour of manual workers from the region and the arid south of Madagascar as well as on educated accountants from the Malagasy highlands. Papan' i Lucien knew many of them by name and remembered some in person, and he could tell stories about their endeavours and activities, families and fates. The places of the colonial logging companies and the local ports from where the wood was shipped became buzzing centres of activity. His own family, however, chose another option.

> At first, we were living close to today's village of Marofototra. There was a *vazaha* [foreigner] who owned the land around there. 'Those of you who don't want to work for me', he said, 'go away from here. You are not allowed to stay here'. And so people left. My father didn't work for him. He didn't want to become a *maromita* (a servant, a bearer of burdens)[2]. And so we moved to Ambanizana.

Many, however, ended up in servitude, just like slaves (*andevo*), Papan' i Lucien insisted, only they were not called 'slaves' anymore.

> The *vazaha* hated the fact that there were *andevo*. '*Andevo* is a bad thing', they said. So they changed that name to *maromita*. But the time when there are no more *maromita* just wouldn't come, up to this day.

The *colons* of the 1930s and 1940s were replaced by others, and these in turn were replaced by others still, until the last left after independence in 1960. Around that time a French-Senegalese company named Les Grands Moulins de Dakar showed up and became involved in logging activities on the Masoala peninsula, including in the region of Ambanizana. 'And now the last one that has come, replacing the others before it, is the *Projet* (the park)', Papan' i Lucien went on, without any probing on my part on the topic of the park anywhere in our conversation thus far. Between the departure of the Grands Moulins sometime in the 1970s and the arrival of the park in 1997, 'there was a little bit of space for the local people (*nalalaka hely ny vahoaka*). And then came, like the Moulins, the ... *Projet*. ... Who will replace them, I don't know, but they will go too, eventually!' Papan' i Lucien concluded, foreshadowing the expected continuation of the history of foreign control over the forests of Masoala. On this and many other occasions, he had nothing positive to say about the park. Instead he repeatedly emphasised how the park was driving people into poverty and hopelessness and, indeed, that it was the very intention of those responsible for it to impoverish the local population.

Papan' i Lucien was particularly disturbed by the fact that the park had taken from the people the land that the Creator of all things, Zanahary, had given to their ancestors:

> Zanahary made all these trees, Zanahary made them. 'This is what will belong to you (Zanahary had said to the ancestors). You know nothing about guns, you know nothing about canons, you don't know how to build ships – you don't even know how to make bicycles.' Concerning these things, the Malagasy are totally ignorant! ... And so when they are confronted with those who are powerful, those who have come with an intention in mind, the Malagasy will be oppressed. The Malagasy get nothing! And so I believe that *fañandevôzaña* will come back in the end. *Fañandevôzaña* will come back (*mbôla hiheriny ny fañandevôzaña*).

The word *fañandevôzaña*,[3] which we may tentatively translate as 'slavery', is employed by people in Masoala when they refer to different historical periods, in particular the era of French colonial rule between 1896 and 1960 but also when they refer to pre-colonial systems of slavery which are said to have been equally harsh and brutal, if not more so. When trying to capture the Malagasy sense of the term *fañandevôzaña*, it is best to understand it as denoting a status of servitude under powerful outsiders, rather than as specifying particular political regimes or historical periods. The term *fañandevôzaña* evokes a life-situation in which one is prohibited from working the fields for one's own livelihood and for the fruitful continuation of one's own kin group, and is forced instead to work for the prosperity of others (Feeley-Harnik 1991: 22, 442; Cole 2001: 156; Cole 2010: 57). *Fañandevôzaña* implies the interruption of the productive process of growth that connects ancestors, living people and future generations of descendants through a kin group's links with the land. Pre-colonial systems of slavery as well as French rule were such times.

'*Fañandevôzaña* will come back', Papan' i Lucien repeated several times.[4] He then continued his narrative by drawing a contrast between, on the one hand, *fañandevôzaña* during pre-colonial times under a group of rulers from western Madagascar who had taken control over the area (see Petit 1967; Toto 2005) and, on the other hand, the present situation. Comparing these two periods, Papan' i Lucien pointed to the possibility of pre-colonial slaves being able to escape the control of their masters by running away to other regions on the peninsula, whereas now there was no such land available any longer because it had all been taken by the park.

> And so if it is the nature of this *projet* to imprison (*migadra*) this land, I am sure that there will be *fañandevôzaña* again very soon from now. The land will be fenced off, the things you need are inside the boundary, and you are left with nothing. 'Let them suffer (*mijaly*)!' That is the park.

In the eyes of this old man, the people in Masoala might soon again be living in a situation of servitude under powerful outsiders, whoever they might be, because the park has taken away from them much of the land upon which their prosperity and growth depend.[5] 'The time when there are no more *maromita* (servants, bearers of burden) just wouldn't come, up to this day', as he had said. 'People in Madagascar don't have strength. We are like *flera* (*fleurs*/flowers)', he ended his reflections – perhaps he meant the delicate flower of the vanilla orchid that, in order to be pollinated, needs to be, and easily is, 'broken'.[6]

When Papan' i Lucien looks at the Masoala National Park, his gaze focuses on the historically charged relations between the people of Masoala and others who have come to the region 'with an intention in mind'. He reflects about the park as a new manifestation of a historical process connecting the past, the present and probably also the future. For Papan' i Lucien, the park represents the continuation of a history of power relations between outsiders from beyond local people's living space (both Malagasy and foreign) and the local people of Masoala, including his own family who had to leave their hamlet near today's village of Marofototra when their land was taken by a *colon* early in the twentieth century. Moreover, among

Photograph 10.1 Papan' i Lucien's sister holding the bones of their mother during the ritual at the 'Island of the Wanderer'

the ancestors who had rested on the Island of the Wanderer was Papan' i Lucien's mother. He was, in fact, one of the very few people I spoke to who had been against moving the tombs. It had saddened him deeply that his mother would have to leave the burial ground where her bones had lain for so long, and he did not fail to make a connection between losing NosindRendra and his family's experience of losing their land near Marofototra many decades previously. Having been pushed from her home as a child, his mother would, now that she was an ancestor, be pushed from her tomb.

'The Vazaha Don't Forget'

Narratives of historical continuity from the time of French colonisation to the present situation were offered by several people in the villages, especially but not exclusively by old people. These narratives included the history of Ambodiforaha.

Ambodiforaha is a small coastal village located halfway between Ambanizana and Marofototra. Its inhabitants very largely depend on fishing and the cultivation of hill rice through slash-and-burn agriculture. Before the French *colons* started to turn up in the area looking for suitable land for their various enterprises, Ambodiforaha is said to have been a sizeable village. But when the *vazaha* came, the farmers had to leave. However, the foreigners who claimed the land in Ambodiforaha for their own purposes gave those who were displaced new land in Ambanizana where the latter settled and henceforth lived. After independence and the subsequent departure of the last *colons* a couple of decades later, two brothers whose forebears had been amongst these previously displaced families 'returned home' (*mody*) to Ambodiforaha where they began to make a living once again. Ambodiforaha's contemporary inhabitants are largely the descendants of these two brothers. With the arrival of the Masoala National Park, the land around Ambodiforaha once again became contested, especially because the village lies in an area that is regarded as particularly important for Nature conservation goals (see Kremen et al. 1999). 'Now the *vazaha* have come back. The people in Ambodiforaha are afraid that they might have to leave once again. One doesn't know, but one can't have any trust', one man in his late thirties remarked. He was by no means the only person who talked about the threat of renewed displacement as a result of the arrival of the park. Many people in Ambanizana, Marofototra and Ambodiforaha itself volunteered such reflections about the potential repetition of history.

The village of Ambodiforaha lies a stone's throw away from the aforementioned tourist lodges. Tourists usually come to Masoala with a view to observing lemurs, birds and other animals inside the park. Until recently, only three such 'eco-lodges' existed, and they were all owned and/or managed by white foreigners. Although two of them were officially co-managed with Malagasy partners, local people clearly perceived them as foreign, *vazaha*-owned enterprises. Moreover, because they had opened in the wake of the creation of the park, they were rightly understood as being somehow connected with it.[7]

Maman' i Jao looked like a very old woman in 2008, though she was probably only in her seventies; she has since died. She was a close relative of the family in Ambanizana with whom I always stay, and she lived in the same compound. One day upon my return to Ambanizana from a visit to Marofototra, we were sitting together drinking coffee and got chatting about Ambodiforaha that I had passed through along my way. Reflecting about the tourist lodges there, Maman' i Jao remarked that there used to be many, many *vazaha* in that area when she was young: 'Then they left, and now they are coming back; the *vazaha* don't forget the places where they once enjoyed good times (*nahavariaña zare*)'.

For her, it was not an accident that the tourist lodges were located exactly in the same spot along the coast where in her youth more than one colonial logging enterprise had been based, and it was obvious to her that these things were connected. She had seen one lot of *vazaha* departing and another coming back to precisely the same place several decades later. For Maman' i Jao, therefore, there existed a direct link between the *colons* of her youth and the foreigners who had returned to Masoala to once again settle and start commercial enterprises. Perhaps the latter were the grandchildren of the former, she pondered, and had in this way got wind of the particular attractions of the area?[8]

It is important to remember in this context, that there are still people around who personally experienced the colonial era which ended in 1960. One man from Ambanizana who was born in 1947, for example, recalled that his uncle still had to carry *vazaha* on a palanquin as did a much younger man of about forty years of age who remembered his father having been among the last to carry *vazaha*. Other reminders of 'the time of the *vazaha*', as the colonial era is often referred to in Masoala, included remains of the rail system for the transport of heavy logs of precious wood along the coast, or Monsieur Fraise's Rock (*Ambatondrafrezy*), the name given to a rock out at sea near Marofototra at which the *colon* of that name is said to have capsized.

While people of all ages perceived the Masoala National Park as a threat to their ability to continue to live off their land, some, especially but not exclusively old people, went one step further by interpreting the park as a new manifestation of a history of foreign control.[9] Papan' i Lucien and Maman' i Jao were amongst these, as were others who commented on 'the gift'.

The Gift

In October 2008, a strange event took place in Ambanizana. News had arrived in the village that a group from Madagascar's capital city, Antananarivo, were to give a *spectacle*. The group who called themselves 'Foniala', Heart of the Forest, and consisted of ten Malagasy men and one white French-speaking woman, arrived one day late in the afternoon, set up quarters at the park's office, and announced their *spectacle* for the next morning at seven o'clock. Nobody knew who exactly these people were or what they wanted, but those who caught a first glimpse of the members of the group were somewhat taken aback, especially by one of them who was sporting long, thick dreadlocks – a highly unusual sight in a village like Ambanizana. 'If I were to meet him in the forest, I'd run away, I'd be scared', one woman remarked to me. Some who had spotted the 'rasta-man', as he soon became known, thought his looks indecent, while others merely found him amusing. The gossip was beginning to do the rounds, later on proven incorrect, that he was not Malagasy but 'African'. Several of the group were wearing dark or reflecting sunglasses which prevented direct eye-contact.

The next morning, people flocked to the village centre at the announced time. After much delay (during which those present started to complain that they were being kept from work for nothing), the first of the group suddenly appeared at the end of the main village street moving towards the crowd on a unicycle. He was followed by another on high stilts and the rest of the troupe carrying juggling clubs and drums. The woman was taking photographs. The audience, especially the children, roared with laughter. Some fifteen minutes passed during which they offered various performances.

Then it was time for a speech during which one of the members of the group explained the purpose of their visit. The speaker began by saying that it was the aim of Heart of the Forest to protect the environment, using a new Malagasy expression for 'environment' which has been coined in the course of the recent conservation efforts in Madagascar and is now also in use in Masoala (see chapter 9, endnote 2). The rest of his ten-minute talk was largely unintelligible to the audience as the speech was delivered in the official Malagasy dialect which most people in Ambanizana do not fully understand. As a result, one of the park employees in the village who acted as host to the group ended up translating what had been said in 'the language of the *vazaha*' (*lelam-bazaha*) into 'Malagasy', that is the local dialect. Note the use of the term *vazaha* in this context; normally the expression 'language of the *vazaha*' would refer to French.

The basic idea that the guests proposed was to enter into an exchange of knowledge. They would show the villagers how to juggle clubs or ride on the unicycle while the villagers were to come forth with whatever *talenta* they had – for example, telling a myth, or perhaps playing a tune on the guitar that Foniala had brought with them? The group was going to stay in the village for two days and those interested in the offer of exchange should write down their name on a list. First, however, the group was to teach the local children at the school, to which purpose the guests then departed.

For many adults, the whole thing had a negative touch from the beginning: the members of the group were felt to be a very distant kind of Malagasy, speaking in *vazaha*-language; some of them looked rather like aliens; and, because they were staying at the local ANGAP (park authority) office and were accompanied by ANGAP staff, they were associated with the park. Upon hearing about the group's plan to take over class instruction while they were in the village, several adults immediately went to the school to fetch their children, for there were rumours – in Ambanizana as well as in other villages as I later learnt – that these strange people from the capital had, in fact, come to Masoala with intent to kidnap children.[10] Some of the village's teachers, for their part, were annoyed because Foniala had not actually asked their permission to go and teach the children; not that they were likely to decline but they should have been asked.

At the school, the members of Foniala wrapped their message concerning the protection of the environment (*fiarovan'ny tontol-iainana*) in entertainment and novelty. The 'rastaman', who quickly became a favourite with the children, taught them how to play the drums while speaking the following rhyming verse as a kind of rap:

> Protect the environment (*Koa arovy ny tontolo*)
> Do not cut it down, do not burn it (*Tsy hovoakapa sy voadoro*)
> Neither the forest nor the animals (*Na ny ala na ny biby*)
> For they are priceless wealth (*Harena sarobidy*)

Another member of the group taught the children a myth about a girl who had saved a bird's egg and was duly rewarded for her good deed. The children then learnt how to draw scenes from the myth with crayons and watercolours, being encouraged to always use 'natural' material for drawings rather than the usual ballpoint pens with their chemical ingredients (in a village where not all children are lucky enough to even have a pen).

Not a single adult enlisted for the proposed exchange of knowledge. 'If they really want to know what our *talenta* is,' one woman remarked sarcastically, 'let us show them how to clear the bush and plant hill rice, as that is what we really know how to do well.' Moreover, the offered skills, like riding on a unicycle, appeared to many adults as too childlike to be worthy of engaging with, as well as being useless, and the group's concept of wrapping their environmental message in entertainment was too obvious not to be noticed. 'They think of us here as children', one man remarked disapprovingly.

In the early evening of the second day of Foniala's visit, the children showed the newly learnt skills to the public in a *gala* in the village's main street. Lots of people gathered to watch the spectacle. Some children had learnt to arrange their bodies to form a pyramid, others had learnt to juggle the clubs, a teenage boy walked around on high stilts, another was riding the unicycle, one boy recounted the myth about the good girl while the real girls were holding up their drawings of it to be admired by everyone present, and a group of children were drumming. The female, white member of the group took photographs, while another made a video recording. At the end, the guests were thanked in an official manner, following Malagasy etiquette.

The show was over but the troupe had something else in store. Before they left Ambanizana to continue their programme elsewhere, they asked the village president, the *Commune*'s mayor (who happened to be present) and the head teacher to come to the municipality bureau of the village as they wanted to offer them a present. 'We thought we were going to be given something valuable,' the village president commented upon his return from the meeting, 'but this is what we were given; it's ridiculous', he continued throwing a strange-looking, round something onto the table (see Photograph 10.2 on the next page).

The gift consisted of a symbolic representation of a spider in a spider's web. Its body was made of a blackened pinecone and its legs of straw, the spider's web was made of rapphia and a metal ring wrapped with string. The overall object was no larger than the width of a stretched out hand. The village president, the *Commune*'s mayor and the school teacher had each been given one such gift. The group had explained, the village president recounted, that the spider was their emblem and why this was so, though he had not quite grasped the reason. It had something to do with the similarity between spiders and the forest. He had understood it thus: 'When a spider loses too many of its legs, it cannot walk anymore just like a forest without trees will die', but he was uncertain whether he had actually understood the rationale behind the emblem. While their shows had been fun to watch and a welcome change to the repetitive rounds of village life, the 'gift' made the laughter stick in people's throats. The toy spider was such an incredibly inappropriate present that it caused a mixture of feelings of bewilderment, disgust and bitter insult among those who set eyes on it.

Photograph 10.2 The gift

The following day, we were celebrating the erection of a new house in our neighbourhood. Large numbers of people were present including several elders, and a ritual meal was consumed. The discussion soon turned towards 'the gift' which was duly fetched to be shown to those who had not yet seen it. The spider was passed around while the same mixture of amusement, offence and incredulity began to be felt. '*This is it?*' people asked, with a look of consternation crossing their faces. Several offered their thoughts as to what the meaning of such a present could possibly be. One man pondered whether it was to be understood as a symbol for human life, as both the spider and people were good at caring for their respective homes? 'No, that is not the point of this present', one of the elders interrupted the previous speaker. 'It's clear what the meaning of this is. They have given us this present to tell us that we are like the spider, caught and constrained in our ability to move, like this spider here caught in its web. That is what they wanted to tell us.' This conclusion was followed by a discussion about the Masoala National Park and how it made people suffer (*mijaly*) and sad (*malahelo*). Several times, I heard the old man murmuring to himself: 'It will come back, it will come back, that is what this present shows'. 'What will come back?' I asked him. My question was answered by another elder: 'The servitude (*fañandevôzaña*) of the Malagasy will come back'. In the course of the following days several adults came to our house specifically to inspect 'the gift' with their own eyes, incredulous at its description by others. Upon reflection of its meaning, one man in his forties said to me: 'The spider represents the park, and we are the insects that get caught in its web. That is what this is about'.

Later on back in Switzerland, I found out more about Foniala and its campaign in Masoala. Since October 2003, that is a few months after the opening of the Masoala exhibit at the Zurich zoo, the management of the Masoala National Park has produced, two or three times a year, a newsletter called *Masoala News*, which is available in French and German. In it, various types of projects carried out by the park management are reported on, as well as other information such as the number of tourists who have come to Masoala in a given year. The director of Zurich zoo and other zoo staff sometimes write editorials or other contributions. In the edition of May 2009, Foniala's visit to Ambanizana (and two other places in the area) was among the chosen topics, with the park staff member responsible for 'environmental education' in Masoala writing about the event.[11] It was reported that the cooperation between Foniala and the park management had been initiated by the Wildlife Conservation Society (WCS), the zoo's partner organisation, and that the visit had been a success. The event was said to have contributed to a number of objectives related to 'the revaluation of the natural and cultural heritage', including learning about 'the foundations of Nature conservation and the role and significance of the environment', the importance of recycling as well as learning about folk tales, myths and traditions, drawing and 'the fine arts', the latter through a workshop about the making of musical instruments from bamboo. Two illustrations accompany the text: a photograph of children forming a human pyramid and one of the drawings of the myth by the children in Ambanizana.

The similarity of Foniala's declared intentions in Ambanizana, on the one hand, and some of the views embraced by adult visitors to the Zurich zoo's exhibit as well as by pupils in Switzerland which I discussed in the first part of this book, on the other, is striking. In both contexts, what is considered to be needed most in Masoala is the education of the farmers. Like many of the people I spoke with in Switzerland, the members of Foniala emphasised in their environmental-educational input in the village that leaving the forest untouched was crucial not only for biodiversity but also for the local population's own future. The forest was presented, as, for example, in the rap the 'rastaman' taught the children, as 'priceless wealth', the loss of which would inevitably lead to more poverty. Just like in Zurich (in public statements by zoo staff and in the media as well as by zoo visitors), Nature conservation was thus represented as 'development' and 'progress'. In the programme of Foniala, such development consisted, besides environmental education, in enhancing local people's cultural wealth by, for example, fostering the telling of myths. Foniala's programme amounted to a 'civilising mission' spotlighting what the farmers were assumed to lack, including not only their alleged lack of knowledge concerning the sustainable use of the forest resources but also their competences in the field of arts and crafts. Thus, like in Switzerland where the Malagasy's reputed lag concerning ecological knowledge has become seen as a manifestation of their civilising backwardness (chapter 5), Foniala intended to enhance the farmers' knowledge both with respect to the environment and with respect to 'culture' (acrobatics, folk tales, playing the guitar, etc.).

Foniala was a group of Malagasy people unconnected to the park who were bringing the same message of Nature conservation to Ambanizana, albeit wrapped in entertainment and novelty, that the people in the village were already familiar with from park staff, representing an example of the adoption of the global agenda of Nature conservation by national elites in countries in the South (cf. Tsing 2005: chapter 4). The members of the juggling troupe were thought of by the people in Ambanizana as very distant to themselves: they were Merina (the ethnic group associated with power and exploitation of the coastal regions; see chapter 9), they were urban, and they looked and behaved oddly. The distance between them and the local people was epitomised in their way of speaking being referred to as 'the language of the *vazaha*' (normally meaning white foreigners) which needed to be translated into 'Malagasy' (the local dialect) in order to be understood.

The movement of knowledge across such distances is anything but smooth. More than anything else, Foniala's visit to Ambanizana exhibited a complete lack of any kind of common understanding between the guests and the hosts. First, as we saw throughout the second part of this book, the environmentalist programme that Foniala carried to the village was perceived by its population as a manifestation of outside power. The foreignness of the group's members and especially the gift only confirmed this, adding insult to injury. Second, Foniala's ideas as to what the people in Ambanizana might be interested in – learning how to ride a unicycle or to juggle clubs – was of no interest to the adults in the village; on the contrary, it made them feel they were being treated like children. And third, Foniala's concept of how to promote the message of Nature conservation in order to make it attractive, namely through an 'exchange of knowledge', was considered by many in the village as hypocritical. 'If they really want to know what our *talenta* is', as one woman had remarked, 'let us show them how to clear the bush and plant hill rice, because that is what we really know how to do well.' Moreover, the way Foniala's visit was later portrayed in the Masoala newsletter, which would also be read by interested people in Switzerland, had nothing to do with how that event had been perceived by those for whose 'benefit' it had been carried out. Thus the transmission of knowledge to and fro was fraught with friction.

Putting the Wheel of History into Reverse[12]

When old people, especially those with personal memories of the colonial era, look at the Masoala National Park, they often look at it through a historical lens seeing the park itself or certain events in connection with it as new manifestations of a history that brought hardship and servitude to the people of Masoala in the past. Examples include the loss of the 'Island of the Wanderer', the establishment of the tourist lodges and 'the gift' by Foniala. This chapter has thus far drawn attention to such interpretations. There is, however, a further aspect of history repeating itself that deserves to be discussed in detail.

Overcoming Slave Descent

Pre-colonial Madagascar knew several forms of slavery, which implied significant differences concerning what it actually meant to be an *andevo* (slave). In some circumstances, to be a slave meant enduring unimaginable physical and social brutality (Graeber 1997: 375–76; 2007: 201–2 226–27). In other contexts slaves were treated almost like junior family members although, of course, they were owned by their masters (Ellis 1859: 173–76; Bloch 1979: 274; 1994a: 71). Regardless of the extent of hardship involved, however, people who were enslaved were permanently torn away from their own kin and from their 'land of the ancestors' where their kin were buried. Slaves were people who had 'been ripped from their ancestral landscapes, left unanchored to any place' (Graeber 1997: 376). Therefore, they could no longer take part in the important rituals through which Malagasy people receive the blessing of their ancestors. Being deprived of ancestral blessing in turn meant that *andevo* stopped being kin – and, possibly, stopped being full people (Bloch 1994b: 135) – because, in Madagascar, kinship is not simply a matter of being related by birth (Bloch 1985, 1993; Southall 1986: 417–26). Rather, to a large degree, it is something continually created through the passage of ancestral blessing from dead to living kin and the joint reception by the living of their ancestors' blessing. Indeed, the status of *andevo* was and is defined in Madagascar as referring to someone whose ties to his or her ancestors have been forcibly severed; an *andevo* is 'a person without ancestors', a person without a *tanindrazana*, 'land of the ancestors' (Feeley-Harnik 1982: 37; 1991: 57–58; Bloch 1994b: 135; Graeber 1997: 374; 2007: 226–27; Cole 1998: 622; Evers 2002).

Thinking back on the story of the Island of the Wanderer, it is hardly surprising that the incorporation of the tombs into the off-limits Hard Core of the park caused such anxiety among the families concerned. As related in chapter 8, local people had heard different kinds of rumours as to what the park authorities or the *vazaha* planned to do with Nosin-dRendra, and some had observed a group of foreigners kayaking to the Island of the Wanderer while being completely in the dark as to the purpose of such a visit. Eventually, people began to worry about losing control over the bones of their ancestors. The worst case scenario of the ancestral remains being thrown away became a real threat in the minds of some. 'It's not as if our bones had any value for the foreigners!', one man had remarked. Given that one's ancestors' physical presence is of utmost importance in Madagascar and that tombs epitomise a kin group's status as 'people with a *tanindrazana*' – people who are *not* of slave descent – even the remotest chance of losing ancestral bones was too high a risk to take. Therefore, the tombs were moved to beyond the park's reach.

Slavery was abolished in the wake of the French conquest at the end of the nineteenth century. However, its legacy has far from disappeared. Being of slave descent continues to be a burden all over Madagascar, although to significantly different degrees in different parts of the country. To this day, in the highlands especially, evidence of slave descent creates an enormous social stigma, and marriage between descendants of slaves and descendants of free people is strongly tabooed and heavily sanctioned if it occurs (see Bloch 1994a: 198–99; Freeman 2001: 27–29; 2013; Evers 2002: 54–71; Somda 2009). Moreover, in the highlands, slave descent is still literally visible in a variety of ways (Evers 2002). This is not so among the populations along Madagascar's east coast, including on the Masoala peninsula, where slave descent has become invisible, with descendants of slaves engaging in the same daily activities and the same ritual practices as those of free descent (Cole 2001: 73–74; Brown 2004; Keller 2005: 31–36). This is largely attributable to two factors (cf. Bloch 1980). First, in Masoala, as the history of Ambanizana and Marofototra illustrates, marriages between descendants of slaves and descendants of free people have regularly occurred in the course of the last several generations. Second, people of slave descent have found access to new land in Masoala. It is the latter aspect that I concentrate on here.

If slaves were constituted as slaves through the severing of their connection to their kin group's 'land of the ancestors', then access to new land was crucial in overcoming slave status, once such an endeavour became possible with the end of slavery (Bloch 1994a: 210–15; Graeber 1997: 377; 2007: 203; Evers 2002: 28–32). Access to land enabled ex-slaves or descendants of slaves to restart creating a kin group rooted in a particular place. Moreover, for people of slave descent to be able to rebuild a 'placed' kin group, they needed the opportunity to engage in that complex and drawn-out process of growth that implies the generation of descendants, the growth of deep roots in the land, the eventual creation of an ancestral burial ground on this land, and the continuation of this process of growth and anchorage through one's descendants. In other words, people burdened with the history of slavery not only needed land for the here and now but they also needed land that their descendants would be able to continue to turn into 'land that enables life' (*tany fivelômana*) and, eventually, into 'land of the ancestors' (*tanindrazana*).

This was precisely what the Masoala peninsula offered. As a largely uninhabited forest frontier area with vast stretches of unclaimed land, it allowed many people of slave descent to root themselves in new land and to progressively turn it into their 'land of the ancestors' over the course of the past several generations. Among those who share a history of successfully shedding slave descent by having created a new *tanindrazana* for themselves through anchorage in the land on the Masoala peninsula are many people who now live in Ambanizana and Marofototra. It is extremely difficult to establish with certainty who is, and who is not, of slave descent. However, on the basis of oral historical accounts about the origin of the different kin groups living in Ambanizana and Marofototra, it is certain that a substantial percentage of the populations of these two (and other nearby) villages is made up of descendants of slaves from different historical backgrounds. Some would be the descendants of the slaves brought to the region by the founders of the village of Ambanizana for the purpose of turning the fertile land along the riverbank into wet rice fields. Others would be the descendants of ex-slaves from the Malagasy highlands who, after the abolition of slavery, moved to Masoala in search of a piece of land of their own (cf. Cassanelli 1987). Still others would ultimately be the descendents of slaves from continental Africa (see Campbell 2005). Many of these Makoa, as people considered to be of African descent are named, came to Masoala as cautchouc workers during the colonial era and later on established themselves as the rightful owners of land; large numbers of people in Ambanizana refer to themselves as Makoa pointing to their very curly hair as evidence. Land available on the Masoala peninsula allowed all these people of slave descent to shed their status as *andevo*. Nowadays, they are no longer people without a *tanindrazana*, and they are no longer people who are deprived of caring for their ancestors and of receiving the latter's blessing in return, because they are no longer people 'left unanchored to any place' (Graeber 1997: 376). They have succeeded in rejoining the process of growth by rooting themselves in Masoala, and that process continues as each generation walks in the footsteps of the one before.

Interrupting the Process

The Masoala National Park threatens to reverse these people's success stories. Although the park puts everyone's future at risk by appropriating much of the available land and leaves many people with a sense of having been defeated, such defeat seems particularly tragic in the case of people of slave descent who have succeeded in, or who are in the process of, overcoming that legacy. By narrowing down people's potential living space, the park stops those of slave descent from continuing the process of rebuilding a kin group rooted in the land that their ancestors re-embarked on after they became free. I should emphasise that this is an analytical comment on a historical process and that, with regard to what people in Ambanizana and Marofototra themselves say about the park, there is no difference between people of slave descent and others.

The story of Michel and Ramama from Marofototra is a striking case in point. Michel's parents were born in the highlands. Probably sometime in the 1920s, when Michel was a small child, they came to Masoala, where Michel's father began to work for a colonial logging company. Both of Michel's parents were buried and exhumed in Ambanizana. This alone is a clear indication that they were of slave descent: They had no 'land of the ancestors' in the highlands to which their bones could be taken for burial in family tombs. Moreover, Michel's parents have been laid to rest with a group of people from highland Madagascar who are undoubtedly of slave descent, a scenario that would be totally unthinkable if Michel's parents had not been of slave descent themselves.

Michel married Ramama. Close to today's village of Marofototra, he found work with a French *colon*, Monsieur Manuel, who had a large logging enterprise in the area until shortly after independence in 1960. While Michel worked as Monsieur Manuel's head mechanic, Ramama ran a shop that Monsieur Manuel had opened for the hundred or so inhabitants of the logging settlement. Partly because of the changes resulting from independence and partly because of a personal family tragedy, Monsieur Manuel went back to France in 1968. He left his entire concession to Michel and Ramama, who had served him so well during so many years. Overnight, they became the owners of a large estate. But misfortune struck soon after that; Michel died, still relatively young. He too was buried in Ambanizana with the same kin group that had already received his parents as 'guests' in its burial ground. Ramama and their many children continued to make a living on the land that Monsieur Manuel had given to them. In 2006, no other family in Marofototra owned even remotely as much land as Ramama – her land included wet rice fields, slopes suitable for hill rice, cash-crop plantations, and as yet uncleared forest – and Ramama was an important local personality, arriving in church every Sunday morning attired in a white dress and hat. With the establishment of the Masoala National Park, however, all of her land was included within the Zone d'Occupation Contrôlée of Marofototra. Since then, it has been subject to the various regulations pertaining to land inside the park, which, among other things, forbid the clearing of forest. As a result, those parts of Ramama's land that are still forested are lost, and she cannot pass them on to her children and grandchildren.

Whether Ramama is of slave descent, I do not know. Michel, however, as the child of slave descendants from the highlands where overcoming slave status is particularly difficult if not impossible, had, through a combination of skill and chance, managed to obtain access to much land on which his descendants would be able to 'pro-gress' and grow – land that might eventually have become their *tanindrazana*, their 'land of the ancestors'. This process has not yet been completed, as Michel's kin group has not yet built its own burial ground in Marofototra. Michel and his parents are still in Ambanizana as 'guests' in another kin group's burial ground because their roots in their land have not yet grown deep enough to make it imaginable as their *tanindrazana*. Had the park not been created, Michel's land might have become the 'land of the ancestors' of his descendants. Two or three generations after him, his descendants might have decided to create a new burial ground on their own land and to bring the ancestral bones of Michel and his parents to their own, new *tanindrazana*. But now that they have become trapped inside the tight limits the park sets on their endeavour of creating a future in Marofototra, this looks unlikely. The process of shedding slave descent, which Michel had begun, has now been interrupted by the Masoala National Park, which has claimed the land on which Michel's descendants were to create a kin group living on its own 'land of the ancestors'.

The Masoala peninsula, with its immense forest and its sparse population, is the epitome of a frontier region (cf. Kopytoff 1987). In the past, it offered marginalised people the possibility to create a livelihood for their families on *tany malalaka*: 'land that nobody had yet claimed as theirs'. By declaring most of the forest an off-limits conservation zone, some of the most vulnerable have lost this frontier.[13]

Notes

1. For a historical analysis of forced labour in the district of Maroantsetra, see Fremigacci 2009.
2. Ellis 1838: 316; Sibree 1915: 24. See also Sodikoff 2012: 35. The Malagasy historian Toto Tsiadino Chaplain, who originates from the area of Maroantsetra and who did research on its pre-colonial history, refers to *maromita* as 'slaves' (2005: 15, footnote 20) and 'les couches les plus basses dans la structure de la vie sociale de l'époque ancienne' (ibid.: 12, footnote 18).
3. From the root *andevo* = slave.
4. In the course of our conversations, Papan' i Lucien used the expression *fañandevôzaña* interchangeably with two other expressions, *fahaverezaña* and *havirezaña*, that stem from the root *very* = 'to be lost'. These latter expressions are also clearly linked to the notion of slavery and servitude. For the sake of clarity of presentation, I only use *fañandevôzaña* here.
5. See Sodikoff 2004 for similar locally perceived continuities between colonial forced labour and present conservation regimes (with regard to the Mananara Biosphere Reserve).
6. *Mamaky flera*, literally: to break the flowers, is the local term for pollinating vanilla, Ambanizana's main cash crop.
7. For years, these three lodges were the only touristic facilities in the area. Since 2011, several other entrepreneurs, among them even a couple of local people, have begun to build similar, if somewhat simpler, accommodations for tourists. As the bulk of my fieldwork was carried out previously, I do not take this latest development into account (it is very unclear what the present boom of building tourist lodges will entail).
8. Similar stories of how 'tourists' come to Madagascar equipped with maps provided to them by their grandparents that indicate where mercury or other valuable commodities might be found circulate among people who live near the Ankarana Nature Reserve in the north of Madagascar (personal communication with Andrew Walsh).
9. The importance of historical references for local residents around protected areas in Madagascar is also highlighted in Paul Hanson's ethnography of the situation in Ranomafana, a region in Madagascar's southern highlands where a national park was established a few years earlier than in Masoala (Hanson 1997, 2007, 2009). Focusing on speech performances during ritualised encounters between foreign scientists, Malagasy park staff and local residents, Hanson shows how speech acts delivered by local residents were saturated with historical references both to pre-colonial and colonial times of hardship. The region's history over the past two centuries was remembered primarily as a succession of running away from powerful outsiders taking away the forest from local residents in order to exploit its resources for their own ends, and the Ranomafana national park was perceived as a continuation of the history of such alienation of land. In contrast to the historicising discourse offered

by the local people around Ranomafana, leading foreigners involved in the establishment of the park and the determination of its parameters focused in their speeches on the present and future cooperation between the park and the local people. Furthermore, Hanson analyses in detail how in the process of multiple translations between languages (Malagasy, French and English) significant mutations occurred both with regard to actual wordings and underlying meanings. This was partly due to insufficient linguistic competence of the people involved and partly to the fact that the 'translation dialectics' (ibid. 2007: 260) involved personal and political agendas of the speakers and translators. For example, Malagasy translators aspiring to job promotion within the conservation system are shown to have adjusted their translations to the foreigners' discourses to what they considered the latter would be pleased to hear, a process which is reminiscent of what people in Masoala refer to as *récitation* (chapter 6). Amongst other things, such mutations had the effect of eliminating 'the ancestral weight' (Hanson 2007: 264) and the historicity of the original discourses delivered by local residents in Malagasy.
10. Fear of heart or liver thieves is widespread in Madagascar (see Jarosz 1994; Freeman 2004).
11. Masoala National Park 2009: 4. Also available from http://www.freunde-masoalas.ch/xml_1/internet/de/application/d3/f25.cfm. See also Alliance Voahary Gasy. Retrieved 5 May 2013 from http://www.alliancevoaharygasy.mg/index.php?option=com_content&view=article&id=143&Itemid=237#
12. This last section of this chapter was first published in the *American Ethnologist* 38(4): 650–64 as part of Keller 2008.
13. Concerning the closing of frontiers due to Nature conservation efforts in Madagascar, see also Hanson 1997: chapter 1; and Pollini 2007: 578–79.

Conclusions

The Masoala rainforest conservation project is conceptualised by park managers in Madagascar and zoo managers in Switzerland as a partnership between 'Big Masoala' – the park in Madagascar – and 'Little Masoala' in Zurich. The project is represented as creating a connection not only between two geographically very distant places but also between the people living in these places. In this book, I have examined the nature of this connection as it is perceived by 'ordinary folk' at both ends of the partnership. I have examined what and who visitors to the Zurich zoo's Masoala exhibit reflect about when they look at the Masoala rainforest conservation project presented to them at the zoo, on the one hand, and what and who Malagasy farmers reflect about when they look at the same project that has led to the creation of a strictly protected conservation area on their doorstep, on the other. '[U]niversal aspirations must travel across distances and differences' (Tsing 2005: 7). Following Tsing, I have 'take[n] this travel as an ethnographic object' (ibid.: 7).

The Masoala National Park is, indeed, an entity that both the farmers in Masoala and the zoo visitors engage with thus apparently establishing a point of contact between them. However, as this book has shown, it would be an illusion to think that when looking at this partnership project, the Malagasy and the Swiss are actually seeing anything like the same thing or reflecting about the same issues. It is as if they were engaged in two completely different stories, following different plots and starring different protagonists.

Two Different Stories

The Swiss story is about Nature and especially the moral duty to conserve it in as pristine a state as possible. Visitors tend to look at what is presented to them at the Masoala exhibit primarily as an appeal to moral introspection. Their gaze is turned inward towards their own moral duty and their desire to do the right thing – very much, in fact, in the tradition of the Protestant ethic (Weber 1988). Within the Swiss story, the Malagasy people are hardly visible, and when they are imagined, it is as representatives of a 'kind' of people – a kind thought to be characterised by a cluster of features merging into what I term the 'coconut schema' – to be found in many distant places in the world. Madagascar and especially the Malagasy people are thereby practically obliterated from the visitors' perceptual lens.

I am not talking about the *intentional* negation of the presence of forest dwellers for the sake of gaining control over land such as, for example, reported in a study of the construction of a pipeline in the Amazon (Sawyer 2003). The perceptual erasure of Malagasy people I have examined in the first part of this book is much more subtle and happens probably largely unconsciously. Subtle as it may be, it is nonetheless dramatic. The case at hand demonstrates that internationally monitored Nature conservation interventions may result in the people who live in areas targeted for conservation being erased from the picture. Most of these areas lie in the southern hemisphere.

Descola (2005) suggests that there are four principal ways in which people around the world relate to their non-human surroundings. One of these is Western 'naturalism', a gaze which is characterised by distant observation through an objectifying lens, epitomised in the study of a plant or animal under the microscope. If we extend this concept to the perception of human beings, the zoo visitors can be said to be looking at the Malagasy people through a naturalist lens which denies any social relationship between observer and the 'subject under study'. Moreover, the very fact of Madagascar and the Malagasy people being presented at a *zoo* encourages such a distancing look (cf. Rothfels 2002).

In Masoala, local farmers tell a different story. Their reflections in connection with the Masoala National Park have very little to do with forests and lemurs or Nature conservation but everything with land, kinship and aspired human growth. Their gaze onto the issues at stake is not directed inward. Instead it focuses on social relationships: the relationship among kin and the relationship between the people of Masoala and others from beyond. In the very same project that for the visitors to the zoo's exhibit represents a genuine and urgent attempt to act morally by saving Nature, the Malagasy farmers see the continuation of historical inequalities and the exertion of power. Instead of seeing a site of endangered biodiversity and the moral obligation to rescue it when looking at the park, the farmers in Masoala perceive a string of interrelated experiences linking the past, the present and most likely the future. Their story is not a tale about morality but a tale about the continuation of long-established power relations and a comment about their own powerlessness.

It might be argued that talking about the horrors of slavery or the injustice of being pushed from one's own land also amounts to a discourse on morality. From an outsider's perspective, this may be so. But for the people in Ambanizana and Marofototra, to talk about these issues is, more than anything else, to talk about history and power. Similarly, the ethos of growth does represent Malagasy morality. It would, therefore, not be wrong to conclude that while the Masoala National Park is seen by the zoo visitors as a highly moral enterprise, for the Malagasy farmers it is a monstrosity in terms of their moral standards. However, from the point of view of the latter, to relate to one's ancestors and to make one's family 'pro-gress' on the land is not primarily a moral issue but is simply to engage in the purpose of life.

The divergent views of the farmers in Masoala and the zoo visitors are also modelled on completely different visions of how people ought to engage with their non-human surroundings. From the environmentalist perspective embraced by the zoo visitors, humankind ought to walk gently and carefully on the land, thereby barely scratching its surface and leaving as few and as shallow footprints as possible. From the perspective of the Malagasy farmers, the land is inseparable from human society, and socially meaningful people are *in* the land to which the marks they leave behind testify (Bloch 1995). In the Malagasy story, success manifests itself in a productive rice field or an ancestral burial ground. In the Swiss story, success manifests itself in a landscape in which the existence of humankind is barely discernible.

The Masoala rainforest conservation project makes visitors to the Zurich zoo reflect about what they perceive as the intrinsic and timeless value of Nature, a value that is, by virtue of being intrinsic, detached from social relations. While their gaze is almost void of social relationships, the Malagasy farmers' view of the same project excludes almost everything except the historically charged social relationships involved and the threat these pose to local people's aspiration to make their families grow. Living next to, and thinking about, the park makes the farmers reflect about former forms of servitude and the possible return of *fañandevôzaña* in a new guise, that is about the park as a continuation of the history of domination by powerful outsiders, both Malagasy and foreign. In the Malagasy story, history serves as a key tool for analysing the presence of the park and the intentions of those thought to be responsible for its creation and endorsement.

While the farmers in Masoala have a strongly historicised understanding of the park, the view of the zoo visitors is fundamentally ahistorical. The only 'history' that comes into play in the latter's reflections about the

Masoala project is a generalised, evolutionist trajectory of humankind. Within this framework, knowledge about the sustainable use of natural resources as defined by the canonical Nature conservation discourse has emerged as a sign of progress, whereas the transformation of forest into productive, cultivated land – progress for the Malagasy – is seen as testifying to a less advanced position along this trajectory. The key difference between the story told by the farmers in Masoala and the story told by the visitors to the zoo's Masoala exhibit lies in the place that social relationships and history occupy in each. One is a story of specific people in social history, the other is a story of a generic people outside history. These differences are exemplified by the concepts of 'the *vazaha*' and of 'natives' respectively.

The Natives and the Vazaha

For the farmers in Masoala, the park is a continuation of the relationship between 'us' and 'them'. 'Them' stands for a somewhat nebulous consortium of state and other organisations and individuals 'from the outside', both Malagasy and foreign, including 'the *vazaha*'. Here, I only consider the latter. Recall that the word *vazaha* is used in Masoala and elsewhere in Madagascar to refer to outsiders that are perceived as very distant to oneself, typically (but not exclusively, as the example of the juggling troupe Foniala illustrates) white Europeans and North Americans. From the perspective of the people in Ambanizana and Marofototra, the park is a new manifestation of the historically charged relationship between the people of Masoala and the *vazaha* who established themselves in Masoala during the colonial era and who have now come back to secure their access to the peninsula's resources once again. As such, the Malagasy farmers interpret the park in terms of a relationship with a *specific* other.

The notion of the *vazaha* lacks any differentiation between, say, the Swiss, the French and the Americans; all white people are thought of as *vazaha*. Moreover, throughout Madagascar, ideas associated with *vazaha* have an essentialising flavour in that 'the *vazaha*' as a group are perceived to be characterised by certain features that have always been their mark and always will be their mark, especially the fact of having access to knowledge that is thought to be far superior to the knowledge of the Malagasy, for reasons of something like *vazaha*-essence. This imagination of *vazaha*-superiority goes hand in hand with the imagination of the lands where the *vazaha* live being under their full control and thus void of forests, mud, perhaps also free from storms, and certainly not populated by farmers toiling the soil – instead these 'lands beyond the sea' (*andafy*) are imagined by some as being comprised entirely of concrete streets and open space (cf. Stepan 2001). Such openness and clarity[1] is thought of as a manifestation of *vazaha*-power over things that in Madagascar are the business of Zanahary, the Creator. 'Never challenge a *vazaha*,' I remember one friend saying, 'you can never win! The *vazaha* have something that we Malagasy do not have. We will never catch up with them.' When I showed people in Ambanizana and Marofototra photographs of the outside and the inside of the greenhouse at the Zurich zoo, they generally observed two things: the tarred visitors' path, in view of the lack of any 'such good road' anywhere on the Masoala peninsula; and, more importantly for the present discussion, the waterfall rushing down natural-looking rocks. Upon learning that all of this had been built artificially, those looking at the photographs interpreted the information as confirming *vazaha*-superiority, because in Madagascar making things like waterfalls was clearly the realm of the Creator.

In the imagination of the people in Masoala, the *vazaha* are not historically, culturally or otherwise differentiated. *Vazaha* refers to a group in which white people from anywhere abroad are conflated. This may partly be due to the fact that many people in rural places where opportunities for formal schooling are very limited have little knowledge about the geography of the world. Many people I have met over the years imagine the world beyond Madagascar to consist of a number of islands including 'France', 'Amérique' and 'Suisse', and some imagine all *vazaha* coming from one country – one big island perhaps – subdivided into areas akin to Malagasy provinces. But even those people in Ambanizana and Marofototra who do have precise knowledge of continents, countries and Madagascar's location on the globe talk of 'the *vazaha*' as one group.

However, despite the fact that the idea of 'the *vazaha*' involves a process of conflation, when the farmers in Masoala imagine the people involved in establishing and supporting the park, they see in their mind's eye not a *type* of people *like* the *vazaha* but a specific group referred to as THE *vazaha*. The *vazaha* are not representatives of a category of people, and they are not substitutable by any other group. They are perceived as a specific 'other', a particular group of human beings with whom the people on the Masoala peninsula have had a long-standing relationship ever since 'the time of the French' (the colonial era). They are perceived as a group with a face.

When the farmers in Masoala think of 'the *vazaha*', they see a clear counterpart. Such an outlook provides an apt framework for socio-historical reflection. In the zoo visitors' imaginations of the Malagasy, in contrast, the latter are seen as representatives of a generic type of people rather than a specific group as discussed in detail in chapters 4 and 5. The imagination of 'natives' does not offer a clear 'vis-à-vis' to think about and interact with, nor does it encourage socio-historical contemplation.

Putting the imagination of 'the *vazaha*' and the imagination of 'natives' side by side, one discerns a process of conflation in both cases. However, the groups that emerge from each of these processes are very different. The 'natives' imagined by the zoo visitors are not imagined in terms of one's relationship with them. Indeed, one *cannot* have a relationship with a category of people. For the people in Ambanizana and Marofototra, on the other hand, the idea of 'the *vazaha*' is not thinkable outside a specific, historically charged relationship or, in the case of young people with little historical awareness, outside a specific relationship of unequal power.

Imagining the Other Within One's Own Story

The Swiss and the Malagasy people whom I have talked about in this book are engaged in two entirely different stories when reflecting about the Masoala Nature conservation project and when imagining the people involved in it. Yet, both imagine the other to share their own story.

The farmers in Ambanizana and Marofototra imagine that the *vazaha*, and by inclusion the Swiss, are consciously acting within a story of historical continuity. Recall, for example, the remark by Maman' i Jao: 'The *vazaha* don't forget the places where they once enjoyed good times', she had said, commenting on the fact that today's tourist lodges are located in the very spot where many of the *colons* of her youth used to live. This fact she interpreted as demonstrating a direct connection between the latter and today's tourist entrepreneurs, as if the old *colons* had told their grandchildren to go back to Masoala to continue their grandparents' endeavours. Moreover, many local people feel that the *vazaha* and others involved in the park are intentionally continuing the exertion of power, that the ultimate goal of what they are up to is to gain possession of the peninsula's riches – some even suggest that it is the intention of 'those behind the park' to render the local people poor – and that all the talk about the forest and the lemurs is little more than masquerade.

The zoo visitors, for their part, imagine that the farmers in Masoala are acting within a story of Nature conservation. As discussed in chapter 3, three scenarios explaining deforestation in Madagascar are brought to bear: (a) The farmers in Masoala use the forest without realising its finiteness, hence requiring the latter's education concerning methods of sustainable land use; (b) Despite their wish to do so, the people in Masoala cannot afford to preserve the forest due to their poverty and lack of alternatives to their present way of making do; and (c) The forest resources on which the farmers depend are depleted by unscrupulous logging companies, and so the farmers must be supported against such exploitation. Note that the reference point in all these scenarios is 'the forest'. In other words, the zoo visitors imagine that the farmers in Masoala, too, are within a story about the forest and its protection. Thus both sides imagine that 'the others' are thinking about the same things that they themselves are thinking about.

A Broken Bridge

It would be a misrepresentation to conclude that the various issues raised in Masoala and in Zurich in connection with the Masoala National Park weigh differently with the farmers in Madagascar and the visitors to the zoo's exhibit. It would be a misrepresentation to say that the Malagasy foreground social relations while paying less attention to Nature conservation, whereas the Swiss foreground Nature conservation while paying less attention to the social history brought to bear through the creation of the park. Such a conclusion would be a misrepresentation because the farmers in Masoala and the visitors to Little Masoala in Zurich do not even share a common understanding as to which issues are at stake. They cannot be said to be in disagreement, because *there are no common issues* to disagree about.

The farmers in Masoala do not fail to value the forest. But, unlike the Swiss we have encountered in this book, they do not aspire to do so because they wish to protect Nature's intrinsic beauty and worth but because the forest offers the possibility of creating human futures. Thus the notion of Nature as an entity that is separate from society but that humankind has a duty to preserve for its own sake[2] makes no sense to the farmers in Masoala. For those who look towards the peninsula through an environmentalist telescope, on the other hand, protecting Nature is an inviolable moral imperative. Thus we are left with the sad conclusion that although the Masoala project appears to bring Swiss and Malagasy people into contact, they can hardly be said to be talking to one another. There is, in fact, no true contact. Instead there is friction, and friction in imagination, taking place within the 'zones of awkward engagement' (Tsing 2005: xi) that have been instigated in Masoala and in Zurich by the global agenda of Nature conservation.

There is little reason to assume that the visitors to the zoo are not a fairly good mirror of Swiss society at large. Nor does the ethnographic in-depth evidence concerning other protected areas in Madagascar indicate that local people's views elsewhere on the island would be fundamentally different to those embraced by farmers in Masoala.[3] If this is so, then the ethnographic examination at both ends of the Masoala partnership project reveals that the flow of ideas in 'this imagined global era' (Tsing 2005: 5) proceeds anything but smoothly, and that 'universal dreams' such as Nature conservation may, in fact, *increase* the distance between alleged partners. In the case of the project examined in this book, the lens of Nature conservation leads to the perceptual erasure of the real people living in the place to be protected, and to a revival of evolutionist imaginations of the history of humankind in the minds of many Swiss people. In the minds of many Malagasy people, on the other hand, images of servitude and foreign rule resurface – images to which, because of the *vazaha* involvement in the park, the Swiss, too, are connected. Rather than offering a bridge for contact and communication between people in the global North and South, the Masoala Nature conservation project, therefore, widens the gap between them.

To say that by strengthening alienating ideas about the 'other', the Masoala rainforest conservation project increases the distance between the 'ordinary' people at both its ends is not, however, to say that there is no connection between them at all. The zoo visitors in Switzerland are immersed in, and their ideas mirror, the tremendously powerful paradigm of Nature conservation as a global agenda. This paradigm travels to Ambanizana and Marofototra along complicated routes, via stopping points such as the headquarters of the Wildlife Conservation Society in New York, the Zurich zoo, the capital city of Madagascar where groups like Foniala are formed and where Malagasy conservation policy is determined under the influence of various national and foreign bodies, and via the headquarters of the Masoala National Park. Along its complicated routes around the globe, contents and implementation strategies derived from the Nature conservation paradigm may be endorsed or refashioned, a process of continuity and transformation that, to do it justice, would require and deserve another thorough study (cf. Walsh 2012). Ultimately, however, the global agenda of Nature conservation, in which visitors to the Zurich zoo partake, translates into the creation of a strictly protected national park in Masoala which leads to subsistence farmers losing their land. Although, of course, the zoo visitors in Switzerland are in no way responsible for concrete conservation measures taken in Masoala by the relevant conservation bodies and authorities, they can, therefore, nevertheless, not be said to be entirely unconnected to what is happening in Masoala.

Notes

1. See Bloch 1995; Keller 2005: 180–81.
2. As has been nicely observed by the philosopher Kate Soper, all environmentalist discourses inevitably separate humans from 'nature': 'Unless human beings are differentiated from other organic and inorganic forms of being, they can be made no more liable for the effects of their occupancy of the eco-system than can any other species, and it would make no more sense to call upon them to desist from "destroying" nature than to call upon cats to stop killing birds' (Soper 1995: 160).
3. See Harper 2002; Kull 2004; Gezon 2006; Hanson 2007, 2009; Kaufmann 2008; Huff 2011; Sodikoff 2012; Walsh 2012.

References

Abinal and Malzac. (1888) 1993. *Dictionnaire Malgache–Français*. Fianarantsoa: Ambozontany.

Agrawal, A., and K. Redford. 2009. 'Conservation and Displacement: An Overview', *Conservation and Society* 7(1): 1–10.

Allnutt, T.F., et al. 2013. 'Mapping Recent Deforestation and Forest Disturbance in Northeastern Madagascar', *Tropical Conservation Science* 6(1): 1–15.

Ammann, R., and D. Müller. 2004. *Globi erlebt Masoala*. Zürich: Globi-Verlag.

Astuti, R. 2000. 'Kindreds and Descent Groups: New Perspectives from Madagascar', in J. Carsten (ed.), *Cultures of Relatedness: New Approaches to the Study of Kinship*. Cambridge: Cambridge University Press, pp. 90–103.

Bartlett, F.C. 1932. *Remembering: A Study of Experimental and Social Psychology*. Cambridge: Cambridge University Press.

Bauert, M., et al. 2007. 'Three Years of Experience Running the Masoala Rainforest Ecosystem at Zurich Zoo, Switzerland', *International Zoo Yearbook* 41: 203–16.

Bidau, C. 2012. 'REDD+, un Mécanism Novateur? Le Cas de la Forêt de Makira à Madagascar', *Revue Tiers Monde* 3(211): 111–130.

Bloch, M. 1979. 'The Social Implications of Freedom for Merina and Zafimaniry Slaves', in R.K. Kent (ed.), *Madagascar in History: Essays from the 1970s*. Albany, CA: The Foundation for Malagasy Studies, pp. 269–97.

———. 1980. 'Modes of Production and Slavery in Madagascar: Two Case Studies', in J.L. Watson (ed.), *Asian and African Systems of Slavery*. Oxford: Blackwell, pp. 100–34.

———. 1985. 'Questions Historiques Concernant la Parenté sur la Côte Est', *Omaly sy Anio* 21/22: 49–56.

———. 1986. *From Blessing to Violence: History and Ideology in the Circumcision Ritual of the Merina of Madagascar*. Cambridge: Cambridge University Press.

———. 1993. 'Zafimaniry Birth and Kinship Theory', *Social Anthropology* 1(1B): 119–32.

———. (1971) 1994a. *Placing the Dead: Tombs, Ancestral Villages, and Kinship Organization in Madagascar*. Prospect Heights, IL: Waveland.

———. 1994b. 'The Slaves, the King, and Mary in the Slums of Antananarivo', in N. Thomas and C. Humphrey (eds), *Shamanism, History, and the State*. Ann Arbor: University of Michigan Press, pp. 133–45.

———. 1995. 'People Into Places: Zafimaniry Concepts of Clarity', in E. Hirsch and M. O'Hanlon (eds), *The Anthropology of Landscape: Perspectives on Place and Space*. Oxford: Clarendon Press, pp. 63–77.

———. 1996. 'Internal and External Memory: Different Ways of Being in History', in P. Antze and M. Lambek (eds), *Tense Past: Cultural Essays in Trauma and Memory*. London: Routledge, pp. 215–33.

———. 2012. *Anthropology and the Cognitive Challenge*. Cambridge: Cambridge University Press.

Boserup, E. (1965) 1993. *The Conditions of Agricultural Growth: The Economics of Agrarian Change under Population Pressure*. London: Earthscan.

Brändle, R. 2013. *Wildfremd, hautnah. Zürcher Völkerschauen und ihre Schauplätze, 1835–1964*. Zurich: Rotpunktverlag.

Broch-Due, V. 2000. 'Producing Nature and Poverty in Africa: An Introduction', in V. Broch-Due and R.A. Schroeder (eds), *Producing Nature and Poverty in Africa*. Stockholm: Nordiska Afrikainstitutet, pp. 9–52.

Brockington, D. 2009. *Celebrity and the Environment: Fame, Wealth and Power in Conservation*. London and New York: Zed Books.

Brockington, D., and R. Duffy (eds). 2010. 'Capitalism and Conservation'. Special Issue of *Antipode* 42(3).

Brockington, D., R. Duffy and J. Igoe. 2008. *Nature Unbound: Conservation, Capitalism, and the Future of Protected Areas*. London: Earthscan.

Brockington, D., and J. Igoe. 2006. 'Eviction for Conservation: A Global Overview', *Conservation and Society* 4(3): 424–70.

Brockington, D., and K. Scholfield. 2010. 'Expenditure by Conservation Nongovernmental Organizations in Sub-Saharan Africa', *Conservation Letters* 3: 106–13.

Brown, M.L. 2004. 'Reclaiming Lost Ancestors and Acknowledging Slave Descent: Insights from Madagascar', *Comparative Studies in Society and History* 46(3): 616–45.

Burney, D. 1997. 'Theories and Facts Regarding Holocene Environmental Change Before and After Human Colonization', in S.M. Goodman and B.D. Patterson (eds), *Natural Change and Human Impact in Madagascar*. Washington, DC and London: Smithsonian Institution Press, pp. 75–89.

———. 2005. 'Finding the Connections between Paleoecology, Ethnobotany, and Conservation in Madagascar', *Ethnobotany Research and Applications* 3: 385–89.

Büscher, B., and W. Whande. 2007. 'Whims of the Winds of Time? Emerging Trends in Biodiversity Conservation and Protected Area Management', *Conservation and Society* 5(1): 22–43.

Campbell, B. 2005. 'Changing Protection Policies and Ethnographies of Environmental Engagement', *Conservation and Society* 3(2): 280–322.

Carrier, J., and P. West (eds). 2009. *Virtualism, Governance and Practice: Vision and Execution in Environmental Conservation*. New York and Oxford: Berghahn Books.

Cassanelli, L.V. 1987. 'Social Construction on the Somali Frontier: Bantu Former Slave Communities in the Nineteenth Century', in I. Kopytoff (ed.), *The African Frontier: The Reproduction of Traditional African Societies*. Bloomington and Indianapolis: Indiana University Press, pp. 216–38.

Castree, N. 2007. 'Neoliberalizing Nature: The Logics of De- and Re-Regulation', *Environment and Planning A* 4: 131–52.

Cernea, M.M. 2006. 'Re-examining "Displacement": A Redefinition of Concepts in Development and Conservation Policies', *Social Change* 36(1): 8–35.

Clark, A. 1997. *Being There: Putting Brain, Body, and World Together Again*. Cambridge, MA: MIT Press.

Cole, J. 1998. 'The Work of Memory in Madagascar', *American Ethnologist* 25(4): 610–33.

_____. 2001. *Forget Colonialism? Sacrifice and the Art of Memory in Madagascar*. Berkeley: University of California Press.

_____. 2010. *Sex and Salvation: Imagining the Future in Madagascar*. Chicago and London: The University of Chicago Press.

Conservation International. 2013. 'Madagascar'. Retrieved 30 April 2013 from http://www.conservation.org/where/africa_madagascar/madagascar/pages/default.asp

Corson, C. 2010. 'Shifting Environmental Governance in a Neoliberal World: US AID for Conservation', *Antipode* 42(3): 576–602.

———. 2011a. 'Territorialization, Enclosure, and Neoliberalism: Non-State Influence in Struggles over Madagascar's Forests', *The Journal of Peasant Studies* 38(4): 703–26.

———. 2011b. 'From Rhetoric to Practice: How High-Profile Politics Impeded Community Consultation in Madagascar's New Protected Areas', *Society and Natural Resources* 0: 1–16.

Corson, C., K.I. MacDonald and B. Neimark. 2013. 'Grabbing "Green": Markets, Environmental Governance and the Materialization of Natural Capital', *Human Geography* 6(1): 1–15.

Covell, M. 1987. *Madagascar: Politics, Economics and Society*. London and New York: Frances Pinter.

Cox, M.P., et al. 2012. 'A Small Cohort of Island Southeast Asian Women Founded Madagascar', *Proceedings of the Royal Society B* (online): 1–8.

Dahl, O.Ch. 1951. *Malgache et Maanjan: Une comparaison linguistique*. Oslo: Egede Instituttet/Arne Gimnes.

D'Andrade, R. 1995. *The Development of Cognitive Anthropology*. Cambridge: Cambridge University Press.

Decary, R. 1939. 'Sépultures Chez les Betsimisaraka du Nord (Madagascar)', *Bulletin de la Société d'Anthropologie de Paris*.

Deschamps, H. 1959. *Les Migrations Intérieures à Madagascar*. Paris: Éditions Berger-Levrault.

Descola, Ph. 1994. *In the Society of Nature: A Native Ecology in Amazonia*. Cambridge: Cambridge University Press.
———. 1996. 'Construction Natures: Symbolic Ecology and Social Practice', in Ph. Descola and G. Palsson (eds), *Nature and Society: Anthropological Perspectives*. London and New York: Routledge, pp. 82–102.
———. 2005. *Par-Delà Nature et Culture*. Paris: Gallimard.
Descola, Ph., and G. Palsson (eds). 1996. *Nature and Society: Anthropological Perspectives*. London and New York: Routledge.
Dewar, R.E. 1997. 'Were People Responsible for the Extinction of Madagascar's Subfossils, and How Will We Ever Know?', in S.M. Goodman and B.D. Patterson (eds), *Natural Change and Human Impact in Madagascar*. Washington, DC and London: Smithsonian Institution Press, pp. 364–77.
Dewar, R.E., and A.F. Richard. 2012. 'Madagascar: A History of Arrivals, What Happened, and Will Happen Next', *Annual Review of Anthropology* 41: 495–517.
Dewar, R.E., et al. 2013. 'Stone Tools and Foraging in Northern Madagascar Challenge Holocene Extinction Models', *PNAS Early Edition*: 1–6.
Duffy, R. 2005. 'Global Environmental Governance and the Challenge of Shadow States: The Impact of Illicit Sapphire Mining in Madagascar', *Development and Change* 36(5): 825–43.
———. 2006. 'Non-governmental Organisations and Governance States: The Impact of Transnational Environmental Management Networks in Madagascar', *Environmental Politics* 15(5): 731–49.
———. 2008. 'Neoliberalising Nature: Global Networks and Ecotourism Development in Madagascar', *Journal of Sustainable Tourism* 16(3): 327–44.
Durrell Wildlife Conservation Trust. 2009. 'Madagascar'. Retrieved 23 February 2009 from http://www.durrell.org/Conservation/Where-we-work/Madagascar/
EAZA. 2010. *Annual Report*. European Association of Zoos and Aquaria.
———. 2011. *Looking at People Looking at Animals: An International Bibliography on Visitor Experience Studies and Exhibit Evaluation in Zoos and Aquariums*. European Association of Zoos and Aquaria Education Committee.
Ellis, W. 1838. *History of Madagascar* (Vol. 1). London: Fisher.
———. 1859. *Three Visits to Madagascar During the Years 1853, 1854, 1856*. New York: Harper and Brothers.
Escobar, A. 1998. 'Whose Knowledge, Whose Nature? Biodiversity, Conservation, and the Political Ecology of Social Movements', *Journal of Political Ecology* 5: 53–82.
———. 1999. 'After Nature: Steps to an Antiessentialist Political Ecology', *Current Anthropology* 40(1): 1–16.
Evers, S.J.T.M. 2002. *Constructing History, Culture and Inequality: The Betsileo in the Extreme Southern Highlands of Madagascar*. Leiden: Brill.
———. 2013. 'Lex Loci Meets Lex Fori: Merging Customary Law and National Land Legislation in Madagascar', in S.J.T.M. Evers, G. Campbell and M. Lambek (eds), *Contest for Land in Madagascar: Environment, Ancestors and Development*. Brill: Leiden and Boston, pp. 119–40.

Evers, S.J.T.M., and C. Seagle. 2012. 'Stealing the Sacred: Why "Global Heritage" Discourse is Perceived as a Frontal Attack on Local Heritage-Making in Madagascar', *Madagascar Conservation and Development* 7(2S): 97–106.
Fairhead, J., and M. Leach. 1998. *Reframing Deforestation. Global Analysis and Local Realities: Studies in West Africa*. London and New York: Routledge.
———. 2003. *Science, Society and Power: Environmental Knowledge and Policy in West Africa and the Caribbean*. Cambridge: Cambridge University Press.
Fairhead, J., M. Leach and I. Scoones. 2012. 'Green Grabbing: A New Appropriation of Nature?', *The Journal of Peasant Studies* 39(2): 237–61.
Falk, J.H., and L.D. Dierking. (1992) 2002. *The Museum Experience*. Washington DC: Whalesback Books.
Feeley-Harnik, G. 1982. 'The King's Men in Madagascar: Slavery, Citizenship and Sakalava Monarchy', *Africa* 52(2): 31–50.
———. 1991. *A Green Estate: Restoring Independence in Madagascar*. Washington and London: Smithsonian Institution Press.
———. 1995. 'Plants and People, Children or Wealth?: Shifting Grounds of "Choice" in Madagascar', *Polar* 18(2): 45–64.
Ferguson, B. 2009: 'REDD Comes Into Fashion in Madagascar', *Madagascar Conservation and Development* 4(2): 132–37.
———. 2010a. 'Madagascar', in O. Springate-Baginski and E. Wollenberg (eds), *REDD, Forest Governance and Rural Livelihoods: The Emerging Agenda*. Bogor Barat, Indonesia: CIFOR (Center for International Forestry Research), pp. 135–72.
———. 2010b. 'Voices from Madagascar's Forests: Improving Representation and Rights of Malagasy Forest Peoples' (Final Conference Report of same name). Norwich, 5–6 June.
Francis, D., M. Esson and A. Moss. 2007. 'Following Visitors and What it Tells Us', *IZE (International Zoo Educators Association) Journal* 43: 20–24.
Freeman, L. 2001. 'Knowledge, Education and Social Differentiation amongst the Betsileo of Fisakana, Highland Madagascar'. Ph.D. dissertation. London: University of London.
———. 2004. 'Voleurs de Foies, Voleurs de Coeurs', *Terrain* 43: 85–106.
———. 2013. 'Speech, Silence, and Slave Descent in Highland Madagascar', *Journal of the Royal Anthropological Institute* 19: 600–17.
Fremigacci, J. 1998. 'La Forêt de Madagascar en Situation Coloniale: Une Économie de la Délinquance', in M. Chastenet (ed.), *Plantes et Paysages d'Afrique. Une Histoire à Explorer*. Paris: Karthala and Centre de Recherches Africaines.
———. 2009. 'De la "Violence Légitime" de l'Etat Colonial: Les Prestations dans la Province de Maroantsetra (1905–1930)', *Tsingy* 11: 64–92.
Galvin, M., and T. Haller (eds). 2008. *People, Protected Areas and Global Change: Participatory Conservation in Latin America, Africa, Asia and Europe*. Perspectives of the Swiss National Centre of Competence in Research (NCCR) North–South, University of Bern, Volume 3. Bern: Geographica Bernensia.
Geiger, D. 2009: 'Turner in the Tropics: The Frontier Concept Revisited', Ph.D. dissertation. Zurich: University of Zurich. Retrieved 30 December 2012 from

http://edoc.zhbluzern.ch/unilu/ediss/unilu_diss_2013_001_geiger_fulltext.pdf

Gezon, L.L. 2006. *Global Visions, Local Landscapes: A Political Ecology of Conservation, Conflict, and Control in Northern Madagascar*. Lanham, MD: Altamira Press.

Ghimire, K.B. 1994. 'Parks and People: Livelihood Issues in National Parks Management in Thailand and Madagascar', *Development and Change* 25: 195–229.

Givaudan. 2001. 'Annual Report 2001'. Retrieved 6 June 2013 from http://www.givaudan.com/Media/Publications/Full+and+Half+Year+Reports/Archive

Gommery, D., et al. 2011. 'Les Plus Anciennes Traces d'Activités Anthropiques de Madagascar sur les Ossements d'Hippopotames Subfossiles d'Anjohibe', *Comptes Rendus Palevol* 10: 271–78.

Graeber, D. 1995. 'Dancing with Corpses Reconsidered: An Interpretation of *Famadihana* (in Arivonimamo, Madagascar)', *American Ethnologist* 22(2): 258–78.

———. 1997. 'Painful Memories', *Journal of Religion in Africa* 27(4): 374–400.

———. 2007. *Lost People: Magic and the Legacy of Slavery in Madagascar*. Bloomington and Indianapolis: Indiana University Press.

Grove, R.H. 1995. *Green Imperialism: Colonial Expansion, Tropical Island Edens and the Origins of Environmentalism, 1600–1860*. Cambridge: Cambridge University Press.

Guyer, J., and P. Richards. 1996. 'The Invention of Biodiversity: Social Perspectives on the Management of Biological Variety in Africa', *Africa* 66(1): 1–13.

Hall, St. 1997. 'The Spectacle of the "Other"', in St. Hall (ed.), *Representation: Cultural Representations and Signifying Practices*. London: Sage Publications, pp. 223–79.

Hanson, P.W. 1997. 'The Politics of Need Interpretation in Madagascar's Ranomafana National Park'. Ph.D. dissertation. Philadelphia: The University of Pennsylvania.

———. 2007. 'Governmentality, Language Ideology, and the Production of Needs in Malagasy Conservation and Development', *Cultural Anthropology* 22(2): 244–84.

———. 2009. 'Engaging Green Governmentality through Ritual: The Case of Madagascar's Ranomafana National Park', *Etudes Océan Indien* 42/43: 1–27.

———. 2012. 'Toward a More Transformative Participation in the Conservation of Madagascar's Natural Resources', *Geoforum* 43(6): 1182–93.

Harper, G., et al. 2007. 'Fifty Years of Deforestation and Forest Fragmentation in Madagascar', *Environmental Conservation* 34(4): 325–33.

Harper, J. 2002. *Endangered Species: Health, Illness and Death Among Madagascar's People of the Forest*. Durham: Carolina Academic Press.

Harries, P. 2007. *Butterflies and Barbarians: Swiss Missionaries and Systems of Knowledge in South-East Africa*. Oxford: James Currey; Harare: Weaver Press; Johannesburg: Wits University Press; and Athens: Ohio University Press.

Harris, P.L. 2000. *The Work of the Imagination*. Malden, MA: Blackwell.

Harris, P.L., et al. 2006. 'Germs and Angels: The Role of the Testimony in Young Children's Ontology', *Developmental Science* 9(1): 76–96.

Harrison, G. 2004. *The World Bank and Africa: The Construction of Governance States*. London: Routledge.
Hatchwell, M. 2003. 'The Founding of Masoala National Park', in A. Rübel et al. (eds), *Masoala – The Eye of the Forest. A New Strategy for Rainforest Conservation in Madagascar*. Stäfa: Th. Gut, pp. 85–108.
Heinzer, P., and G. Strebel. 1995. *Globi und der Madagaskar-Vogel*. Zurich: Globi-Verlag.
Hirsch, E., and M. O'Hanlon (eds). 1995. *The Anthropology of Landscape: Perspectives on Place and Space*. Oxford: Clarendon Press.
Horning, N. 2012. 'Debunking Three Myths about Madagascar's Deforestation', *Madagascar Conservation and Development* 7(3): 116–19. [See also Rabesahala Horning]
Huff, A. 2011. 'Vulnerability and Wellbeing in the *Baintao Lava*, "The Long Wounded Year": Environmental Policy, Livelihoods, and Human Health among Mikea of Southwest Madagascar'. Ph.D. dissertation. Athens: The University of Georgia.
Igoe, J. 2010. 'The Spectacle of Nature in the Global Economy of Appearances: Anthropological Engagements with the Spectacular Mediations of Transnational Conservation', *Critique of Anthropology* 30(4): 375–97.
Igoe, J., and D. Brockington. 2007. 'Neoliberal Conservation: A Brief Introduction', *Conservation and Society* 5(4): 432–49.
Ingold, T. 1993. 'Globes and Spheres: The Topology of Environmentalism', in K. Milton (ed.), *Environmentalism: The View from Anthropology*. London and New York: Routledge, pp. 31–42.
———. 2000. *The Perception of the Environment: Essays in Livelihood, Dwelling and Skill*. London and New York: Routledge.
IRBIS. 2003. *Zeitschrift der Tiergarten-Gesellschaft Zürich, Föderverein des Zoo Zürich* 2003(1): 6–7.
Jarosz, L. 1993. 'Defining and Explaining Tropical Deforestation: Shifting Cultivation and Population Growth in Colonial Madagascar (1896–1940)', *Economic Geography* 69: 366–79.
———. 1994. 'Agents of Power, Landscapes of Fear: The Vampires and Heart Thieves of Madagascar', *Environment and Planning D: Society and Space* 12: 421–36.
Kaufmann, J.C. 2008. 'Lemurs and the People Without History', in J.C. Kaufmann (ed.), *Greening the Red Island: Madagascar in Nature and Culture*. Pretoria: Africa Institute of South Africa, pp. 3–15.
Keller, E. 2005. *The Road to Clarity: Seventh-Day Adventism in Madagascar*. New York and Basingstoke: Palgrave Macmillan.
———. 2008. 'The Banana Plant and the Moon: Conservation and the Malagasy Ethos of Life in Masoala, Madagascar', *American Ethnologist* 35(4): 650–64.
———. 2009. '"Who are *They*"? Local Understandings of NGO and State Power in Masoala, Madagascar', *Tsantsa* 14: 11–20.
Klein, J. 2002. 'Deforestation in the Madagascar Highlands – Established "Truth" and Scientific Uncertainty', *GeoJournal* 56: 191–99.

Klein, J., et al. 2007. 'Conservation, Development, and a Heterogeneous Community: The Case of Ambohitantely Special Reserve, Madagascar', *Society and Natural Resources* 20: 451–67.

Köhler, A. 2005. 'Of Apes and Men: Baka and Bantu Attitudes to Wildlife and the Making of Eco-goodies and Baddies', *Conservation and Society* 3(2): 407–35.

Kopytoff, I. 1987. 'The Internal African Frontier: The Making of African Political Culture', in I. Kopytoff (ed.), *The African Frontier: The Reproduction of Traditional African Societies*. Bloomington and Indianapolis: Indiana University Press, pp. 3–84.

Kraemer, A. 2012. 'Whose Forests, Whose Voices? Mining and Community-based Nature Conservation in Southeastern Madagascar', *Madagascar Conservation and Development* 7(2S): 87–96.

Kratz, C.A., and I. Karp. 2006. 'Introduction', in I. Karp, et al. (eds), *Museum Frictions: Public Cultures / Global Transformations*. Durham, NC and London: Duke University Press, pp. 1–31.

Kremen, C., et al. 1995. 'Proposition des Limites du Parc National Masoala', Unpublished Report. CARE International, Wildlife Conservation Society, and Peregrine Fund. Antananarivo, Madagascar.

Kremen, C., et al. 1999. 'Designing the Masoala National Park in Madagascar Based on Biological and Socioeconomic Data', *Conservation Biology* 13(5): 1055–68.

Kremen, C., et al. 2008. 'Aligning Conservation Priorities across Taxa in Madagascar with High-Resolution Planning Tools', *Science* 320: 222–26.

Kull, Ch.A. 2004. *Isle of Fire: The Political Ecology of Landscape Burning in Madagascar*. Chicago and London: University of Chicago Press.

Kull, Ch.A., et al. 2013. 'Melting Pots of Biodiversity: Tropical Smallholder Farm Landscapes as Guarantors of Sustainability', *Environment: Science and Policy for Sustainable Development* 55(2): 6–16.

Larson, A.M., et al. 2013. 'Land Tenure and REDD+: The Good, the Bad and the Ugly', *Global Environmental Change* 23: 678–89.

Larson, P.M. 1996. 'Desperately Seeking "the Merina" (Central Madagascar): Reading Ethnonyms and their Semantic Fields in African Identity Histories', *Journal of Southern African Studies* 22(4): 541–60.

Li, Tania Murray. 2007. *The Will to Improve: Governmentality, Development, and the Practice of Politics*. Durham, NC and London: Duke University Press.

McCall, J.C. 1995. 'Rethinking Ancestors in Africa', *Africa* 65(2): 256–70.

MacCormack, C., and M. Strathern (eds). 1980. *Nature, Culture and Gender*. Cambridge: Cambridge University Press.

Madagascar National Parks. n.d. Retrieved 20 April 2013 from http://www.parcs-madagascar.com/fiche-aire-protegee.php?Ap=13

Marcus, R.R. 2001. 'Seeing the Forest for the Trees: Integrated Conservation and Development Projects and Local Perceptions of Conservation in Madagascar', *Human Ecology* 29(4): 381–96.

Masoala National Park. 2005. *Masoala News*, January–March 2005.

———. 2009. *Masoala News*, May 2009.

Mercier, J.-R. 2006. 'The Preparation of the National Environmental Action Plan (NEAP): Was it a False Start?', *Madagascar Conservation and Development* 1(1): 50–54.
Merenlender, A., et al. 1998. 'Monitoring Impacts of Natural Resource Extraction on Lemurs of the Masoala Peninsula, Madagascar', *Conservation Ecology* 2(2): Art. 5. Retrieved 5 June 2013 from http://www.ecologyandsociety.org/vol2/iss2/art5/
Messerli, P. 2006. 'Exploring Innovative Strategies for Livelihoods in a Slash-and-Burn Context in Madagascar', *Geographica Helvetica* 61(4): 266–74.
Middleton, K. 2013. 'Land Rights and Alien Plants in Dryland Madagascar', in S.J.T.M. Evers, G. Campbell and M. Lambek (eds), *Contest for Land in Madagascar: Environment, Ancestors and Development*. Brill: Leiden and Boston, pp. 141–70.
Myers, N. 1988. 'Threatened Biotas: "Hotspots" in Tropical Forests', *Environmentalist* 8: 187–208.
Myers, N., et al. 2000. 'Biodiversity Hotspots for Conservation Priorities', *Nature* 403: 853–58.
Nash, R.F. 1989. *The Rights of Nature: A History of Environmental Ethics*. Madison: The University of Wisconsin Press.
Neue Zürcher Zeitung. 2003.'Mahnmal und Augenweide – ein Stück Regenwald in Zürich', *NZZ* special dossier, 27 June.
———. 2008. 'Nur die Tomatenfrösche haben noch keinen Nachwuchs', *NZZ online*, 18 September.
Ormsby, A. 2003. 'Perceptions on the Park Periphery: Resident, Staff and Natural Resource Relations at Masoala National Park, Madagascar', Ph.D. dissertation. Antioch New England Graduate School.
———. 2008. 'Perceptions on the Park Periphery: Resident, Staff and Natural Resource Relations at Masoala National Park', in J.C. Kaufmann (ed.), *Greening the Red Island: Madagascar in Nature and Culture*. Pretoria: Africa Institute of South Africa, pp. 275–99.
Ormsby, A., and B.A. Kaplin. 2005. 'A Framework for Understanding Community Resident Perceptions of Masoala National Park, Madagascar', *Environmental Conservation* 32(2): 1–9.
Ormsby, A., and K. Mannle. 2006. 'Ecotourism Benefits and the Role of Local Guides at Masoala National Park, Madagascar', *Journal of Sustainable Tourism* 14(3): 271–87.
Orwell, G. 1946. 'Marrakech', in G. Orwell, *A Collection of Essays*. San Diego: Harcourt.
Petit, M. 1967. 'Les Zafirabay de la Baie d'Antongil', *Annales de l'Université de Madagascar. Serie Lettres et Sciences Humaines* 7: 21–44.
Petit, M., and G. Jacob.1965. 'Un Essai de Colonisation dans la Baie d'Antongil (1895–vers 1926)', *Annales de l'Université de Madagascar* 3: 33–56.
Pollini, J. 2007. 'Slash-and-Burn Cultivation and Deforestation in the Malagasy Rain Forests: Representations and Realities', Ph.D. dissertation. Cornell University. Retrieved 5 June 2013 from http://www.scribd.com/doc/26790856/Deforestation-in-Madagascar

———. 2008. 'Financing Avoided Deforestation through the Carbon Market – A Contribution to the Debate', *Policy Matters* 16: 69–81.
———. 2009. 'Carbon Sequestration for Linking Conservation and Rural Development in Madagascar: The Case of the Vohidrazana–Mantadia Corridor Restoration and Conservation Carbon Project', *Journal of Sustainable Forestry* 28: 322–42.
Pollini, J., and J.P. Lassoie. 2011. 'Trapping Farmer Communities within Global Environmental Regimes: The Case of the GELOSE Legislation in Madagascar', *Society and Natural Resources* 0: 1–17.
Pro Natura and Océan Vert. n.d. 'Le Radeau des Cimes. Programme Madagascar 2000–2001'. Retrieved 31 December 2013 from http://www.radeau-des-cimes.org/radeau/expe%20mada_fr.pdf
Purtschert, P. 2012. 'De Schorsch Gaggo reist uf Afrika. Postkoloniale Konstellationen und diskursive Verschiebungen in Schweizer Kindergeschichten', in P. Purtschert, B. Lüthi and F. Falk (eds), *Postkoloniale Schweiz. Formen und Folgen eines Kolonialismus ohne Kolonien*. Bielefeld: Transcript, pp. 89–116.
———. 2014. 'The Return of the Native: Racialised Space, Colonial Debris and the Human Zoo', *Identities: Global Studies in Culture and Power*, published online 20 June.
Purtschert, P., and G. Krüger. 2012. 'Afrika in Schweizer Kinderbüchern. Hybride Helden in kolonialen Konstellationen', in M. Menrath (ed.), *Afrika im Blick. Afrikabilder im deutschsprachigen Raum 1870–1970*. Zurich: Chronos, pp. 69–98.
Purtschert, P., B. Lüthi and F. Falk. 2012: 'Eine Bestandesaufnahme der postkolonialen Schweiz', in P. Purtschert, B. Lüthi and F. Falk (eds), *Postkoloniale Schweiz. Formen und Folgen eines Kolonialismus ohne Kolonien*. Bielefeld: Transcript, pp. 13–63.
Quinn, N. (ed.). 2005a. *Finding Culture in Talk: A Collection of Methods*. New York and Basingstoke: Palgrave Macmillan.
———. 2005b. 'Introduction', in N. Quinn (ed.), *Finding Culture in Talk: A Collection of Methods*. New York and Basingstoke: Palgrave Macmillan, pp. 1–34.
———. 2005c. 'How to Reconstruct Schemas People Share, from What They Say', in N. Quinn (ed.), *Finding Culture in Talk: A Collection of Methods*. New York and Basingstoke: Palgrave Macmillan, pp. 35–81.
———. 2011. 'The History of the Cultural Models School Reconsidered: A Paradigm Shift in Cognitive Anthropology', in D.B. Kronenfeld et al. (eds), *A Companion to Cognitive Anthropology*. Oxford: Wiley-Blackwell, pp. 30–46.
Rabesahala Horning, N. 2008. 'Strong Support for Weak Performance: Donor Competition in Madagascar', *African Affairs* 107(428): 405–31. [See also Horning]
Rajaonarimanana, N. 1995. *Dictionnaire du Malgache Contemporain*. Paris: Karthala.
Ramiarantsoa, R., C. Blanc-Pamard and F. Pinton (eds). 2012. *Géopolitique et Environnement. Les Leçons de l'Expérience Malgache*. Collection Objectifs Suds. Marseille: Éditions de l'IRD.

Randriamalala, H., and Z. Liu. 2010. 'Rosewood of Madagascar: Between Democracy and Conservation', *Madagascar Conservation and Development* 5(1): 11–22.

Ratsimbazafy, J., and J.C. Kaufmann. 2008. 'An Experiment in Lessening Cultural Distance', in J.C. Kaufmann (ed.), *Greening the Red Island: Madagascar in Nature and Culture*. Pretoria: Africa Institute of South Africa, pp. 33–47.

Rival, L. (ed.). 1998. *The Social Life of Trees: Anthropological Perspectives on Tree Symbolism*. Oxford and New York: Berg.

Robbins, J. 2006. 'Properties of Nature, Properties of Culture: Ownership, Recognition, and the Politics of Nature in a Papua New Guinea Society', in A. Biersack and J.B. Greenberg (eds), *Reimagining Political Ecology*. Durham, NC and London: Duke University Press, pp. 171–91.

Rosch, E. 1977. 'Human Categorization', in N. Warren (ed.), *Advances in Cross-Cultural Psychology*, Vol. 1. New York: Academic Press, pp. 1–49.

Rothfels, N. 2002. *Savages and Beasts: The Birth of the Modern Zoo*. Baltimore and London: The Johns Hopkins University Press.

Rübel, A. 2003a. *Masoala Regenwald. Ein Naturschutz-Projekt des Zoo Zürich*. Zurich: Zoo Zürich.

———. 2003b. 'Wir brauchen einen Bewusstseinswandel', *Neue Zürcher Zeitung*, 27 June, B9.

———. 2004. 'Editorial', *Zooh-news*, November.

———. 2011. 'Der Zoodirektor als Manager und Verkäufer', *Neue Zürcher Zeitung online*, 12 July 2011.

Rübel, A., et al. 2003. *Masoala – The Eye of the Forest: A New Strategy for Rainforest Conservation in Madagascar*. Stäfa: Th. Gut.

Said, E. 1979. *Orientalism*. New York: Vintage.

Savaresi, A. 2013. 'REDD+ and Human Rights: Addressing Synergies between International Regimes', *Ecology and Society* 18(3): 5.

Sawyer, S. 2003: 'Subterranean Techniques: Corporate Environmentalism, Oil Operations, and Social Injustice in the Ecuadorian Rain Forest', in C. Slater (ed.), *In Search of the Rain Forest*. Durham, NC and London: Duke University Press, pp. 69–100.

Scales, I.R. 2011. 'Farming at the Forest Frontier: Land Use and Landscape Change in Western Madagascar,1896–2005', *Environment and History* 17: 499–524.

Seagle, C. 2013. 'Discourse, Development and Legitimacy: Nature/Culture Dualism of Mining Engagements in Biodiversity Offsetting and Conservation in Madagascar', in S.J.T.M. Evers, G. Campbell and M. Lambek (eds), *Contest for Land in Madagascar: Environment, Ancestors and Development*. Brill: Leiden and Boston, pp. 187–220.

Sibree, J. 1915. *A Naturalist in Madagascar: A Record of Observation, Experiences, and Impressions made During a Period of Over Fifty Years' Intimate Association with the Natives and Study of the Animal and Vegetable Life of the Island*. London: Seeley.

Simsik, M.J. 2002. 'The Political Ecology of Biodiversity Conservation on the Malagasy Highlands', *GeoJournal* 58: 233–42.

Slater, C. 2003. 'In Search of the Rain Forest', in C. Slater (ed.), *In Search of the Rain Forest*. Durham, NC and London: Duke University Press, pp. 3–37.

Sodikoff, G. 2004. 'Land and Languor: Ethical Imaginations of Work and Forest in Northeast Madagascar', *History and Anthropology* 15(4): 367–98.

———. 2005. 'Forced and Forest Labor Regimes in Colonial Madagascar, 1926–1936', *Ethnohistory* 52(2): 407–35.

———. 2007. 'An Exceptional Strike: A Micro-history of "People versus Park" in Madagascar', *Journal of Political Ecology* 14: 10–32.

———. 2012. *Forest and Labor in Madagascar: From Colonial Concession to Global Biosphere*. Bloomington and Indianapolis: Indiana University Press.

Somda, D. 2009. *Et le réel serait passé. Le secret de l'esclavage et l'imagination de la société en Anôsy (Sud est de Madagascar)*. Ph.D. dissertation. Paris: Université Paris ouest Nanterre.

Soper, K. 1995. *What is Nature?* Oxford (UK) and Cambridge, MA: Blackwell.

Southall, A. 1986. 'Common Themes in Malagasy Culture', in C.Ph. Kottak et al. (eds), *Madagascar: Society and History*. Durham, NC: Carolina Academic Press, pp. 411–26.

Sperber, D. (1985) 1996. *Explaining Culture: A Naturalistic Approach*. Oxford (UK) and Cambridge, MA: Blackwell.

Stepan, N. 2001. *Picturing Tropical Nature*. Ithaca, NY: Cornell University Press.

Strauss, C. 2005. 'Analyzing Discourse for Cultural Complexity', in N. Quinn (ed.), *Finding Culture in Talk: A Collection of Methods*. New York and Basingstoke: Palgrave Macmillan, pp. 203–42.

Strauss, C., and N. Quinn. 1997. *A Cognitive Theory of Cultural Meaning*. Cambridge: Cambridge University Press.

Thomas, Ph. 1997. 'The Water that Blesses, the River that Flows: Place and the Ritual Imagination among the Temanambondro of Southeast Madagascar', in J.J. Fox (ed.), *The Poetic Power of Place: Comparative Perspectives on Austronesian Ideas of Locality*. Canberra: Research School of Pacific and Asian Studies, Australian National University, pp. 22–41.

Toto, T.Ch. 2005. 'La Baie d'Antongil au XVIIIème Siècle: Récits et Mémoires sur l'Hégémonie Zafindrabay', *Tsingy* 2: 9–20.

Tsing, A. Lowenhaupt. 1993. *In the Realm of the Diamond Queen*. New Jersey and Chichester: Princeton University Press.

———. 2005. *Friction: An Ethnography of Global Connection*. Princeton, NJ and Oxford: Princeton University Press.

Tucker, B., et al. 2011: 'When the Wealthy are Poor: Poverty Explanations and Local Perspectives in Southwestern Madagascar', *American Anthropologist* 113(2): 291–305.

UNESCO. 2003. 'Tripling Environmental Protection Plan in Madagascar'. Retrieved 30 April 2013 from http://portal.unesco.org/culture/en/ev.php-URL_ID=14248&URL_DO=DO_PRINTPAGE&URL_SECTION=201.html

United Nations 2011. 'Madagascar: Photographer completes 20-year project on the "Noah's Ark of Diversity"'. Retrieved 29 April 2013 from http://www.unep.org/NairobiConvention/Information_Center/News_Events_January2011.asp

Virah-Sawmy, M. 2009. 'Ecosystem Management in Madagascar during Global Change', *Conservation Letters* 2: 163–70.

Walsh, A. 2004. 'In the Wake of Things: Speculating In and About Sapphires in Northern Madagascar', *American Anthropologist* 106(2): 225–37.

———. 2012. *Made in Madagascar: Sapphires, Ecotourism, and the Global Bazaar*. Toronto: University of Toronto Press.

Weber, M. (1904/5) 1988. 'Die Protestantische Ethik und der Geist des Kapitalismus', in M. Weber, *Gesammelte Aufsätze zur Religionssoziologie I*. Tübingen: J.C.B. Mohr, pp. 17–206.

West, P. 2005. 'Translation, Value and Space: Theorizing an Ethnographic and Engaged Environmental Anthropology', *American Anthropologist* 107(4): 632–42.

West, P., J. Igoe and D. Brockington. 2006. 'Parks and Peoples: The Social Impact of Protected Areas', *Annual Review of Anthropology* 35: 251–77.

Wildlife Conservation Society. 2012. 'Wildlife Conservation Society/Makira, Madagascar'. Retrieved 30 April 2013 from http://www.coderedd.org/redd-project/wildlife-conservation-society-makira-madagascar/

———. 2013. 'Madagascar: Makira-Masoala Landscape'. Retrieved 30 April 2013 from http://www.wcs.org/saving-wild-places/africa/madagascar-makira-masoala.aspx

Wohlhauser, S., and P. Kistler. 2002. 'Etude de Faisabilité pour la Mise en Place d'un Programme de Recherches Appliquées au Développement des Zones Périphériques du Parc National de Masoala'. Unpublished report commissioned by ANGAP (Association Nationale pour la Gestion des Aires Protégées, Madagascar).

Woolley, O. 2002. *The Earth Shakers of Madagascar: An Anthropological Study of Authority, Fertility and Creation*. London and New York: Continuum.

World Association of Zoos and Aquariums (n.d.). 'Masoala Conservation'. WAZA Conservation Projects. Retrieved 11 March 2013 from http://www.waza.org/en/site/conservation/waza-conservation-projects/overview/masoala-conservation

Zavada, M., et al. 2009. 'The Significance of Human Induced and Natural Erosion Features (lavakas) on the Central Highlands of Madagascar', *Madagascar Conservation and Development* 4(2): 120–27.

Zurich Zoo. 2003. *Zooh Magazine* 2003(1).

———. 2004. Jahresbericht 2004.

———. 2005. *Zooh Journal* 2005.

———. 2006. *Zooh Journal* 2006(4).

———. 2007. 'Masoala National Park to be Inscribed on World Heritage List'. Press release of 26 June 2007. Retrieved 30 June 2007 from http://www.zoo.ch/xml_1/internet/de/application/d342/d1590/f344.cfm

———. 2008. *Zooh Journal* 2008.

———. 2010a. 'Zoo Zürich äusserst besorgt über illegalen Holzschlag im Masoala Nationalpark'. Press release of 25 March 2010. Retrieved 6 June 2013 from http://www.zoo.ch/xml_1/internet/de/application/d342/d1590/f344.cfm

———. 2010b. 'Geschäftsbericht Zoo Zürich'. Press release of 2 June. Retrieved 7 June 2013 from http://www.zoo.ch/xml_1/internet/de/application/d342/d1590/f344.cfm

———. 2011a. 'Masoala Mediendokumentation'. August Edition. Retrieved 5 August 2012 from www.zoo.ch

———. 2011b. *Zooh Journal* 2011.

———. 2012. *Zooh Journal* 2012.

———. 2013a. *Zooh Journal* 2013.

———. 2013b. 'Ein Meilenstein in der Entwicklung des Zoo Zürich zum Naturschutzzentrum'. Press release of 26 March 2013. Retrieved 27 March 2013 from http://www.zoo.ch/xml_1/internet/de/application/d342/d1590/f344.cfm

Index

absence of people, chapter 4; 53, 112n1, 223. *See also* animation film; Ur-; wilderness
Africa, 64, 73, 86, 90, 96, 100
Ambanizana
   convention of, 129–30, 133–34, 140
   description of, 118–20
   history of, 118, 148, 197–99, 211 (*see also* slavery)
   See also Marofototra; Masoala; Masoala National Park
ancestors
   and blessing, 155, 156, 162, 171n3, 178, 179, 209–10, 212
   and loss of bones, 177, 210
   rituals for, 120, 155–56, 159–62, 171n1, 175–76, 178, 209, 210 (*see also* funerary practices; Island of the Wanderer)
   and taboos, 156, 176, 177, 210
   transferral of bones of, 155–56, 170, 171n1, 179–82, 184n6, 188, 201 (*see also* funerary practices; Island of the Wanderer)
   See also burial ground; children; kinship; land of the ancestors; process of growth; *tany fivelômana*
ANGAP
   and authorisation for hill rice, 139
   and compensations for loss of land, 129, 135–36, 143, 164
   and cooperation with foreigners and the state, 3, 176–77, 179, 182, 185–86, 188, 193, 195
   history of, 3, 123, 150n6
   and negotiations with villagers, 143
   staff of, 138, 146–47, 149, 152n21, n23, 175, 189, 203–04 (*see also* Marofototra: Comité de Surveillance of)
   and surveillance, 138, 188 (*see also* Marofototra: Comité de Surveillance of)
   See also Masoala National Park: boundary of
animation film, 80–84, 97, 100
Astuti, Rita, 153, 167

biodiversity, 1, 3, 10, 17n4, 25, 40, 54, 109, 144, 163, 190, 207, 217
Bloch, Maurice, 12, 19n16, 152n20, 155–56, 171n1, 172n10, 209–11, 218, 224n1
Boserup, Ester, 18n8, 172n9
Brockington, Daniel, 2, 3, 17n5, 18n8, n11, 19n15, n17, n20, 47, 92n4, 151n15
burial ground, chapter 8; 154–62, 170, 200–01, 211, 212–13, 218. *See also* ancestors; Island of the Wanderer; kinship; land of the ancestors
Burney, David A., 18n8

Campbell, Ben, 10, 19n26, 152n22, 172n8, 211
canonical narrative. *See under* Nature conservation: canonical narrative of
cash crops, 119, 164, 168
children, 153–62. *See also* process of growth
coconut schema, chapter 5 (esp. 94–97, 101–6, 109–12); 217. *See also* schemas
Cole, Jennifer, 151n13, 155, 171n3, 172n6, n12, 189, 194, 199, 210
colonial era, 196n4
   and displacement, 152n20, 197, 201 (*see also* Masoala National Park: and displacement)

240 | Index

colonial era (*cont.*)
  and forced labour, 151n9, 152n20, 197, 214n1, n5
  memories of, 178, 188, 194, 199, 201–02 (*see also* Masoala National Park: as continuation of historical power relations; slavery)
  reference at Zurich zoo to, 37, 52
  See also logging
community committee (V.O.I.), 139–40
conservation. *See under* Nature conservation
Conservation International, 17n7, 18n11
Corson, Catherine, 2, 3, 18n9, 19n19, n20, n24, 121, 148, 151n6, n16

Decary, Raymond, 183n3
deforestation, 4, 36, 40, 43, 45, 54, 61, 70–71, 72, 94, 100, 102, 106–9
  causes of, 41, 46, 67, 71, 72–74, 100, 103, 108, 221–22
  and visit to Masoala exhibit, 106–7, 108, 109
  See also logging; perception of Malagasy people: as ignorant, and poverty; slash-and-burn agriculture; traditionalism
Descola, Philippe, 16n2, 19n14, 162, 172n7, 217
Dewar, Robert E., 2, 17n6, 18n8
Duffy, Rosaleen, 2, 3, 17n5, 18n8, 19n17, n19, n23, 148, 151n6, n15, 195

emotions, 13, 27–28, 74–75
Evers, Sandra J.T.M., 19n16, n22, 122, 151n12, 155, 184n4, 210, 211
evolutionism, 7, 32, 47, 106, 110–12, 208, 219, 223. *See also* coconut schema; perception of Malagasy people: as backward, as ignorant; traditionalism

Fairhead, James, 18n8, n9, 19n20, n25, 150n3, 152n18, 172n8, 195
Feeley-Harnik, Gillian, 155, 156, 159, 199, 210
Foniala (juggling troupe), 203–09
forest conservation. *See under* deforestation

Fremigacci, Jean, 18n8, 142, 151n9, 152n20, 196n4, 214n1
friction, 8–9, 162–63, 171, 209, 222
funerary practices, 171n5, n6, 174, 181, 183n3. *See also* ancestors; burial ground; Island of the Wanderer

generification, chapter 4; 112n1, 219–21. *See also* Ur-
Gezon, Lisa L., 148, 224n3
globalisation, 1, 8, 16, 162–63, 208, 222–23
  and agency, 8, 148, 152n22
  and environmental governance, 2, 10, 18n9, 188, 195
  See also Nature conservation: and power inequalities
Globi, 6, 47–56, 60, 85, 94, 110. *See also* Nature conservation: and adventure, and science
Graeber, David, 19n16, 155, 171n3, 194, 209, 210, 211, 212

Hanson, Paul W., 19n17, n24, 214n9, 215n14, 224n3
Harper, Janice, 149, 196n6, 224n3
Harris, Paul L., 83–85

Igoe, James, 2, 3, 17n5, 18n8, 19n15, n17, n20, 47, 92n4, 151n15
implicit and explicit knowledge, 12–13
Ingold, Tim, 10, 19n14
Island of the Wanderer, chapter 8
  as burial site: 173–75
  and Masoala National Park, 175–83, 188, 193, 200–01, 210
  See also ancestors: transferral of bones of; burial ground; land of the ancestors

jungle, 31, 33, 35, 49, 50, 63, 80–81, 85, 88, 95, 96. *See also* animation film; tropics; wilderness

keywords, 13, 15, 94
kinship, chapter 7 (esp. 153–62); 209–10
  and land, 9, 19n16, 128, 162, 171, 176, 199, 217, 218
  See also ancestors; burial ground; children; land of the ancestors;

process of growth; slavery; *tany fivelômana*
Kopytoff, Igor, 156–58, 166, 213
Kremen, Claire, 2, 3, 121–24, 129, 142, 150n2, n3, n4, n5, 201
Kull, Christian A., 2, 17n4, 18n8, n9, 19n24, 128–29, 172n9, 224n3

land. *See under* kinship: and land
land of the ancestors (*tanindrazana*), chapter 7 (esp. 154–62); 19n16, 181, 209–10, 211–13. *See also* burial ground; kinship; process of growth; slavery; *tany fivelômana*
Leach, Melissa, 18n8, n9, 19n20, n25, 150n3, 152n18, 172n8, 195
Li, Tania M., 77–78, 103
logging, 17n7, 40, 142
    during colonial era, 43, 152n19, 197–98, 202, 212
    illegal, 34, 40, 67, 68n5, 71, 72, 108, 141, 221–22

mandimby, 159–62. *See also* kinship
Marofototra
    Comité de Surveillance of, 144
    description of, 141–45 (*see also* Masoala National Park: zones of)
    Dina of, 143–45; 152n20, 164 (*see also:* Masoala National Park: and legal framework)
    history of, 142, 198, 212–13
    marine park of, 145
    See also Ambanizana; Masoala; Masoala National Park
Masoala
    and biodiversity, 3 (*see also* biodiversity)
    and colonial era (*see under* colonial era)
    and external control over resources, chapter 9 (*see also* Masoala National Park: as continuation of historical power relations)
    as frontier, 156–58, 166, 211, 213, 215n3
    history of slavery in (*see under* slavery)
    meaning of word, 117–18
    population of, 150n2
    tourism in, 5, 19n12, 42, 60, 62, 87, 147, 152n23, 164, 167–68, 177, 186, 191, 192, 201–02, 214n7, n8, 221 (*see also* Island of the Wanderer; *vazaha*)
    See also Ambanizana; Marofototra; Masoala National Park
Masoala exhibit, 3–4, 11, 163
    effect of visit to, 66, 92, 94, 98, 106, 107, 108–9
    greenhouse, 26–31, 33
    information centre, 36–44
    'little house' (kitchen), 28–33, 98–100
    research camp, 33–35
    restaurant, 35–36
    tunnel, 24–26
Masoala National Park
    benefits from, 147–50
    boundary of, 121–24, 126–27, 129–30, 135, 144–45, 149, 163, 164–65, 187, 194
    and colonial era (*see under* colonial era)
    and compensations for loss of land, 134–36, 143, 164
    and consultation/participation, 121–22, 126–27, 140, 143, 151n16, 166
    as continuation of historical power relations, chapter 9; 10, 188,198, 201–02, 217–18, 221
    description of, 120–27
    and displacement, 122, 134–35, 143–44, 201 (*see also* colonial era: and displacement)
    history of, 3, 120–21, 195n1
    and implication of foreigners, 5, 177–79 (*see also vazaha*)
    and land tenure, 122, 127–29, 133, 164
    and legal framework, 124, 144, 151n10, 189–90 (*see also* Marofototra: Dina of; rice cultivation: hill rice)
    and loss of burial ground (*see under* Island of the Wanderer)
    and loss of land, 127–34, 149, 164 (*see also* kinship; land of the ancestors; process of growth; *tany fivelômana*)
    and penalties, 124, 136–38, 145, 189–90
    and sense of defeat, 165–70, 179–82, 212
    and slavery (*see under* slavery)

Masoala National Park (*cont.*)
  and state control, 186, 188, 189–90, 193–95
  as threat to livelihood, 123, 133, 134, 138, 140, 149, 150, 164, 166, 167, 170, 177, 183, 197, 201, 202, 210, 218
  and uncertainty, chapter 9; 127, 129, 140–41, 144, 149, 177–79
  and *vazaha* (*see under vazaha*)
  zones of, 124–27 (*see also* Marofototra: description of)
  See also Masoala; process of growth
media, 12, 45, 46, 59–60, 75, 78n4, 107, 108, 109, 110, 208. *See also* animation film; Globi
Merina, 37, 194–95, 208
morality, chapter 3; 80, 90, 103, 105, 109, 110, 111, 163, 216–17, 222. *See also* perception of Malagasy people: as in need of education
Myers, Norman, 1, 17n3, n4, 25

Nash, Roderick F., 16n2, 76
Nature conservation, 1, 4
  and adventure, 53, 55, 60, 62 (*see also* Globi)
  canonical narrative of, 2, 17n5, n7, 18n8, 172n8, 219
  and displacement, 10, 134–35 (*see also* Masoala National Park: and displacement)
  and friction with process of growth, 162–65, 170–71
  and morality, 53, 55, 60, 62 (*see also* morality)
  paradigm of, 10, 75, 76, 110–12, 223 (*see also* process of growth: and friction with conservation paradigm)
  and participation, 10
  and power inequalities, 10, 77–78, 148, 165
  public discourse of, 45, 52, 66
  and science, 52, 53, 54, 55, 60, 61–62 (*see also* Globi)
  transcendental quality of, 75–77, 162
  See also globalisation
non-governmental organisations, 2, 10, 18n9, n11, 151n6, 195
Nosin-dRendra. *See under* Island of the Wanderer

Ormsby, Alison, 19n12, 121, 150n2, 152n23, 195n1
othering, 32, 90–91, 112n1. *See also* postcolonial studies; tropics

paradigm. *See under* Nature conservation: paradigm of
participant observation, 11, 12
perception, 62. *See also* schemas
perception of Malagasy people
  as backward, 73, 85, 86, 91, 95, 98–99, 102, 105, 106, 110–11, 208
  as cannibals, 32, 89
  and clothing, 94–95, 101, 102, 109
  as deficient, 55, 94–95, 98, 102, 105, 109
  as in need of education, 58–61, 71, 77–78, 103–4, 105, 109, 110, 163, 171, 207, 221 (*see also* morality)
  as Eingeborene (*see under* Ur-: Ureinwohner/Urvolk)
  and houses, 88, 89, 95, 96, 98, 99, 100, 102, 109
  as hunters and gatherers, 90, 95, 100, 102, 103, 109
  as ignorant, 73, 78, 95, 103, 104, 105, 108, 110, 111 (*see also* morality)
  as natives, chapter 4; 31, 47, 86, 100, 219–21 (*see also* Ur-: Ureinwohner/Urvolk)
  and poverty, 32, 40, 67, 71, 73, 80, 85–86, 94, 95, 98, 100, 102, 103, 104, 108, 109, 221
  as savages, 86, 102
  See also evolutionism; generification; jungle; traditionalism; wilderness
Pollini, Jacques, 2, 17n5, 18n8, n9, 19n18, n21, n24, n25, 148, 151n6, 152n18, 172n9, 215n14
population growth, 162. *See also* process of growth
postcolonial studies, 32, 52. *See also* othering
process of growth, chapter 7 (esp. 154–62); 176, 181, 183, 199–200, 211–12, 217–18
  and friction with conservation paradigm, 162–65, 170–71, 181, 183
  See also children; kinship; land of the ancestors; *tany fivelômana*
protected areas agency. *See under* ANGAP

protected areas in Madagascar, 3, 42, 186–87, 189, 195, 222
Protestant ethic, 72, 217
Purtschert, Patricia, 24, 32, 35, 46, 52, 57n15, 112n1

Quinn, Naomi, 12–14, 64–65, 74–75, 85, 94, 96, 97, 98

(Rabesahala) Horning, Nadia, 16n1, 18n8, n9, 19n25, 194
récitation, 123, 215n9
responsibility. *See under* morality
rice cultivation
　hill rice, 119, 122, 124, 126, 127, 129, 133, 139, 140, 143–40, 144, 150n5, 166, 168–69, 187, 189, 201, 204 (*see also* Masoala National Park: and legal framework; slash-and-burn agriculture)
　wet rice, 118–19, 122, 126, 144
Richard, Alison F., 2, 18n8
Rothfels, Nigel, 32, 57n16, 70, 217

schemas, 6, 16, 63–67, 74, 78n3, 85, 96–98, 108, 111. *See also* coconut schema
school classes, 15, 93
science. *See under* Nature conservation: and science
slash-and-burn agriculture, 2, 17n7, 36, 37, 40, 42, 43, 46, 61, 71, 72, 108, 163. *See also* rice cultivation: hill rice
Slater, Candace, 76
slavery
　history in Masoala of, 118, 148, 198–201, 209–13, 214n2
　and kinship, 209–13
　and marriage, 210
　and Masoala National Park, 118, 198–201, 206–07, 209–13, 218, 223 (*see also* Masoala National Park: as continuation of historical power relations)
　reference at Zurich zoo to, 37
　See also land of the ancestors; kinship
Sodikoff, Genese M., 119, 149, 151n9, 152n21, 195n2, 214n2, n5, 224n3
Soper, Kate, 16n2, 224n2
Sperber, Dan, 78n3, 97

Stepan, Nancy L., 16n2, 68n3, 90–91, 112n2, 220
Strauss, Claudia, 12, 13, 16, 64–65, 74–75, 85, 94, 97, 101, 111

tanindrazana. *See under* land of the ancestors
tany fivelômana, 165-66, 168–70, 172n12, 211. *See also* kinship; land of the ancestors; process of growth
tourism in Masoala. *See under* Masoala: tourism in
traditionalism, 37, 39, 47, 61, 67, 73, 78, 103, 104, 106, 108, 110, 207. *See also* evolutionism; perception of Malagasy people: as backward
tropics, 63, 68n3, 74, 90. *See also* jungle; wilderness
Tsing, Anna L., 1, 8–9, 19n13, n14, 76, 148, 162, 208, 215n12, 216, 222, 223

uncertainty. *See under* Masoala National Park: and uncertainty
UNESCO, 3, 124, 187–88, 193
Ur-, 86, 95
Ureinwohner/Urvolk, chapter 4; 31, 100, 102, 104 (*see also* perception of Malagasy people)
Urwald, 43, 70, 73
See also generification

vazaha, 188, 219–21
　Malagasy as, 188, 194, 196n8, 203–04, 208
　in Masoala, 190–95, 198, 201–03, 210, 219
　See also Masoala: tourism in; Masoala National Park: and implication of foreigners
visitors to Masoala exhibit
　and attention span, 34, 35–36, 44–45
　background of, 15–16, 69–70, 105
　See also Masoala exhibit
Völkerschauen, 32

Walsh, Andrew, 19n23, 87, 191, 214n8, 223, 224n3
Weber, Max, 72, 217
West, Paige, 19n15, n17, 47, 92n4, 151n15, 152n22
wilderness, 64, 82–84, 87, 91. *See also* animation film; jungle; tropics

244 | *Index*

Wildlife Conservation Society (WCS), 3, 17n5, 18n11, 34, 42, 60, 117, 121, 123, 139, 150n1, n3, n6, 185, 190, 192–93, 195, 207, 223. *See also* Zurich zoo: partnership with WCS
World Wildlife Fund (WWF), 18n11, 104, 106–7, 123

Zurich zoo
    and Foniala (juggling troupe), 207
    Little Masoala (*see under* Masoala exhibit)
    in Masoala, 147–48, 177, 185, 190
    Masoala exhibit at (*see under* Masoala exhibit)
    and Masoala newsletter, 207, 209
    as Nature conservation centre, 4, 58–59
    partnership with WCS, 4, 34, 42, 117, 123, 193 (*see also* Wildlife Conservation Society)
    and support of Masoala National Park, 4, 35, 47, 54, 60, 68n2, 165, 195
    and UNESCO, 124, 188

Studies in Environmental Anthropology and Ethnobiology

Volume 1
The Logic of Environmentalism
Anthropology, Ecology and Postcoloniality
Vassos Argyrou

Volume 2
Conversations on the Beach
Fishermen's Knowledge, Metaphor and Environmental Change in South India
Götz Hoeppe

Volume 3
Green Encounters
Shaping and Contesting Environmentalism in Rural Costa Rica
Luis A. Vivanco

Volume 4
Local Science vs Global Science
Approaches to Indigenous Knowledge in International Development
Edited by Paul Sillitoe

Volume 5
Sustainability and Communities of Place
Edited by Carl A. Maida

Volume 6
Modern Crises and Traditional Strategies
Local Ecological Knowledge in Island Southeast Asia
Edited by Roy Ellen

Volume 7
Traveling Cultures and Plants
The Ethnobiology and Ethnopharmacy of Human Migrations
Edited by Andrea Pieroni and Ina Vandebroek

Volume 8
Fishers and Scientists in Modern Turkey
The Management of Natural Resources, Knowledge and Identity on the Eastern Black Sea Coast
Ståle Knudsen

Volume 9
Landscape Ethnoecology
Concepts of Biotic and Physical Space
Edited by Leslie Main Johnson and Eugene Hunn

Volume 10
Landscape, Process and Power
Re-Evaluating Traditional Environmental Knowledge
Edited by Serena Heckler

Volume 11
Mobility and Migration in Indigenous Amazonia
Contemporary Ethnoecological Perspectives
Edited by Miguel N. Alexiades

Volume 12
Unveiling the Whale
Discourses on Whales and Whaling
Arne Kalland

Volume 13
Virtualism, Governance and Practice
Vision and Execution in Environmental Conservation
Edited by James G. Carrier and Paige West

Volume 14
Ethnobotany in the New Europe
People, Health and Wild Plant Resources
Edited by Manuel Pardo-de-Santayana, Andrea Pieroni and Rajindra K. Puri

Volume 15
Urban Pollution
Cultural Meanings, Social Practices
Edited by Eveline Dürr and Rivke Jaffe

Volume 16
Weathering the World
Recovery in the Wake of the Tsunami in a Tamil Fishing Village
Frida Hastrup

Volume 17
Environmental Anthropology Engaging Ecotopia
Bioregionalism, Permaculture, and Ecovillages
Edited by Joshua Lockyer and James R. Veteto

Volume 18
Things Fall Apart?
The Political Ecology of Forest Governance in Southern Nigeria
Pauline von Hellermann

Volume 19
Sustainable Development
An Appraisal from the Gulf Region
Edited by Paul Sillitoe

Volume 20
Beyond the Lens of Conservation
Malagasy and Swiss Imaginations of One Another
Eva Keller

Volume 21
Trees, Knots, and Outriggers
Environmental Knowledge in the Northeast Kula Ring
Frederick H. Damon

Volume 22
Indigenous Revival and Sacred Sites
Conservation in the Americas
Edited by Fausto Sarmiento and Sarah Hitchner

www.ingramcontent.com/pod-product-compliance
Lightning Source LLC
Chambersburg PA
CBHW072149100526

44589CB00015B/2151